THE AUTHENTIC
GEORGIAN DOLLS'
HOUSE

BRIDGE END HOUSE, TWEEDMOUTH
BERWICK-UPON-TWEED

A Georgian house in a provincial town, showing greater
individuality and charm than any city houses of the period.
You probably know a town and a house like this one.

THE AUTHENTIC GEORGIAN DOLLS' HOUSE

BRIAN LONG

GUILD OF MASTER CRAFTSMAN PUBLICATIONS LTD

First published 2001 by
Guild of Master Craftsman Publications Ltd
Castle Place, 166 High Street,
Lewes, East Sussex BN7 1XU

ISBN 1 86108 187 1

A catalogue record for this book is available from the British Library.

Edited by Stephen Haynes
Book and cover designed by Ian Hunt Design

Set in Stone Serif, Trajan and Frutiger

Colour origination by Viscan Graphics (Singapore)
Printed and bound by Kyodo Printing (Singapore)

MEASUREMENTS

Since the builders of Georgian houses worked in feet and inches, and the
scales used by miniaturists are designed with imperial measurements
in mind (in 1/12 scale, for example, 1 inch represents 1 foot), we have
not thought it appropriate to include metric equivalents in the measured
drawings. Where metric conversions are given in the text, they have been
rounded up or down as convenient. Most miniaturists work to 1/12 scale,
but interest in smaller scales is growing. To cater for all eventualities, the
drawings of the smaller items are given with full-size measurements.

When working in these scales, it is sometimes necessary to use measurements such as ½ or ⅛in, which will not be found on an ordinary ruler.
One solution is to use a scale rule which is actually marked with 1/12
(or 1/24) scale measurements. These are available on the miniatures market;
one that I know of is supplied by Black Country Miniatures. Architects' rules
with various scales, including 1/12 and 1/24, can sometimes be found.

CONTENTS

ABOUT THE AUTHOR vi

INTRODUCTION

Never dishonour the eye 1

PART I
THE GEORGIAN HOUSE

1 GEORGIAN STYLE

Period styles • Windows • Roofs 5

PART II
YOUR KIND OF HOUSE

2 TOWN AND COUNTRY

House types • Town houses • A provincial
town house: Bridge End House 29

3 RESEARCHING YOUR MODEL

Field work • Ladythorne House
Northumberland farmhouse of 1788 • Penparcau
tollhouse • Slate worker's cottage 48

4 SOME UNUSUAL HOUSES

Harbour Master's House • The gatekeeper's
lodges at Ewart • The Needle's Eye
Baby houses 67

5 USING INFORMATION FROM
WRITTEN SOURCES

Inventories • Period literature • Dates and signatures
Fire marks 88

PART III
SERVICES, FIXTURES AND FITTINGS

6 LIGHT AND WATER

Lighting • Exterior ironwork • Sanitation • Water
supply • Rainwater goods 106

7 HEATING AND COOKING

Kitchens • Reception rooms • Fire screens, chimney
boards and dummy boards • Stoves • Portable
heaters 126

8 KITCHENS

The Georgian kitchen• Ovens • Dressers
Kitchen accessories 142

9 DECORATION AND FURNISHINGS

Walls • Floors • Ceilings • Colour schemes • Blinds
and curtains • Protective coverings 172

10 AND SO TO BED

Beds • Bedwarmers 183

EPILOGUE

The Georgian World 196

FURTHER READING 198

PLACES TO VISIT 199

INDEX 200

ABOUT THE AUTHOR

Brian Long has worn many hats in his time, starting out as a coal miner, then training as a teacher of ceramics and graphics, followed by a long spell as a forest officer. He has restored three period houses and one garden, as well as a Gothic Revival castle. In his spare time he was Secretary, Editor, then Chairman of the Association of Northumberland Local History Societies. A book on the castles of Northumberland and many papers on villages and period houses were to follow. Today he is to be found at specialist miniatures fairs, where he retails his own authentic yet unusual miniatures and freely dispenses information to other enthusiasts.

INTRODUCTION

Never dishonour the eye

The world of a Georgian gentleman and his family was one of order and grace. He lived in an age of higher civilization than had ever been achieved before. Architects, builders and interior decorators ensured that the sense of sight was never dishonoured: houses and furniture were constructed within strict rules of proportion to achieve a visual perfection which would announce to the world at large that these were the homes of exquisites. These 'period homes' were the latest in the field of domestic arts and science – places where a well-ordered and comfortable life could be achieved, using the latest ideas and equipment.

The Georgians nevertheless accepted, as we do, the inevitable smells of the street – in their day, horses' sweat, dung and urine, to name but a few. Indoors, they used vast quantities of perfume and scented waters to banish, or at least obscure, the ever-present body odour from their fine apartments.

'PLAN OF A ROOM, – SHEWING THE PROPER DISTRIBUTION OF THE FURNITURE'

by George Hepplewhite
(by courtesy of Dover Publications, Inc.)

———

Owners of fine furniture were advised to draw a plan to show the 'manner of properly disposing of the same', which meant placing most pieces against the walls; as a rule, only the dining table was allowed to escape this rigid regime. This drawing appeared in *The Cabinet-Maker and Upholsterer's Guide*, first published by Hepplewhite's widow in 1788.

Plan of a Room, – shewing the proper distribution of the Furniture.

Underclothes were worn more to protect the rich outer garments from their own unwashed bodies than anything else.

The surviving houses from this period have evolved over the intervening years to suit new ideas of comfort and fashion, and in this way they have continued to serve the requirements and tastes of successive owners in a changing world. To cut out draughts which the Georgians had found acceptable, subsequent owners would seal a door, or hang curtains where previously taste decreed there would only be shutters. Lighting changed from rush lights and candles to oil, then gas, and today electricity – all simple changes, yet over the years making a great difference to an elegant Georgian home. Fireplaces have been altered to improve their efficiency and cut out down-draughts, only to be replaced by central heating.

The endless list of 'improvements' means that existing Georgian homes have accumulated a great deal of later clutter. To furnish and equip a period dolls' house correctly we have to learn to identify the elements that remain true to period, then look to other sources to find the missing pieces of the

> ## A FAMILY IN AN INTERIOR TAKING TEA
> *English school, c.1740*
> *(© Christie's Images Ltd 2001)*
>
> ━━━━━
>
> Drinking tea from Chinese tea bowls, a servant on hand with fresh hot water – this scene should be a set piece in every Georgian dolls' house. The mistress of the house displays her valuable tea caddy at her feet. All ladies of quality aspired to such heights.
>
> The décor of the room is also worthy of note. Green-painted wooden panelling is still in fashion. The fireplace houses a basket rather than a hob grate, and has no mantel shelf; there is not even a chimney breast, as the chimney is on the outside of the house.
>
> This was a conventional pose for eighteenth-century group portraits, and examples can be found in many collections.

jigsaw. It is only in specialist museums (some of which are listed on page 199) that you will find rooms or houses furnished, equipped and decorated in a particular period style, without the accumulated improvements of later generations of proud owners. In short, miniaturists have to become house detectives.

We in the dolls' house world, like the exquisites of the period, tend to think in a blinkered way as though elegant houses were the norm. We furnish and equip our models in a style that is often far above their station, turning our backs on the more numerous houses of lesser standing – the abodes of labourers and artisans who toiled to enable their betters to live as they did. These masses of ordinary working people lived in very different circumstances, and their humble homes provide us miniaturists with a varied selection of challenges. Some lived in purpose-built rows of cottages, others in estate villages designed to reflect the taste of their owners; many of these were designed by well-known architects and built by craftsmen. Lower down the social scale, homes were built by the occupants themselves using local materials. In some parts of coastal Britain, poor fisherfolk lived

in rather curious houses (described by Dickens in *David Copperfield*) formed out of redundant boats turned upside down – a truly challenging project for them, and for the miniaturist as well.

These various types of home present us with a wide choice of architectural style, social class, size and shape. If you are willing to be adventurous,

WORKERS' HOUSES: LLAINFADYN COTTAGE, ST FAGANS, CARDIFF

Simple cottages like this housed people with insufficient land to live off – typically farm labourers, craftsmen or quarrymen. This one-roomed example of 1762 (see pages 65–6) was home to a quarryman and his family. In common with the working classes in much of upland Britain, what little privacy they had was gained by the clever use of box or cupboard beds to form small self-contained bedrooms, with a half-loft above for the smaller children.

you can design and build a miniature Georgian home to fit whatever space you have available in a busy modern house, and in a way that complements your décor. Don't hide it – flaunt it! Use it to surprise and stimulate your guests and family as did the exquisites of the eighteenth century.

No matter what your initial area of interest is – interior decoration, architecture, fashion, social history or model-making – the pursuit of your ideal dolls' house will be an absorbing and addictive pastime for many years.

Brian Long
Wokingham, 2000

Loch Long, Susie's Castle Portincaple

CHAPTER ONE

GEORGIAN STYLE

Period styles • Windows • Roofs

INFLUENCES

The Georgian era was preceded by what we now know as the Restoration period, which is often considered to start about 1640, though its defining point is the re-establishment of the monarchy in 1660; Restoration styles continued to influence architecture until about 1745. This period saw the development of Palladianism – the architectural movement inspired by the classical ideas of Andrea Palladio (1508–80) – and the birth of the extravagant Baroque style, both of which were to reach their climax under the Georgians. The reign of Queen Anne (1702–14) brought in a quieter, more homely style which influenced many smaller houses of the early eighteenth century, and was subsequently resurrected by the Edwardians at the beginning of the twentieth century.

The Georgian period itself, calculated in regnal years, began on 1 August 1714 with the accession of George I and ended over a century later with the death of George IV on 26 June 1830. Naturally, artistic taste, style or fashion did not begin and end with the death of a monarch: influences from the previous period continued to develop, while other features which we think of as typically Georgian would in turn continue into the Victorian era. Georgian style, like any style, was not static, and the 1,100,000 houses built between 1714 and 1830 which still exist today are united not by their architectural style but by their quality and attention to detail. The Georgian era was truly an age of elegance whose like has not been seen since, and its buildings drew on influences as varied as Palladianism, Gothic Revival, Chinoiserie and Regency – some of which remained in vogue well into the nineteenth century.

QUEEN ANNE

Though it still retained hints of the earlier Tudor and Jacobean styles, Queen Anne was, at its best, a neat, symmetrical style characterized by classical shapes and proportions. Many windows still had the mullions and transoms typical of an earlier era. Fitted into these were hinged casements – usually with square panes by this time, though sash windows had begun to appear by about 1670. Diamond-shaped quarries were still used for dormers, basement windows and other service areas. It was common for window heads to be made in classical form, but in rural areas the old Tudor hood-mould was still used.

The fine hoods built over front doors, both to protect and to decorate them, are the one element of the Queen Anne style that strikes most people today. Some were most ornate and took the form of huge seashells supported on large decorative brackets. Rectangular hoods were much more common, but don't have the same charm. Other classical motifs were used to great effect. Twisted columns inspired by Solomon's temple flanked front doors, and staircase balusters were enriched in a similar style. After about 1640, strapwork ceilings were replaced by deeply moulded beams or ovals, the favoured décor of the late seventeenth century. The spaces between the beams or mouldings could be painted or left blank to emphasize the central feature.

Roofs were commonly hipped, with their gutters hidden away and carried by projecting wooden brackets or *modillions* – a feature which was eventually to be outlawed in the Building Act of 1707. This was one of a rash of building acts, initially applying only to London, designed to reduce the

THE GEORGIAN ERA

This chronological table shows that regnal years are only a rough guide to the overlapping stylistic periods.

| 1680 | 1690 | 1700 | 1710 | 1720 | 1730 | 1740 | 1750 | 1760 | 1770 | 1780 | 1790 | 1800 | 1810 | 1820 | 1830 | 1840 | 1850 |

REGNAL YEARS

Anne
1702–1714

George II
1727–1760

REGENCY
1811–1820

George IV
1820–1830

Victoria
1837–1901

William & Mary
1689–1702

George I
1714–1727

George III
1760–1811

William IV
1830–1837

STYLISTIC PERIODS

RESTORATION
1640–1745

EARLY GEORGIAN
1705–85

LATE GEORGIAN
1740–1810

REGENCY
1785–1845

EARLY VICTORIAN
1800–60

PRIME MOVERS IN ARCHITECTURE AND DESIGN

- Sir Christopher WREN 1632–1723
- Sir John VANBRUGH 1664–1726
- Colen CAMPBELL 1676–1729
- William KENT 1685–1748
- Giacomo LEONI (translator of Palladio) c.1686–1746
- John WOOD of Bath, the elder 1704–54
- The GILLOW family:
  Robert I 1704–72
  Richard I 1734–1811
  Richard II 1772–1849
  Robert II 1747–?

- Thomas CHIPPENDALE 1718–79
- John CARR of York 1723–1807
- John WOOD the younger 1728–81
- Robert ADAM 1728–92
- George DANCE the younger 1741–1825
- Henry HOLLAND 1745–1805
- James WYATT 1746–1813
- Thomas SHERATON 1751–1806
- Humphry REPTON 1752–1818
- John NASH 1752–1835
- Sir John SOANE 1753–1837
- Sir Jeffrey WYATTVILLE 1766–1840
- John WILSON of Guernsey fl. 1816–25
- Lancelot 'Capability' BROWN 1716–83
- George HEPPLEWHITE d. 1786
- James PAINE 1717–89
- Horace WALPOLE, 4th Earl of Orford 1717–97

ARTISTIC AND LITERARY FIGURES

- Daniel DEFOE c.1660–1731
- George Frederick HANDEL 1685–1759
- Dr Samuel JOHNSON 1709–84
- Laurence STERNE 1713–68
- Sir Joshua REYNOLDS 1723–92
- Thomas GAINSBOROUGH 1727–88

- William BLAKE 1757–1827
- Robert BURNS 1759–96
- William WORDSWORTH 1770–1850
- Jane AUSTEN 1775–1817
- J. M. W. TURNER 1775–1851
- John CONSTABLE 1776–1837
- Charles DICKENS 1812–70

HISTORICAL AND ARTISTIC EVENTS

- 1690–9 Window tax
- 1707 First fire engine
- 1728 John Gay's Beggar's Opera
- 1745 Jacobite Rebellion
- 1746 Battle of Culloden
- 1746 Window tax reintroduced
- 1768 Capt. James Cook lands in Australia
- 1773 Boston Tea Party
- 1776 American Independence

- 1784 Mail coaches introduced
- 1787 John Cary's New and Correct English Atlas
- 1789 French Revolution
- 1805 Battle of Trafalgar
- 1815 Battle of Waterloo
- 1818 Duelling prohibited
- 1825 Stockton & Darlington Railway
- 1834 Tolpuddle Martyrs transported

QUEEN ANNE STYLE

Queen Anne is characteristically a symmetrical style, with classical shapes and dimensions to doors and windows (though still using the traditional mullions and transoms), and the newly fashionable massive, balanced chimneys. The drawing is based on Ashdown House, Oxfordshire.

SHELL HOODS

Queen Anne and Early Georgian doorways were protected by elegant hoods; most are rectangular, but the graceful shell-shaped varieties are especially characteristic.

Shell hood with simple brackets, Ledbury, Hereford & Worcester

Shell hood with ornate scrolled brackets, Wokingham, Berkshire

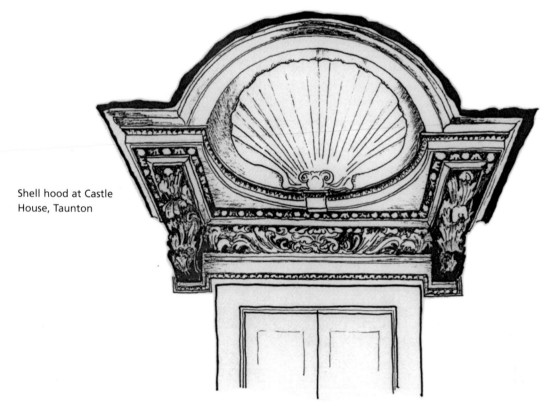

Shell hood at Castle House, Taunton

risk of fire following the Great Fire of 1666. Massive, well-balanced external chimneys which soared skyward were an essential feature of the period, and many elements of the Queen Anne style were still considered fashionable and in good taste well into the eighteenth century.

EARLY GEORGIAN

The Early Georgian style, fashionable from about 1705 to 1785, has its roots in the reign of Queen Anne; it takes the vigorous, often crude, ornament of the Baroque and refines it to produce a much more sophisticated whole. Palladian values based on Roman architecture were much in demand in fashionable circles, and the convenient layout of kitchens and other service areas was sacrificed in the search for symmetry and style. Plans for a new house at Ewart in Northumberland, thought to be by the great Robert Adam (1728–92), have the kitchens 10 yards away over an open court, and this arrangement was not unusual at the time.

The south front of Capheaton Hall, a fine example of a baroque country house built for a local family by a local architect

Speculative building was not new, but now there was an explosion of brick terraced housing in the major cities. In our dolls' houses we usually ensure that every room has a window, but this was not the case in real life, and minor 'dark' rooms were often used as sleeping quarters for domestics. Robert Adam built a village at Lowther (just south of Penrith in Cumbria) to house workers at a carpet manufactory, and many of the houses had no windows to the first-floor bedrooms. Nevertheless, interiors in general became brighter and more

PROVINCIAL BAROQUE

Capheaton Hall, north of Newcastle upon Tyne, was begun in 1667 and the decorators moved in in 1674. It illustrates the lively, often untutored, but charming ornament of the Baroque which contributed much to the Early Georgian style. According to Sir Nikolaus Pevsner, 'The character is that of the provincial and endearing Baroque . . . indulged in by those who would not give in to the academic virtues of Jones, Pratt and Wren.'

A rich man
at home

A poor man at
his door

The south door of Capheaton Hall, with delightfully
unsophisticated ornament by local masons

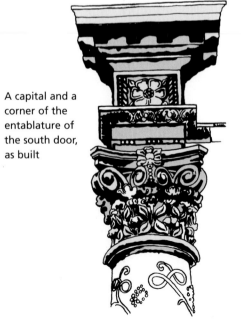

A capital and a
corner of the
entablature of
the south door,
as built

colourful; the extremely expensive 'brighter'
colours (using mainly earth-based pigments) and
the new wallpaper were found even in middle-class
homes. Imported softwoods replaced the native
hardwoods for joinery, so paint was now important as a preservative.

Water companies did exist, but used wooden
pipes which could not withstand the pressure
required to raise water above the ground floor; and
even then, piped supplies were available only at
certain times on prescribed days. A lead cistern or
a large wooden 'buck' stood in the kitchen or in
the front service court or 'area', and was tanked up
when supply allowed. Other areas of the house
were supplied by means of buckets or, in a few
instances, through lead pipes via a hand pump.

Lighting, by rush lights and candles, was an expensive luxury. The best rooms in the best houses would have had a chandelier of wood or wood and metal, with perhaps some crystal drops. Wall brackets or sconces were to be found in most rooms; the best were made from silver, but brass, pewter, gilded wood and tin were all used. Free-standing girandoles were also widely used in elegant houses. Lanterns hung in draughty halls, and if you had one of the fashionable fanlights above your front door it might incorporate a lantern; there are many good examples of these in Dublin. Fanlights were originally made of wood, then iron, followed by iron with lead. The earliest examples are quite simple; they became more fanciful by about 1720, returning to a more sedate style after, say, 1735.

The most important feature of the main façade of a house was the front door. Though in some better houses the doorcase was of stone, in most it was the work of the joiner. The fine brackets of Queen Anne were by now on the way out, and columns and pilasters based on the five orders of classical architecture – Tuscan, Doric, Ionic, Corinthian and Composite – were commonly used. The door itself was always panelled, using robust fielded (bevel-edged) panels, except for the lower panels which were flush on the outside so as to repel rain. Interior doors were matched to the status of the room or office, starting with double doors for the best rooms and ending as far down the scale as

MID-GEORGIAN DOORWAYS

Typical elements include the fanlight over the door and the experimental use of classical detail.

Fine masonry on a house in Merrion Square, Dublin

A robust provincial example: Kingston House, Bradford on Avon, Wiltshire

Merrion Square, Dublin, c.1760

planked examples in some lower service areas. Main entrance doors tended to be flush on the back, and the same is true in situations where the thickness of the wall required two sets of doors; but the doors from the hall to the reception rooms would be fielded and decorated back and front.

Homes in the country may have continued to use casement windows, but in town or the better country houses the sash was predominant, the preferred configuration being six lights over six, set in rather heavy glazing bars of simple pattern. The sash boxes were at first positioned flush with the outside face of the wall; but in London, the Building Act of 1709 (whose scope was extended in 1724) stipulated that at least the ground-floor ones had to be set back 4in (one brick) from the wall surface. Later, windows on all floors had to be set back, and after the 1774 Act they had to be rebated so that the sash box was not fully exposed to view from the outside. Shutters were more common than curtains, being much more

The Royal Society of Antiquaries of Ireland, Dublin

A simple yet elegant Dublin example

A pair of mid-Georgian doorways, Dublin

secure against burglars, draughts, sunlight and prying eyes.

With the demise of the overhanging wooden eaves, parapets were not unusual for the better class of house; the position of the eaves was shown on the outside of the parapet by a simple string course or cornice. Chimneys were, as previously, at the sides of the house, but by now they were built inside rather than outside. This resulted in alcoves either side of the fireplace, which were used for cupboards or display shelves.

LATE GEORGIAN

The Late Georgian style is usually reckoned to last from about 1740 to 1810, overlapping considerably with the Early Georgian. Late Georgian houses are less reliant on a procession of classical details such as pilasters and entablature; the emphasis is on well-proportioned façades of plain brick relieved by string courses, with equally well-proportioned windows and an elegant doorway.

Terraces, even though built by several concerns, were now visually one unit with what is known as a 'palace' façade, the central block being delineated by large pilasters and a pediment. The best examples of this type of development are the Circus and the Royal Crescent in Bath.

A patent 'Roman Cement' or stucco, introduced in 1796, was used to simulate stonework, at least on the basement and ground-floor façade. This fashion reached its peak in the Regency with John Nash's Regent's Park terraces. From 1775 onwards another artificial material, Coade Stone, was widely used to cast architectural ornament; it is best known today by the many keystones, with faces on them, above front doors.

Doors had changed little over the years; the best were made from fine woods, but pine, painted black or dark green, was becoming much more common. The fanlight over the front door was by this time commonplace, and windows flanking the door were fashionable (again, there are many good examples in Dublin), but it is rare to find glass in the door itself. After 1770 the panels of interior doors were often painted with Pompeian motifs.

Windows became taller – so much so that first-floor windows often came down to floor level and opened onto a balcony. Glazing bars were much finer than before, and arched window heads were a favourite decorative feature. By 1780 French doors were used at first-floor level to make access to the balcony easier.

Houses were still cold places if you moved away from the fire, so stoves were introduced into entrance halls; many of these had underfloor flues, a feature that makes them ideal for dolls' houses as no apparent chimney breast is required.

PROVINCIAL GEORGIAN HOUSES

Local masons, using local materials, produced unique buildings with a distinctive regional character and considerable charm; these two examples of the mid-eighteenth century are to be found in the small town of Bradford on Avon, Wiltshire.

Flush toilets, of sorts, were being installed in only the best of houses, so it would be wrong to rush to put one in your dolls' house. The water supply in most areas was inadequate for flushing, and special arrangements were required.

The London Building Act of 1774 set out new minimum standards for terraced houses; a degree of order and dignity in new developments was one of its consequences. Though not binding on the rest of Britain, the provisions of the Act were adhered to as good practice. It specified structural dimensions and divided new terraced houses into four 'rates', defined as follows:

- First rate (great), occupied by the nobility, with a value of over £850 and occupying over 900 sq ft

- Second rate (large), occupied by merchants, with a value of £300–850 and area of 500–900 sq ft

- Third rate (medium), occupied by clerks, with a value of £150–300 and area of 350–500 sq ft

- Fourth rate (small), occupied by mechanics, with a value of up to £150 and area of up to 350 sq ft.

The diagram on page 30 gives an idea of the differences in size and design between these four classes of house.

REGENCY

'The Regency is a quiet backwater off the main stream of artistic history. In its sheltered calm something beautiful came into being and the seeds of it have flowed out into the stream ever since' – so said Professor Bruce Allsopp, founder of the Oriel Press.

Regency builders and decorators harvested the best of the earlier eighteenth century and, with the advantage of a more advanced industrial base, took it to greater, more refined heights. Carpets were now much more in use; wallpaper, while still expensive, was used by a larger section of society; and, thanks to the invention of the power loom, great swathes of curtains could at last be hung in many homes.

A REGENCY FARMHOUSE

Beltingham, just south of the Roman wall near Hexham in Northumberland, is an architect-built house in a rural situation. The windows are now wider and divided into three parts, and the fanlight above the door is no longer fan-shaped.

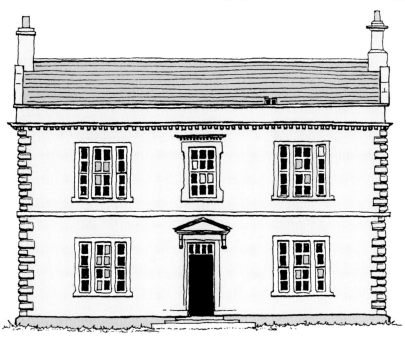

Though wooden modillions had been outlawed earlier in the century, modillions in both stone and wood came back to support wide projecting eaves, and stucco was now used to cover the whole of the main façade of the house, not just the ground floor. Pelmets, housing blinds, were mounted on the outside of windows, which frequently had narrow 'margin lights' of red or blue glass. Semicircular bay windows often rose the full height of the

REGENCY BALCONIES

First-floor balconies of cast or wrought iron are a typical Regency detail. The balcony of this house in Wokingham, Berkshire, has Gothic detail in the railings and a Chinese-style canopy. The French windows, with a central mullion, open inwards and have slim margin lights. These features are all trademarks of the Regency period.

house. But the chief glory of the period was the ironwork: cast iron was taking over from the more expensive wrought iron, and arched porches and pergolas decorated many entrances. Balconettes and multi-arched verandas with pagoda roofs were commonly found gracing the façades of terraces and villas alike, with distinct regional variations.

While the mainstream tended towards simple grace and elegance, there were exceptions – including the Prince Regent himself, who indulged his taste for fantasy in Brighton Pavilion with its Indian exterior and Chinese interior. The pseudo-rustic *cottage orné* style used by Nash at Blaise Hamlet near Bristol was a very different manifestation of the fanciful approach. Even the Egyptians had their day, with John Foulston's houses in Penzance and Devonport (a suburb of Plymouth) being the best-known examples.

However, if your house was not Grecian, then it was most likely to be in the intermittently fashionable Gothic style, the preferred period being Perpendicular. On display would be a battlemented parapet and pointed or square-headed windows with tracery and hood or drip moulds. Doorways were enriched by clusters of narrow engaged (composite) shafts, instead of the robust columns

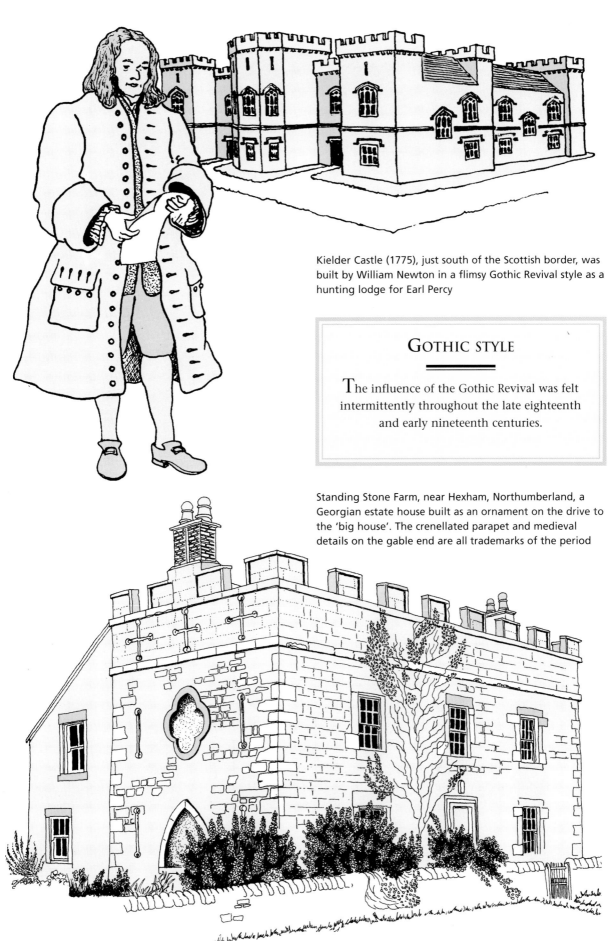

Kielder Castle (1775), just south of the Scottish border, was built by William Newton in a flimsy Gothic Revival style as a hunting lodge for Earl Percy

GOTHIC STYLE

The influence of the Gothic Revival was felt intermittently throughout the late eighteenth and early nineteenth centuries.

Standing Stone Farm, near Hexham, Northumberland, a Georgian estate house built as an ornament on the drive to the 'big house'. The crenellated parapet and medieval details on the gable end are all trademarks of the period

Embleton, on the Northumbrian coast, a Gothic Revival house of 1825 showing considerable scholarship and greater understanding of the style

or pillars of the Greek style. The Gothic Revival gradually moved away from the flimsy pastiche style of Walpole's Strawberry Hill and became more scholarly; serious research and not fancy was to be the norm.

No matter what style they adopted, Regency houses had a dainty elegance which was soon to be overtaken by a rash of ill-digested styles made available through numerous tradesmen's hand-books and the more up-market pattern books; the Victorian age had arrived with a bewildering choice of styles available to all, and the Georgian style was no more – until elements of it were resurrected in modern estates and developments.

PERIOD STYLES

These thumbnail sketches indicate some of the key features of the successive styles.

Kitchen end

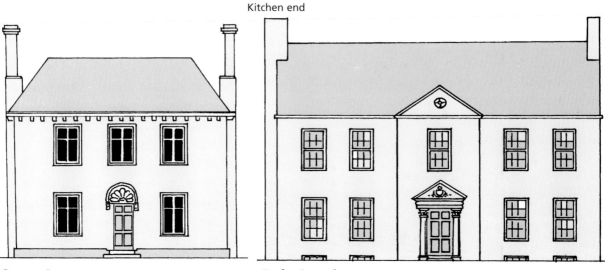

Queen Anne　　　　　　　**Early Georgian**

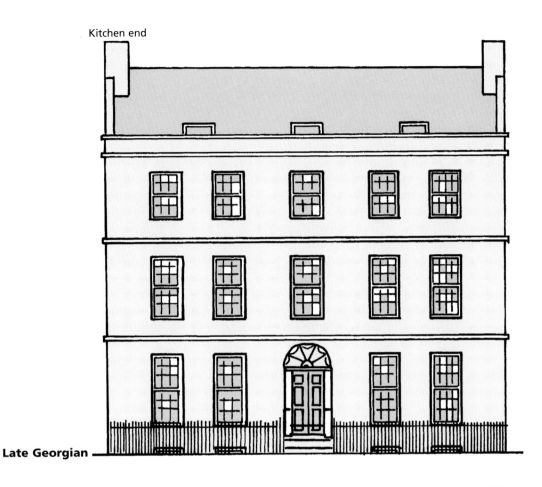

Kitchen end

Late Georgian

Regency villa

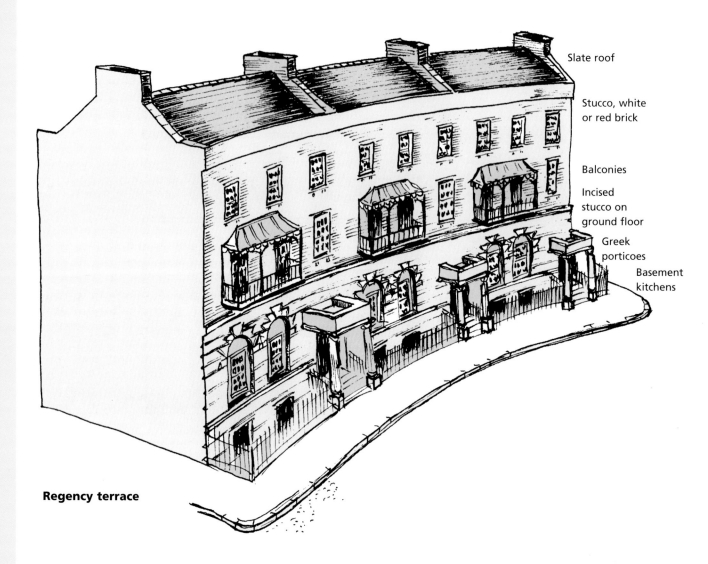

Regency terrace

Slate roof

Stucco, white or red brick

Balconies

Incised stucco on ground floor

Greek porticoes

Basement kitchens

WINDOWS

The mullioned and transomed casement window was pre-eminent in the seventeenth century and was still used sometimes in basements and attics of the eighteenth century. An angular hood mould, or drip mould, as shown in my first drawing of the 1788 farmhouse (page 61), is often found in conjunction with this type of window.

Britain and Holland are the only countries which have a preponderance of sash windows. The origin of the sash window is uncertain, the word *sash* or *chassis* being first used to denote a wooden frame, as opposed to iron and lead. In 1393 two workmen at Ripon Minster in North Yorkshire were paid for the making and fixing of 'saches'. The earliest known record of sash windows with weights and cords refers to those installed in 1673 for the Duke of Lauderdale at the palace of Whitehall. In 1685 and the following two years, windows and frames with 'weights lynes and pulleys' were erected at Windsor Castle. But the invention of the sliding sash may be older than this, as in some houses of the early eighteenth century sash windows are found that never had weights. In these, the upper sash was fixed, with only the lower one sliding up and down. Dr Johnson in his *Journey to the Western Isles of Scotland* of *c*.1770 reported that

their windows do not open upon hinges, but are pushed up and down in grooves, yet they are seldom accommodated with weights and pulleys. He that would have windows open, must hold it with his hands, unless, what may be found amongst contrivers, there be a small nail which he may stick into a hole to keep it from falling.

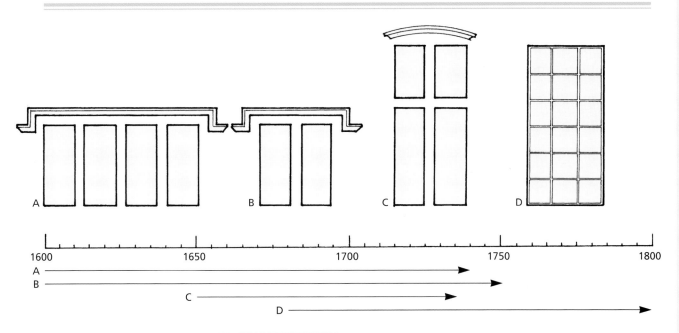

1600   1650   1700   1750   1800

A

B

C

D

DEVELOPMENT OF THE GEORGIAN WINDOW

The Tudor type of mullioned window (A and B) continued in use well into the eighteenth century in cottages and in service areas of large houses. Type C was fashionable in the late seventeenth and early eighteenth centuries; later, the mullions and transom were often removed and type D window frames inserted.

Sash windows rapidly superseded casements, with both vertically sliding and horizontally sliding variations being used – the latter in cottages or in the service areas of large houses, where questions of taste and proportion were not so important. In formal buildings, great attention was paid to proportion and symmetry: next time you visit Hampton Court, notice how Wren varied the size of the panes of glass to emphasize the importance of some windows in the façade.

The later Palladians had strict rules regulating the size and shape of windows. Edward Hoppus in his *Gentleman's and Builder's Repository* of 1737 proposes as ideal the use of round windows, and square windows proportioned so that the sum of their sides is equal to the circumference of the round one. A taller window is achieved by extending the square to form a rectangle, so that the long side of the rectangle is equal to the diagonal of the original square; this shape is known as a √2 (root-2)

WINDOW SHAPES BASED ON A CIRCLE
after Edward Hoppus, 1737

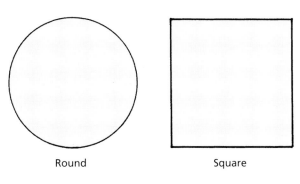

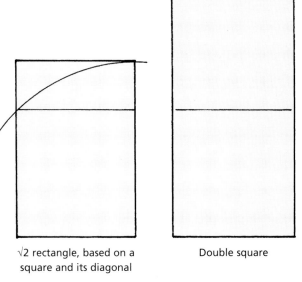

| Round | Square | √2 rectangle, based on a square and its diagonal | Double square |

rectangle, and is easily constructed by using the diagonal of the square to describe an arc. Taller windows may be made the height of the original square plus two-thirds, then the height of the square plus three-quarters, then finally a double square. The language of these old pattern books is a little long-winded, but the proportions of the resulting houses are gems of British architecture.

Period plans and elevations seldom show any details of the woodwork or glass, but it was usual in the earlier part of the century (c.1715–60) for the proportions of the individual pane to match those of the complete unit. In later practice (c.1750–90) the panes were made somewhat squarer, so that

PROPORTIONS OF WINDOW PANES

In this example the window is a double square, so the ratio between its long and short sides is 4 : 2 (or 2 : 1), while the individual panes have the ratio 3 : 2. The proportions of the pane therefore correspond to the width of the whole unit by three-quarters of its height.

Woodwork was heavy at first, but painting the putty black made glazing bars look narrower.

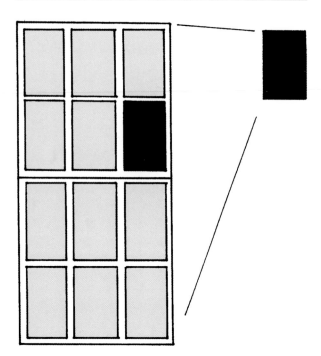

TYPICAL PROFILES OF GLAZING BARS

At first the bars were quite stout and the glass was thick, but over the period both bars and glass grew thinner. In some early examples the putty was painted black to give the impression of more delicate woodwork.

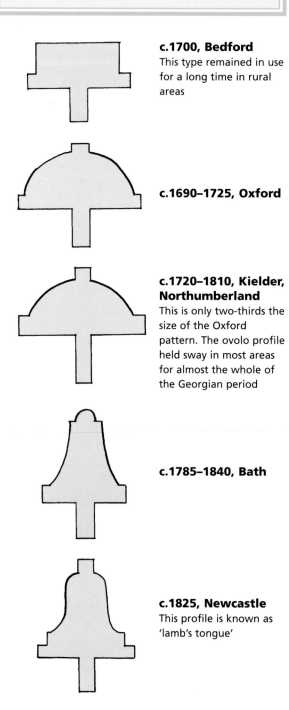

c.1700, Bedford
This type remained in use for a long time in rural areas

c.1690–1725, Oxford

c.1720–1810, Kielder, Northumberland
This is only two-thirds the size of the Oxford pattern. The ovolo profile held sway in most areas for almost the whole of the Georgian period

c.1785–1840, Bath

c.1825, Newcastle
This profile is known as 'lamb's tongue'

REGENCY COTTAGE WINDOWS OF TYPICAL THREE-PART DESIGN

Three-part windows were high fashion between about 1790 and 1830. The photograph shows an original example of this period. Note the lack of a projecting 'horn' or stop under the upper sash; this invariably indicates either pre-Victorian woodwork or a well-informed restoration.

their proportions corresponded to the width of the window by three-quarters of its height. Glazing bars were thick at first, and sash boxes were carved out of solid lengths of timber, but both were gradually refined towards the end of the century. Bear in mind that it could take as long as 25 to 30 years for what was fashionable in the city to reach more rural areas, resulting in some delightful, if 'incorrect', provincial houses.

The Georgian house, more than any other style, depends for its elegance on the arrangement of its windows. The many sham windows – some in relief, some painted – were not all the result of window tax: they were often added for the sake of symmetry, to satisfy the new desire for a harmonious whole. When the window tax was finally repealed in 1851, detached houses began to be built with windows in all walls, as if in revolt against the restrictions that had forced the building of houses with no side windows but only plain brick walls.

Dormer windows were an important element on the elevations of houses of the late seventeenth and early eighteenth centuries, but were later concealed behind parapets, and positioned for reasons of internal comfort rather than visual impact. In spite of this, they were made in many shapes, with segmental, semicircular, triangular or flat heads; they almost always contained casements, rather than sashes.

The Venetian window, consisting of an arched window flanked by two rectangular ones, is a much-used element, giving extreme elegance to many houses. The only 'rule' was that all three sections should be of the same width – a rule that was bent and bent again by architects and builders alike. Normally only one such window was built into an elevation, but houses in the towns of Berwick-upon-Tweed and Ludlow have many variations; some elevations there consist wholly of Venetian windows, which gives them a naïve charm. Circular, bull's-eye and elliptical windows could also be used to great effect in pediments, dormers and other locations.

It was virtually unheard-of to have glass in a door so, to light the entrance hall, simple rectangular fanlights were placed above the door frame but below the canopy or hood. Later, around 1730, the familiar semicircular fanlight with its many variations came into use; Dublin has the best selection on view.

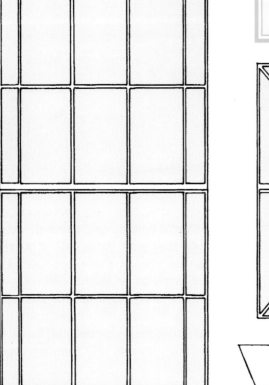

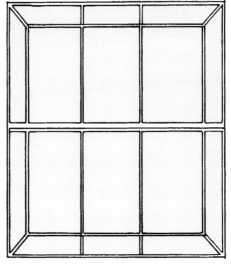

REGENCY WINDOWS
c.1790–1820/30

Glass is by now of much better quality, and the woodwork of the frames much more delicate. The narrow margin lights often had glass of blue or red.

LATE REGENCY WINDOW
c.1820 onwards

Pilasters or mullions separate the central sash from the smaller side ones, a style with its roots in the Venetian window as shown on pages 46 and 72.

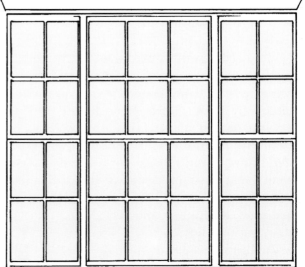

BULL'S-EYE AND THERMAL (OR DIOCLETIAN) WINDOWS

The central bay of this late eighteenth-century house has a pedimented porch supported by Tuscan columns, and above it a semicircular window based on those in the Thermae (baths) of Diocletian, Rome. The ox-eye or bull's-eye window in the pediment gives a touch of elegance, and a view from the dormer behind it.

'THE GARDENER'S HOUSE' LEMMINGTON, NEAR ALNWICK, NORTHUMBERLAND

A Georgian cottage, built around 1780 by William Newton of Newcastle, with none of the usual rectangular windows: instead, there are Venetian windows on the ground floor and rose windows carved out of single stones on the first floor. The line A–A shows how little headroom there was in the bedrooms when the cottage was first built.

A nice touch when building a town house was to arrange the panels on the door in the same order as the windows: medium height at the bottom, then tall in the centre and small at the top.

The first windows or 'wind eyes' were openings to allow ventilation of the house, letting light into the rooms and permitting views from within. By the Georgian period, the availability of cheap glass windows gave some protection from the icy blast; but the windows were themselves fragile and required protection by shutters. Storm shutters could be fitted to the outside, but more fashionable

Configuration of doors reflecting that of windows

Exterior doors, like most others, had fielded (bevel-edged) panels, except that the lower ones were made flat to prevent rain from penetrating, and were marked out by a narrow bead. Builders of taste designed their doors so that the configuration of panels matched that of the windows in the front of the house.

ones were on the inside, where they still protected the interior from winter draughts, valuable paintings and fabrics from harmful sunlight, the occupants from unruly crowds or villains, and helped to retain heat. Many windows, even in quite fine rooms, never had curtains but relied on shutters alone. Shutters, when closed, were held in place by stout wrought iron-bars, never by ordinary bolts, as a further protection from forced entry.

WINDOW TAX

A window tax was introduced for a short time in 1690–9, but only became a significant factor in the mid-eighteenth century. In 1746 it was 9s. 4d. per hundredweight of glass, but it was increased at various times to bolster the Exchequer in time of war. It was raised in 1777 to fund the British forces in America, and again in 1812 to support the efforts against Napoleon. Few records now survive, but those that do are held by county records offices.

At first the tax was to cover the cost of reminting damaged coins, and to a large extent it replaced the hearth tax. Each household paid a basic tax of 2s., with larger houses (10–20 windows) paying a further 8s. The Act of 1746–7 stipulated that houses with 10–14 windows paid 6d. per window on top of the basic rate, and those with 15–19 windows paid 9d. If you had more than 19 windows, then the excess was 1s. per window. In 1825, those who had fewer than 8 windows were exempted, and the tax was abolished in England in 1851; houses in Scotland and Ireland had been exempt since 1707. With this little bit of information you can keep your dolls' house in its correct socio-economic group, remembering that 74% of the population earned under £50 per annum per household, with most earning less than £15 per annum.

ROOFS

There were set rules for obtaining the pitch of a roof, which resulted in three basic forms:

- **Gothic pitch** was arrived at by using rafters the same length as the span to be roofed, so that the roof void or loft area was an equilateral triangle. This early style was ideal for thatch and for porous pantiles, both of which needed to shed rainwater quickly.

Gothic pitch

True or common pitch

Pediment pitch

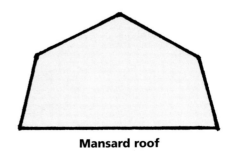

Mansard roof

- **True or common pitch** was the product of rafters whose length was ¾ of the span, and was used for plain tile or slate roofs.

- **Pediment pitch** used a more complex ratio, the height of the ridge from the line of the ceiling or base of the roof being ⅖ of the span. Such roofs were commonly covered in lead.

Mansard roofs were invented by François Mansart (1598–1666) and were late on the scene in Britain, arriving about 1760. This is perhaps the roof type most used by miniaturists, as its distinctive double slope allows plenty of headroom in the attic.

POINTS TO REMEMBER

By far the majority of houses were roofed with thatch (except in places where the Building Acts applied); but stone tiles (as distinct from slate) were the preferred roofing material in many areas from the Tudor period until the first quarter of the nineteenth century. Normally the larger ones were at the wall head, reducing to smaller ones at the ridge. The ridges of stone-tiled roofs were usually made from stone chiselled into shape and bedded in lime mortar. The length of these ridge stones could be anything from 2 to 4ft (0.6–1.2m).

The same type of ridge was common on slate roofs too, but in the traditional slate areas of Britain 'wrestler' slates were used. These are so called because they interlock at the ridge: slots were cut into the sides of each slate approximately 2in (50mm) below the top to engage with similar slates on the obverse slope. As with stone ridges,

all that was now required was a good bed of lime mortar.

Welsh slates were used to cover the Governor's House in Williamsburg, Virginia in 1709, but only became widespread in Britain in the reign of George III, when the Brothers Adam used them in their London houses. At this time the areas in which slates could be used were dictated by waterways, as they were carried by coastal ships and barges. A heavy tax on slate was not removed until 1831, when it at last started to take over from thatch. These two requirements – proximity of waterways and sufficient funds to pay the tax on slate – dictated who could have a slate roof. Slate was only introduced into many tile and thatch areas following the advent of railways, which transported many thousands of tons beyond the reach of the eighteenth-century waterways.

Pantiles, with a double-curved or S-shaped section, were used in many parts of Britain. They were made in Britain only from the seventeenth century (though a few may have been imported before then), so a pantile roof in an Elizabethan or earlier context will usually be a replacement of the original flat tiles. It was during the reign of George I that the size of pantiles was fixed at 13½ x 9½ x ½in (343 x 241 x 13mm).

'WRESTLER' SLATES

Interlocking 'fish-tailed' slates bedded in lime mortar were used to complete ridges in traditional slate areas.

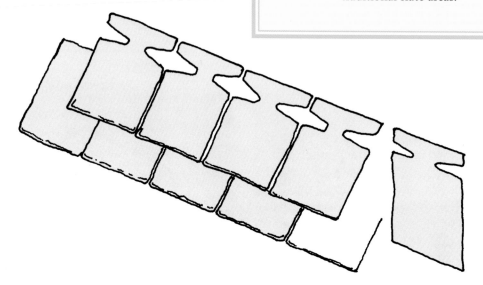

CHAPTER TWO

TOWN AND COUNTRY

House types • Town houses • A provincial town house: Bridge End House

What kind of house would you like to build? Houses of the eighteenth century come in all shapes and sizes, and there must be one out there that would suit you. Any awkward corner can be used to house and display your dream house, and careful positioning can make it a most important and striking part of your décor. Whether you plan to fit it into the void under the stairs, in a redundant fireplace, on a large mantel shelf, or use it as a room divider, there is a house just the shape you require – you just have to look. The Georgians are famous for their elegant town houses, but they also built follies of all shapes, sizes and styles, from a pineapple to a pyramid. Lodges and gatekeepers' cottages were built singly and in matching pairs, and there are many fantastic one-off creations, built on a whim by eccentric landowners.

BRIDGE END HOUSE

The original of Bridge End House sits on the south bank of the Tweed at the end of the Old Tweed Bridge, Berwick-upon-Tweed – hence its name. I first knew it as no. 4 High Street, then Bridge House, then Bridge End House; the present owners call it Tweedmouth House. Name changes like this are not unusual, but can make research a little difficult. The house is unusual for Berwick in being rendered or 'harled', but its Georgian symmetry jumps out at you.

Many of these structures are well recorded: their plans and other relevant details, including builders' accounts, are held in estate offices or deposited in county records offices. The staff of these establishments are often very helpful. Give them a ring, or pop in and tell them what you are interested in. You will often find that the history of the building helps you to decide how it should be furnished or equipped. In later chapters we shall be looking closely at some of this archive material and the uses that can be made of it.

course, built in much larger numbers, and in many styles. Town houses were divided into the four 'rates' mentioned earlier, to house the nobility while in town (I), ship owners and merchants of some standing (II), clerks and men of the cloth (III), and 'mechanics' and superior craftsmen (IV). ('Inferior' craftsmen lived in rented rooms in older houses, or in simple one-roomed cottages out of town.) The diagram below, depicting the four rates, is based on numerous conflicting accounts, but I hope it gives a reasonable consensus of the facts.

TOWN HOUSES

In later chapters we will explore some of the more unusual types of house to be found in the eighteenth century; but conventional houses were, of

SCHEMATIC DIAGRAMS OF TERRACED HOUSES
as stipulated in the Building Act of 1774

Rate and grade of house	First rate, 'great'	Second rate, 'large'	Third rate, 'medium'	Fourth rate, 'small'
Value	over £850	£300–850	£150–300	up to £150
Size	over 900 sq ft	500–900sq ft	350–500 sq ft	up to 350 sq ft
Occupants	gentry	ship owners and merchants	clerks and men of the cloth	superior craftsmen and 'mechanics'

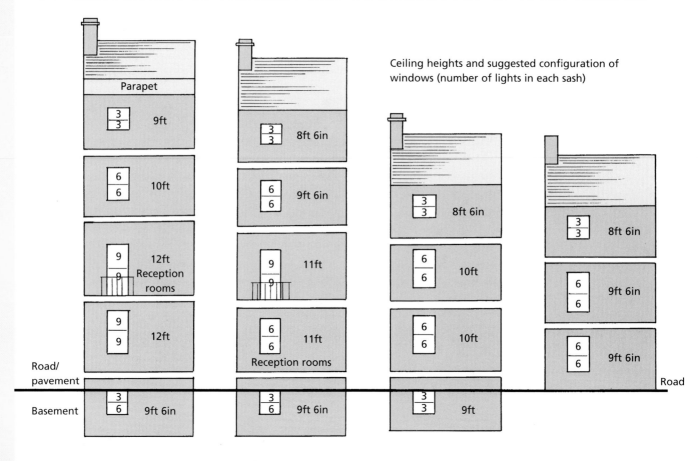

Ceiling heights and suggested configuration of windows (number of lights in each sash)

The first rate had its reception rooms on the first floor, while the others had them (or it) on the ground floor. Rates I, II and III had basements and front service areas, while IV did not; and ceilings got lower as you went down the scale or up the stairs. Windows were larger in the best rooms, whatever floor they were on; the least important rooms had the smallest windows. A look at the stipulated room heights shows that most dolls' house ceilings are too low – so do take care when

THE GOTHIC BEDROOM
AT BRIDGE END HOUSE

This view shows the chimney breast (the fire basket by Neil Butcher is just visible) and, on the shelf above, Staffordshire figures by R. J. Williams. The walls are papered above the dado rail with a 'dragged' pattern produced by specialist makers Small Interiors.

building or buying your house. Remember that a 'small' house in the terms of the Act was large by comparison with some of the buildings described in Chapter 4, and that most working people lived in one-roomed cottages until well into the nineteenth century.

These town houses were built on restricted sites, but most had back gardens, however small. In the country, or in country towns, lower land prices allowed houses to spread out more, presenting fine frontages and with more space for kitchens and other offices. Bridge End House and Ladythorne (see pages 33–47 and 48–55) are from this latter group, the former in a small town and the latter in the country just outside it.

The first-rate Georgian town house has always been a firm favourite with dolls' house enthusiasts, yet for over 90% of the population in the eighteenth century such a house was only a dream. It was home – or second home – to only a privileged few, and in privileged circles it was taken for granted and often abused. While it is all well and good to have a dolls' house in this style, ask yourself who would have lived in it and how they

The Dining Room at Bridge End House

The carved wood fireplace from Bespaque is a little out of date for a house of c.1760, but would still have been acceptable in the provinces. The bold use of a paper border would be slightly unusual for a mid-Georgian room, but the screen next to the pot cupboard of the sideboard was not – otherwise a visit to the toilet might deny you the pleasure of the punch-line to the tale being spun at the table.

As in the reception/withdrawing room, the floor is of random hardwoods – a good flooring for a not too rich owner.

would have furnished it. Some of these fine houses were furnished purely for pleasure and entertaining: Lord Cholmondeley's house in Piccadilly, London (1740–50), was built to display his large collection of paintings and other works of art.

To help us find out more, most of the larger British towns and cities have a system of commemorative plaques – like the well-known 'blue plaques' of London – to tell us who lived, lodged, supped or died in a particular house, or where some important event or diabolical plot was hatched or enacted.

The conveniently compact city of Bath has a bronze plaque system, and was host in the eighteenth century to some of the most important people in the country. This makes it a good example to use when looking for the kind of people who would have lived in such fine houses. Those who wanted to be seen purchased fine houses in Bath

and other spa towns, but for the most part would only visit them 'in season'; for the rest of the year they would let the house to friends or relations, or people of the kind they wished to be associated with. The same held true of their hunting lodges and shooting boxes situated in deep rural locations: here they would spend a few days, starting on the 'Glorious Twelfth', then depart for home or for a spa town, leaving a depleted wine cellar and grouse moor to their friends.

The Bath architect John Wood the younger, who lived at 41 Gay Street, like most speculative builders of the day would have incorporated many of the latest innovations in his own house, which he would use like a present-day show house to impress his clients. It would be his home, his drawing office and his pride and joy – a suitable subject for any miniaturist. His more eccentric father was an even more interesting man, living a life of near-fictional quality at no. 24 Queen Street.

In 1796 the Duke of York, second son of George III and grandson of Frederick, Prince of Wales, rented no. 16 Royal Crescent for the huge sum of £5,000, for which he got a furnished house with stabling for 16 horses. A gambler and a womanizer, it was he who became the subject of the nursery rhyme 'The grand old Duke of York' – now here is a tenant to set you thinking.

Thomas Gainsborough lived and worked at 17 The Circus, where he would have had his lodgings, a studio and a gallery to display his works. Think of his clients – who were able to have their portraits painted by one of our greatest artists, when we have to make do with photographs – and you will begin to understand what fine houses these were. The accomplished William Hoare would produce a cheaper pastel portrait for the less wealthy visitor, or for those who did not have the time to sit for an oil. If it was a fine view or a landscape you required, you would visit Thomas Barker at Doric House to view his work.

Mrs Piozzi (formerly Mrs Hester Thrale) was a writer and local gossip of advanced years who 'lived in a state of rampant senility' at 8 Gay Street. She, like anyone in Georgian society, could behave as badly as she wished, but the furnishings of her home were of the finest workmanship. Contemporary engravings show some of the most ugly of human beings, yet the furniture on view is never ugly. How would you furnish and populate a house like this?

No. 19 New King Street was home to Sir William Herschel, a successful musician and composer who was often to be found conducting and playing the oboe in Linley's Pump Room. An amateur astronomer, he discovered Uranus in 1781 – the first such discovery for many centuries. His brilliance in this field of science earned him the title of Court Astronomer to George III. His home is now the William Herschel Museum, and would make a truly fascinating project for a miniaturist.

The playwright Richard Brinsley Sheridan lived at 9 New King Street. He married Elizabeth Linley, the 'maid of Bath'; reputed to be the most beautiful woman in England, she previously lived in Linley House (how grand can you get?), Pierrepont Place. This was a stormy relationship involving two marriages and two duels (not between husband and wife), yet it is one of our greatest love stories. A beautiful singer and a flamboyant writer living in a fine town house – how might it have been furnished?

This is just a small selection of the rich and famous who lived in fine houses in one particular town; but it serves to show that these large town houses were not the homes of average people with 2.5 children and a dog. They belonged to people of standing who lived life with flair – with a passion that must have been reflected in the way they decorated and furnished their homes.

First learn all you can about the inhabitants of your intended dolls' house, then furnish it for *them* and that will give *you* great pleasure.

BRIDGE END HOUSE, A PROVINCIAL TOWN HOUSE

My own current project is Bridge End House, Berwick-upon-Tweed, Northumberland. This was chosen because it has an attractive front and is of a countrified Georgian type, peculiar to small provincial towns remote from high society. It is a house of rustic charm that I had passed many times on my way over the old bridge to deliver lectures, but had never stopped to look at; now I am engrossed. There may be just such a house in a town that you know, which you would like to shrink to grace your lounge; it would give you greater pleasure than television and, like the wealthy ladies of Georgian society, you could entertain and enthral your guests with it.

Details of the model's construction are given on the following pages, and views of the interior can be found throughout the book. It is made with two opening doors at the front and one at the back. The portico, with the music room on the first floor, is made separately and is detachable to give access to the hall and landing. The model was made to my specifications by the Camno Workshop, and is furnished with miniatures from a wide variety of sources. The décor is consistent with a date of around 1760 – bearing in mind that a provincial house such as this is unlikely to have reflected the very latest developments in metropolitan taste.

BRIDGE END HOUSE
BERWICK-UPON-TWEED

The photographs of the real Bridge End House (now Tweedmouth House Nursing Home) appear by courtesy of the present owners, Mr and Mrs C. Thomlinson. When working from photographs, take pictures from all angles, recording as much detail as you can.

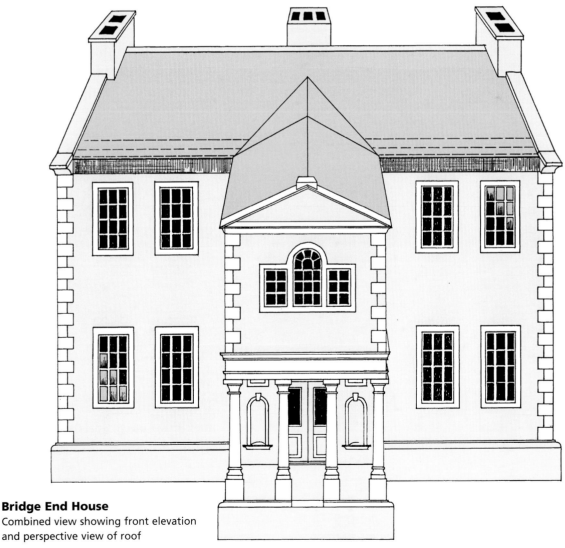

Bridge End House
Combined view showing front elevation
and perspective view of roof

Bridge End House

Perspective views of ground floor and first floor showing
layout and dimensions for 1/12 scale

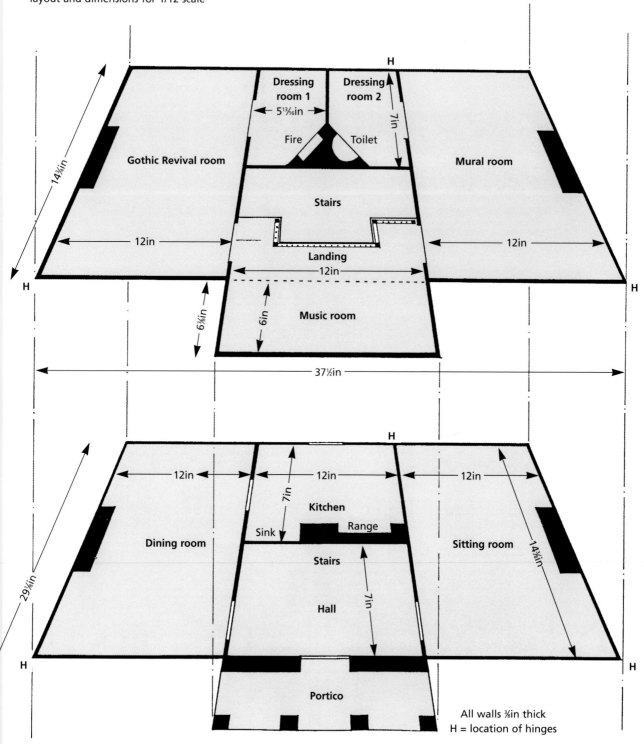

Dressing room 1

Dressing room 2

5¹³⁄₁₆in

7in

Fire

Toilet

Gothic Revival room

Mural room

14⅜in

Stairs

12in

12in

Landing

12in

6⅜in

6in

Music room

37½in

Kitchen

12in

12in

12in

7in

Sink

Range

Dining room

Sitting room

Stairs

14⅜in

29⅛in

Hall

7in

Portico

All walls ⅜in thick
H = location of hinges

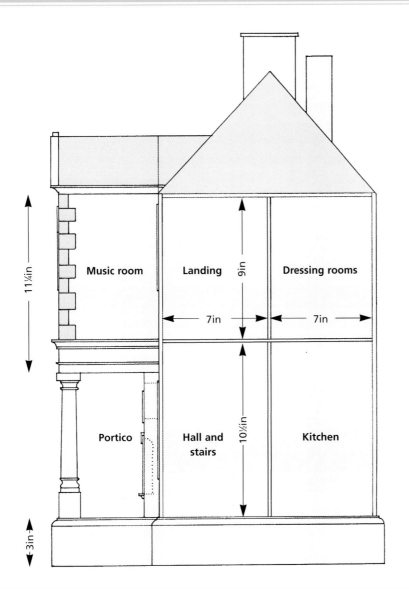

Bridge End House
Side elevation of portico and
cross section of body of house

11¼in

Music room

Landing

9in

Dressing rooms

7in   7in

Portico

Hall and
stairs

10½in

Kitchen

3in

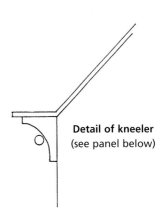

Detail of kneeler
(see panel below)

KNEELERS

The gabled ends of a building had to be protected against water penetration from the roof. In less refined buildings the slates or tiles above the gable were tilted towards the main body of the roof to encourage rainwater to run that way and not down the wall. More polite houses used coping stones or 'skews' to cover the top of the wall, but these were liable to slip unless they were firmly held in place. They could be secured by metal clamps, or by large stones known as 'kneelers' or 'skew putts', which became a vehicle for decoration from an early time.

Simple examples were just large rectangular blocks of stone bonded into the wall head; others incorporated the lowest coping stone as part of their design. The decoration of kneelers is as a rule quite simple, but now and again a true craftsman has been at work and emblems, perhaps indicating the family trade, are to be seen. The barrel-shaped one may have belonged to a wine merchant.

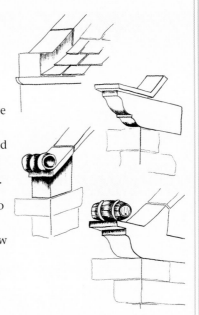

Bridge End House
List of cut parts (not to scale)

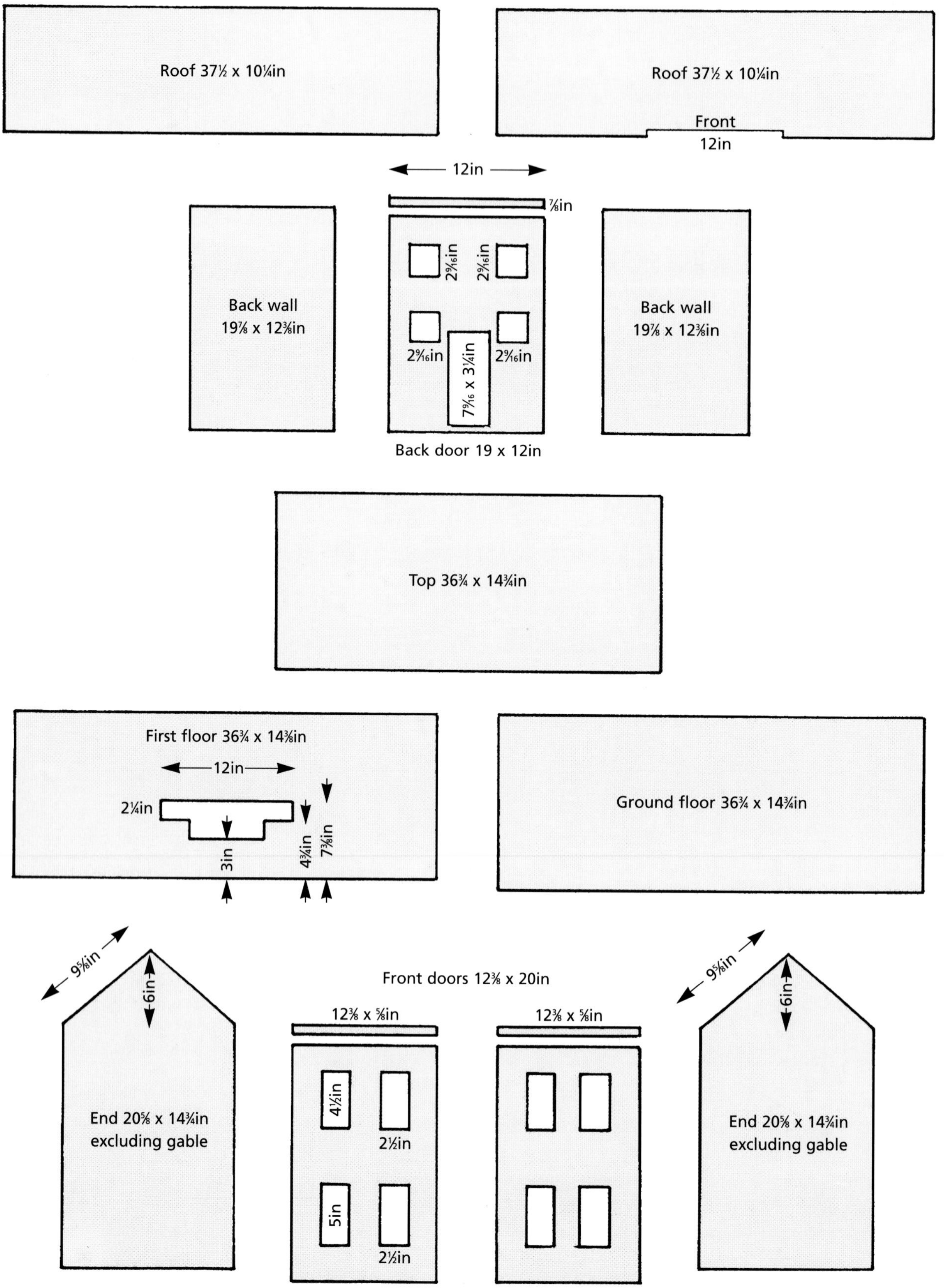
Roof 37½ x 10¼in
Roof 37½ x 10¼in
Front
12in
12in
⅞in
Back wall
19⅞ x 12⅜in
2 9/16in
2 9/16in
2 9/16in
2 9/16in
7 7/16 x 3¼in
Back door 19 x 12in
Back wall
19⅞ x 12⅜in
Top 36¾ x 14¾in
First floor 36¾ x 14⅜in
12in
2¼in
3in
4¾in
7⅜in
Ground floor 36¾ x 14¾in
9⅝in
6in
End 20⅝ x 14¾in
excluding gable
Front doors 12⅜ x 20in
12⅜ x ⅝in
4½in
2½in
5in
2½in
12⅜ x ⅝in
9⅝in
6in
End 20⅝ x 14¾in
excluding gable

Inside walls

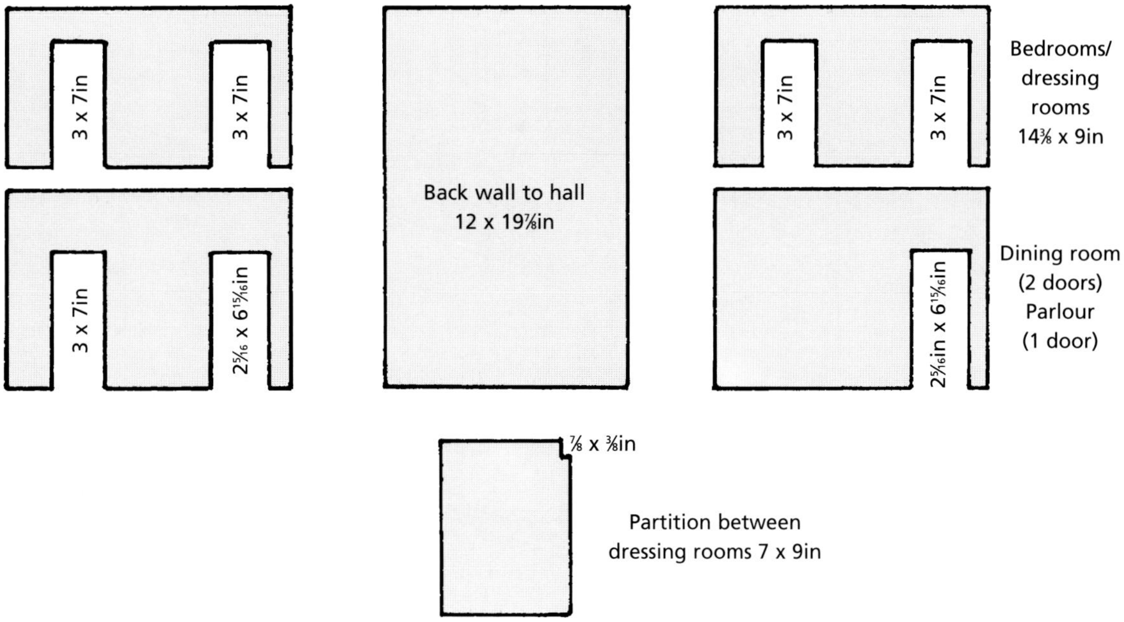
3 x 7in
3 x 7in
Back wall to hall
12 x 19⅞in
3 x 7in
3 x 7in
Bedrooms/
dressing
rooms
14⅜ x 9in
3 x 7in
2 5/16 x 6 15/16in
2 5/16in x 6 15/16in
Dining room
(2 doors)
Parlour
(1 door)
⅞ x ⅜in
Partition between
dressing rooms 7 x 9in

Portico

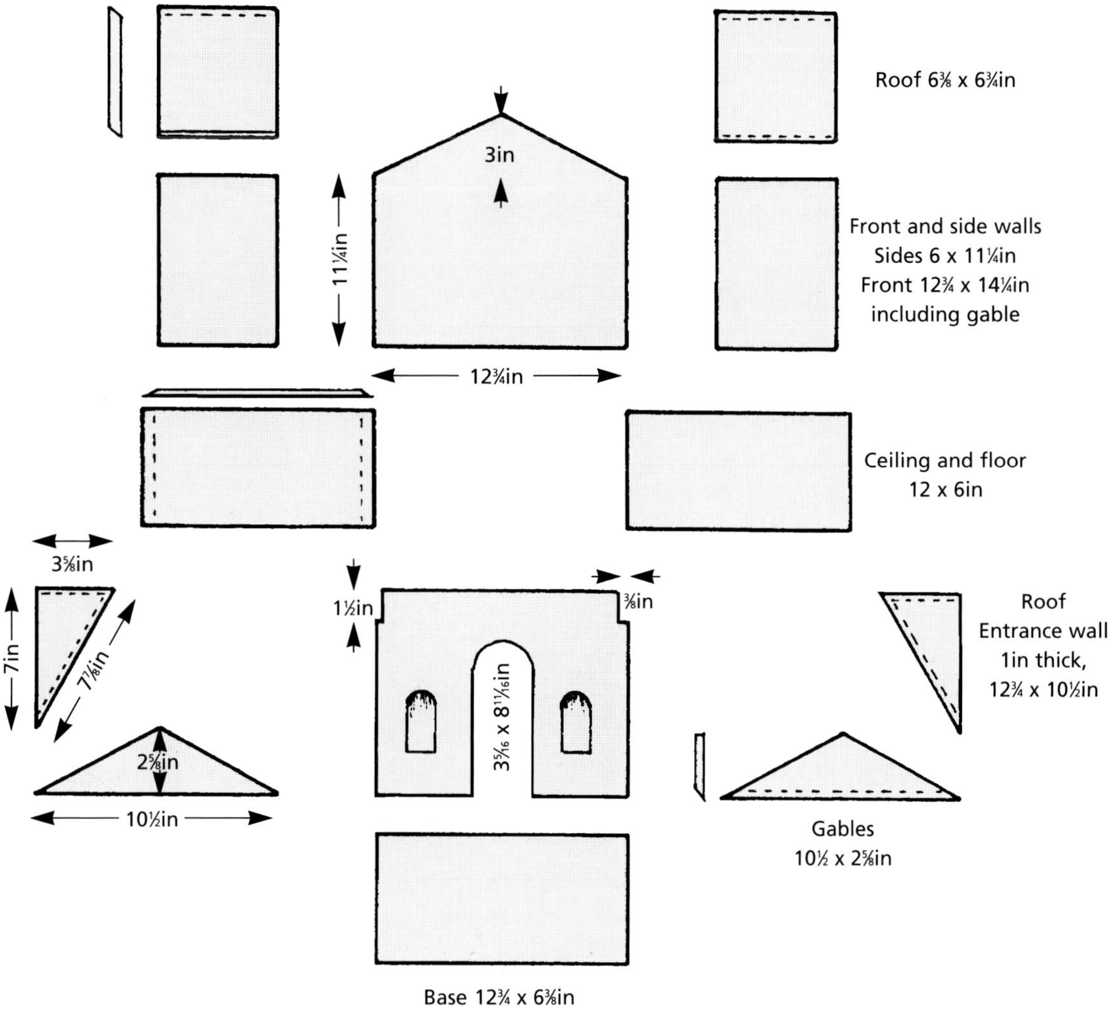
Roof 6⅜ x 6¾in
3in
11¼in
Front and side walls
Sides 6 x 11¼in
Front 12¾ x 14¼in
including gable
12¾in
Ceiling and floor
12 x 6in
3⅝in
7in
7⅞in
2⅝in
10½in
1½in
⅜in
3 5/16 x 8 11/16in
Roof
Entrance wall
1in thick,
12¾ x 10½in
Gables
10½ x 2⅝in
Base 12¾ x 6⅜in

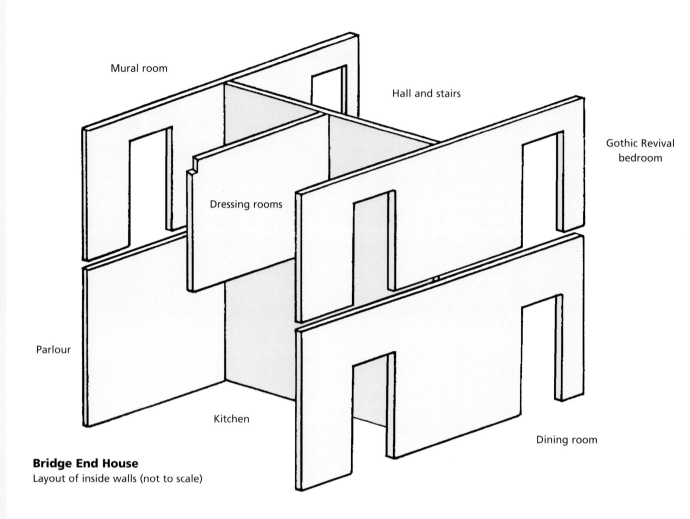

Mural room

Hall and stairs

Gothic Revival bedroom

Dressing rooms

Parlour

Kitchen

Dining room

Bridge End House
Layout of inside walls (not to scale)

Glue and nail all parts in the following order:

1 Working from the back of the house, fix the gable ends to the floor, using the back panels to act as braces and hold them firmly in place. It may be worth using a temporary brace to ensure that the two back panels are in the same plane.

2 Next fix the first-floor ceiling, then leave all glued joints to set prior to starting on the interior walls.

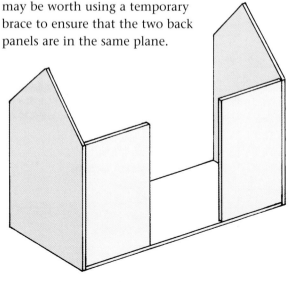

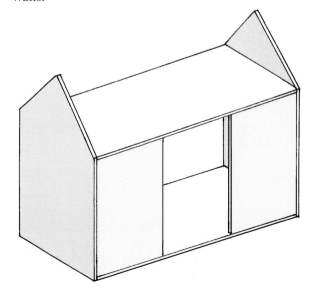

3 Now working from the front, insert the internal walls to the dining room and parlour. Use the back wall to the hall as a template to ensure the correct location.

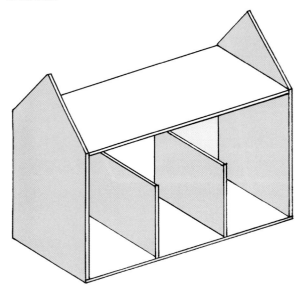

4 Slide the first floor part way in and insert in the hole left for the stairwell the panel which forms the back wall to the hall. Push both parts home, then glue and nail.

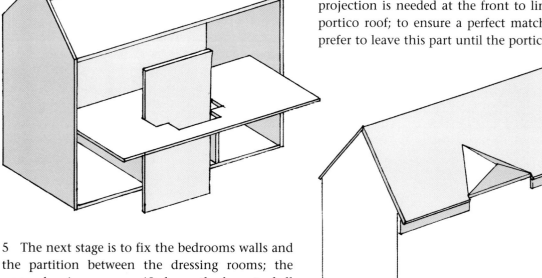

5 The next stage is to fix the bedrooms walls and the partition between the dressing rooms; the upper drawing on page 40 shows the layout of all the internal partitions, with the first floor and ceiling omitted for clarity. The lintel for the hinged door at the back, which gives access to the kitchen and dressing rooms, should now be fitted to the underside of the first-floor ceiling, between the partition walls and flush with the outside. Now fit, on the outside, the strips which will form the lintels for the two hinged doors at the front.

The doors can be left off until the bulk of the interior fitting and decoration is well advanced, but this is up to you. When you do decide to fit them, use lengths of piano hinge, fitting it to the door first, then to the body of the house.

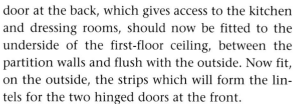

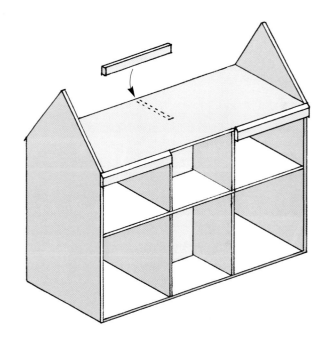

6 The main roof should now be fitted. A small projection is needed at the front to link it to the portico roof; to ensure a perfect match, you may prefer to leave this part until the portico is ready.

The next major step is to make up the portico. A small porch could be built onto one of the front doors of the house, but the portico of Bridge End House is too large for this treatment and is best made as a separate unit.

7 Having first made the doorway and arched recesses in the 1in-thick (25mm) front entrance wall, fix this to the base of the portico and to the floor of the music room.

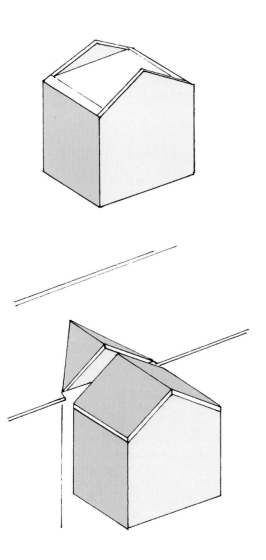

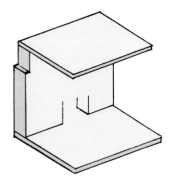

8 Now fit the side and front walls of the music room, making sure they are in alignment with the partition walls in the main body of the house. You may wish to support the portico at this stage by tacking a temporary stay from the front to the base.

FINISHING OFF

The main part of the house is now complete and you have the pleasure of adding the finishing touches which add so much to its character.

The bottom edge of the portico is at the moment only ⅜in (10mm) thick, and needs to be at least ¾in (19mm) to take the capitals of the supporting columns. I achieved this by inserting three strips of wood to thicken the part of the walls which lies below the music room floor, as shown on the opposite page. It is best to decorate the ceiling inside the portico at this stage, before the columns get in the way.

The columns at the front of the house are an important element and can be made up with broom shank and blocks of wood – or you may wish to have them turned by a friend with a lathe. Good ready-made ones are available from some miniaturists' shops, but you will still have to make

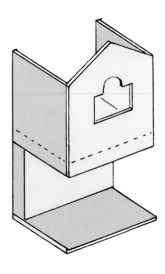

9 You are now ready to fit the music room ceiling, followed by the inner gable and roof. When these are set, line up the whole assembly with the front of the house and fit the additional section of roof that ties the portico in to the house.

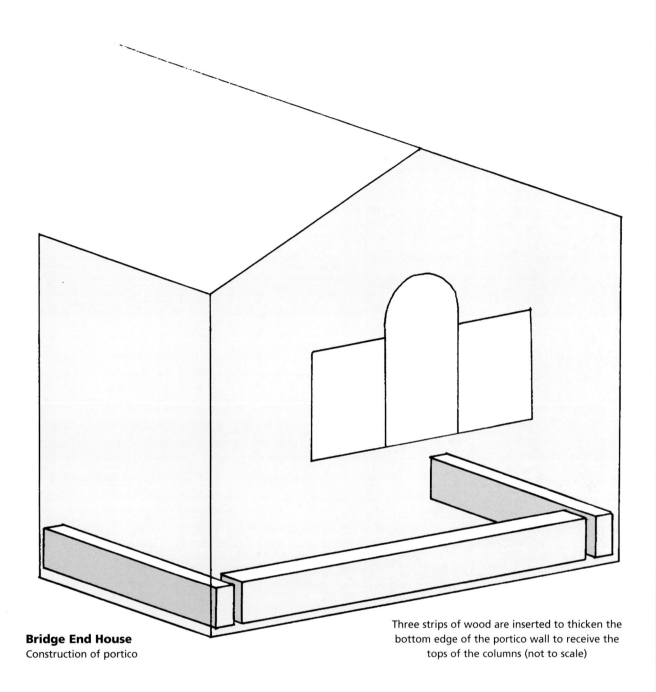

Bridge End House
Construction of portico

Three strips of wood are inserted to thicken the
bottom edge of the portico wall to receive the
tops of the columns (not to scale)

the bases and capitals to build up the appropriate
height – you should not find this too difficult,
compared to what you have done so far.

The ½in (13mm) moulding on the portico
serves to hold the doors closed, so it needs to be
made ⅜in (10mm) shorter than the portico sides to
allow for the thickness of the doors.

The real house stands on quite a high plinth of
five steps, so for the model I made a strong
platform with brass carrying handles. This gives
the house greater impact, and the handles make
life easier when it comes to spring cleaning. The
materials used were 3in x 1in (76 x 25mm) dressed

wood, ⅜in (10mm) plywood and ⅜in moulding.
Remember that the plinth will need to be ¾in
(19mm) larger than the ground floor of the house
in all directions.

Unusually for Berwick, Bridge End House is rendered, and has been since it was built. Most of the
Georgian houses in the town are built using pink
sandstone dressed to a high standard. The quoins
(see panel on page 44) are made from material ⅛in
(3mm) thick, the small ones measuring ¾in
(19mm) square and the larger ones ¾ x 1½in (19 x
38mm). Good-quality card can be used, and it is
best to paint them prior to gluing them on.

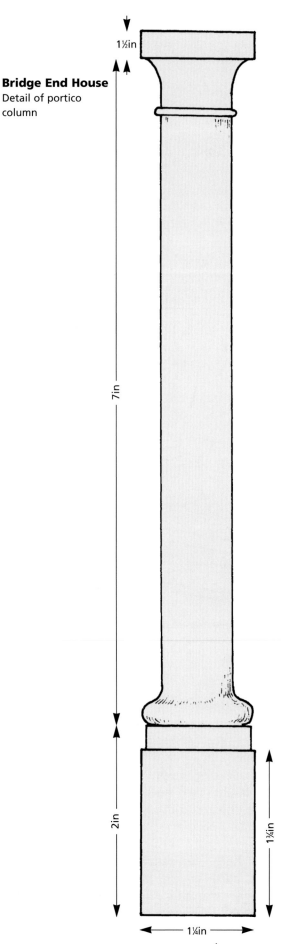

Bridge End House
Detail of portico
column

1½in

7in

2in

1¾in

1¼in

QUOINS OR CORNER 'STONES'

A large number of nice houses are not quite
what they seem: the 'bricks' are not bricks but
tiles, and the large quoins and decorative
mouldings are painted wood rather than stone.
No. 33 High Street, Lewes, East Sussex, has real
bricks on its main front but, to cut down on the
brick tax, the gables are of brick tiles. While
these so-called 'mathematical' tiles helped
overcome the tax problem, they made finishing
off the corners difficult, so the builders did what
miniaturists have to do: they made their quoins
out of wood, painted to look like stone.
On a brick house the quoins would be three or
four bricks high, the smaller ones being square
and the larger ones a double square. Those used
on Bridge End House are based on the three-
brick unit, which makes them 9 x 9in (23 x
23cm) and 18 x 9in (46 x 23cm) – in 1/12 scale,
¾ x ¾in (19 x 19mm) and 1½ x ¾in (38 x 19mm).
The use of tiles and weatherboarding was given
an incentive by the brick tax of 1784, but just as
quickly faded away when it was repealed in
1850. Remember this when choosing the
covering for your house.

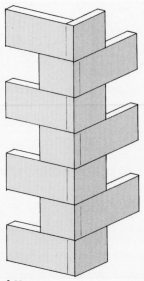

Bridge End House
Quoins

The shorter pieces are square, the longer ones two
squares long. Overlap at the corner as shown

MAKING THE STAIRS

The stairs rise from the back right-hand corner of the hall, and start with a small platform or dais in the corner, ⅜in (10mm) thick. This is followed by nine steps rising up against the back wall, then the last four steps are winders, turning through 90° to reach the landing.

The ⅜in dais can be cut from plywood. The rest of the steps are all ¾in (19mm) high, and the straight ones have ¾in treads. These can be made from a 3ft 6in or 1m length of 1½ x ¾in (38 x 19mm) dressed timber, which can be purchased from most do-it-yourself stores.

Start by cutting nine lengths at 2¼in (57mm), then glue and nail them together, overlapping them to give the required tread width of ¾in (19mm). All nails should be on the underside, as in the diagram. The top four steps, turning the corner, require more care and should be cut as in the diagram, allowing an overlap so that you can glue them together. The last one is the most important,

as it has to marry up with the landing. Don't rush, and take care.

The underside of the stairs will be quite rough and unsightly, and should be boxed in, with a cupboard or arched recess built into the void.

It was rare for Georgian stairs to have carpets, so finish them with a good wood stain or paint them to look like stone. Applying a simple moulding to each riser will give your stairs a professional look.

MAKING THE WINDOWS

All the windows have a bold stone dressing or frame to them, made from ⅛in thick wood ⅖in wide (3 x 10.5mm) glued to the outside.

The arched section of the window above the entrance may be easiest cut from one piece, by fretwork, to get a nice semicircular head to it. All other glazing bars should be made from ⅛in (3mm) square-section material, and when the frames are complete they should be glued flush with the outside face of the wall.

Bridge End House
Plan of stairs
Make up in three stages:
1 the dais
2 the nine straight steps
3 the four turning steps
Dimensions are for 1/12 scale

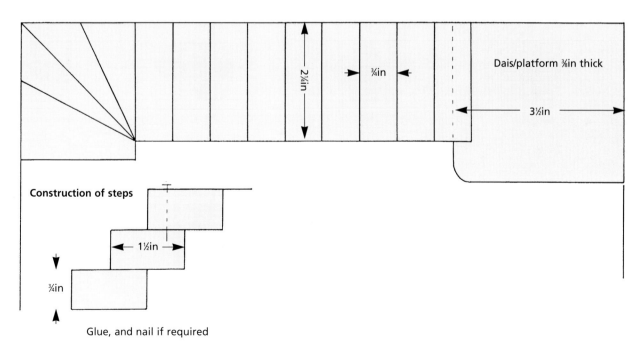

Construction of steps

Glue, and nail if required

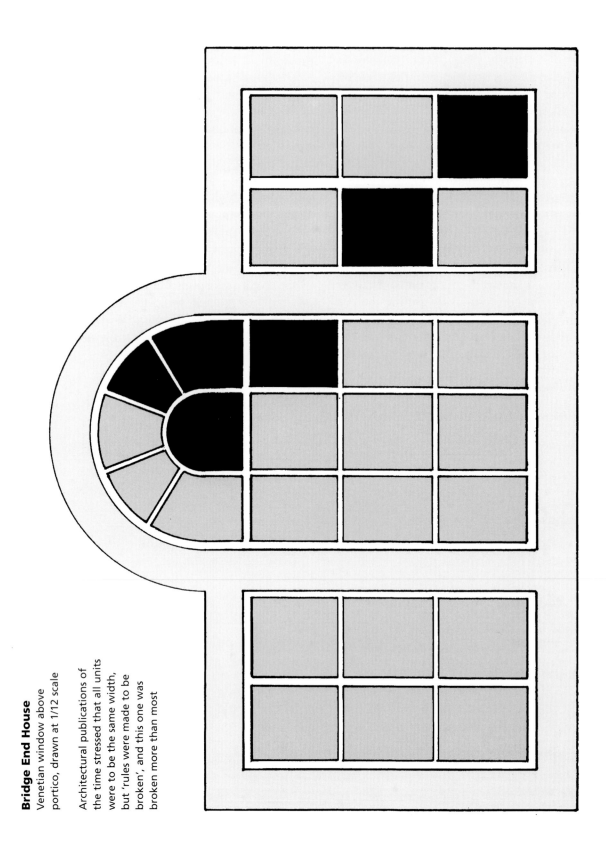

Bridge End House
Venetian window above
portico, drawn at 1/12 scale

Architectural publications of
the time stressed that all units
were to be the same width,
but 'rules were made to be
broken', and this one was
broken more than most

The portico of Bridge End House

The portico is here shown detached from the house, revealing the front door and the music room with its Venetian window. This is the only window in the house to have curtains (not shown in the photograph), and they would be non-working ones, just for decoration. On the table is a silver candelabra (in eighteenth-century usage, *candelabrum*) from Simply Silver; the table itself is a copy by Peter Lane of one owned by the author. The floor is of imported red oak planks of a uniform width, and is intended to impress.

CHAPTER THREE

RESEARCHING YOUR MODEL

Field work • Ladythorne House • Northumberland farmhouse of 1788
Penparcau tollhouse • Slate worker's cottage

Miniaturists fall into three main groups, and many progress through all of these to achieve their ultimate ambition. First are those who work from kits, or buy commercially produced houses; second, those who buy the more specialist models made by craftsmen in much smaller runs. The third stage, which may become an all-consuming passion, is making a one-off replica of a house of your choice, selected either for its good-looking frontage or, perhaps, for its family associations. The following chapters will look at the latter group – the one-off – and I hope they will give you the courage to take this step.

We will look at various ways of gaining the information required to build an accurate copy of a period house: working from photographs and drawings made in the field, using original drawings, and even using written accounts to draw a plan and elevation.

FIELD WORK

The first step in researching a house which appeals to you is to take photographs: good general views from all angles, and more detailed snaps of windows, doors, front steps, roof, chimneys and any gates or period ironwork. (It is advisable to ask the owner's permission first – otherwise your interest might be thought suspicious.) If you like drawing, then make sketches, paying attention to the details. Counting the number of bricks in the height of a window or door will help you in scaling the house down, especially if you have measured one of the bricks; or you might prefer just to work to the standard brick size of 9 x 3 x 4in

(228 x 76 x 102mm), allowing ½in (13mm) for mortar. With Bridge End House I worked from photographs (the front door is a ready-made one, and this dictated the size of the other elements on the front of the house), but the drawings of Ladythorne House on pages 50–1 show what I mean.

First draw a rough outline, with notes on the number of bricks and the bond used in various parts of the house (see the drawings opposite). Follow this with details of any stone dressing to the windows, door heads, tops of walls, etc. A mixture of photographs, drawings and notes is useful, but do whatever you are best at. From these you can work out the size of the completed model at the scale of your choice, and if your lounge can take it, then this is the one for you.

LADYTHORNE HOUSE, NORTHUMBERLAND

Ladythorne House is Early Georgian, with a date of 1721 on one of its ceilings; it was originally used as a shooting box in season, so it could be furnished and equipped as such, or as a comfortable home of the period.

Though the roof of Ladythorne is of slate now, it would have been of local tiles when first built. At this time it was normal for the roof to be high and steep, but the exceptionally steep slope in this case tells us that it was built by someone who was used to thatched roofs, which require a quick run-off for rain. (Roofs were discussed in more detail on pages 27–8.)

The chimney stacks, as in most old houses, have been rebuilt several times and do not match, so we must choose whether to follow the drawing or make them both the same. My own feeling is that they would have had stone dressing at the top to match the parapet.

To convert my sketches of Ladythorne to approximate full-size dimensions you must count the bricks, then multiply this figure by 9½in

(241mm) for the length of one brick plus mortar or 3½in (89mm) for the height. (The sizes of old bricks are variable, so if you wish you may make them anything from 9 to 11in (228–279mm) long.)

As Ladythorne is 50 bricks wide, the width comes out at 475in (12.065m), or at 1/12 scale, 39½in (1.003m or 1003mm).

To work out the height will require two basic calculations: one to give us the height from the ground floor to the eaves or ceilings of the bedrooms, and another to give the height of the roof above this. Counting bricks again gives us 75¼ bricks from the base of the parapet to the top of the stone plinth the house stands on. The resulting calculation makes this 263⅜in (6.69m) high (assuming each brick is 3½in high) or, at 1/12 scale, 22in (559mm). The height to the ridge of the roof from the foot of the parapet is 42½ bricks, which gives 148in (3.76m) or, at 1/12 scale, 12¼in (311mm).

The parapet itself is 18½ bricks high, plus an allowance of 5 bricks for the height of the stone base and coping stones, so we have a total parapet height equivalent to 23½ bricks, giving us 82¼in

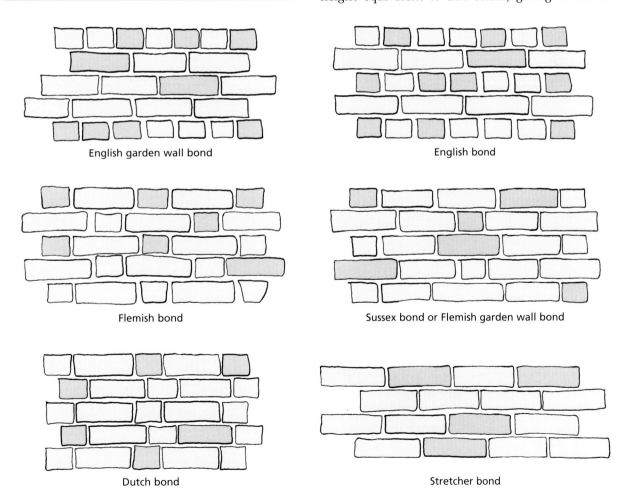

English garden wall bond

English bond

Flemish bond

Sussex bond or Flemish garden wall bond

Dutch bond

Stretcher bond

LADYTHORNE HOUSE
NEAR BERWICK-UPON-TWEED

The field drawing includes notes to remind me of the various details so that a 'proper' drawing could be made later. The numbers on the drawing indicate the number of bricks in each part of the elevation. Take photographs, make sketches and notes to help you remember details.

The finished drawing shows all the bricks in place. Bricks can be as good as a tape measure, as long as you know the size of one, and help you get the scale and proportions correct.

Field drawing

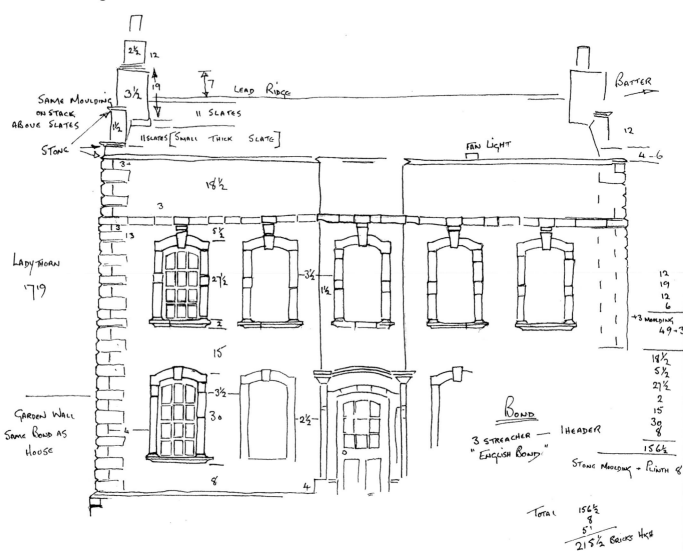

(2.09m) full size, or 6⅞in (174mm) in 1/12 scale. The stone plinth the house stands on is two steps high – say 1½in (38mm) in 1/12 scale – but a higher one would make the model more imposing.

How deep to make the house depends on the space you have to display the model, or on how much room you require in it to display your miniatures; a good minimum size in 1/12 scale would be 14–15in (355–380mm) deep.

Internal arrangements are now up to you; your imagination is your main tool, but be guided by contemporary documents when you furnish it (more on this in Chapter 5).

CONSTRUCTION OF LADYTHORNE HOUSE

The diagrams overleaf show the basic dimensions and method of constructing the house. Note that:

- The front elevation is based on the calculations given on page 49, with the projection of the central bay being just the thickness of one piece of ⅜in (9mm) ply fixed to the front.

- The base could be made slightly greater in length and depth than the main part of the house. It could be constructed as a stand, fitted with legs of a type befitting the period – either cabriole legs as used on Georgian furniture, or in a rusticated architectural style; the choice is yours, and may depend on your own décor.

Finished drawing

Ladythorne House
Details of model construction

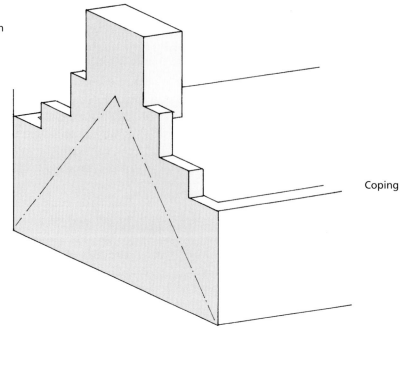

Coping

Gable and parapet

Wall heads are 1in thick and should be built up in two layers with a cavity, as shown in the detail below

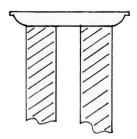

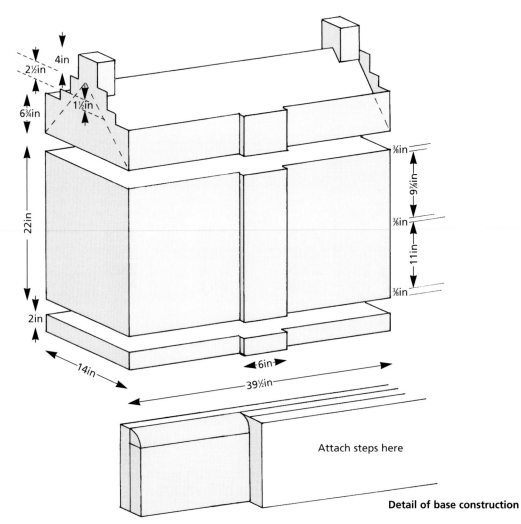

4in

2½in

6¾in

1½in

⅜in

9⅝in

⅜in

11in

⅜in

22in

2in

14in

6in

39½in

Attach steps here

Detail of base construction

- The parapet and roof section are of the same plan as the body of the house; the gable ends show a Dutch influence and are stepped.

- The shape of the gable end and the pitch of the roof depend on how deep you decide to make the model, but the vertical measurements hold true no matter what you decide. If space only permits a shallow model, you might choose to make only the front slope of the roof.

- The short quoins or corner stones are 1¼ bricks long by 3 high, while the long ones are 3 bricks long by 3 high; in 1/12 scale this converts to ¾in high x 1in long (19 x 25mm) or ¾in high x 2²⁄₁₂in long (19 x 59mm) respectively. The string course at the base of the parapet is also ¾in (19mm) high.

- The windows come out at 5 bricks wide by 24 high, or, in 1/12 scale, 4 x 7in (102 x 178mm), excluding the sills but including all other stonework.

- The central bay with the door in it is 8 bricks wide, or 6³⁄₈in (161mm), the door complete with its surround being 35 bricks high, or 10¼in (260mm).

Ladythorne House
Quoins at 1/12 scale

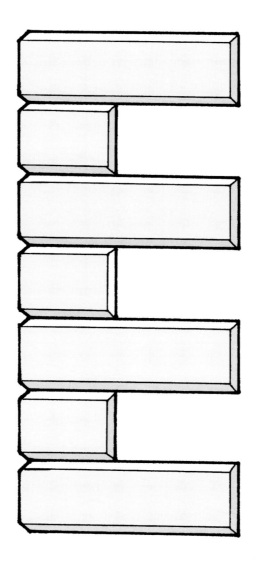

Ladythorne House
Windows at 1/12 scale

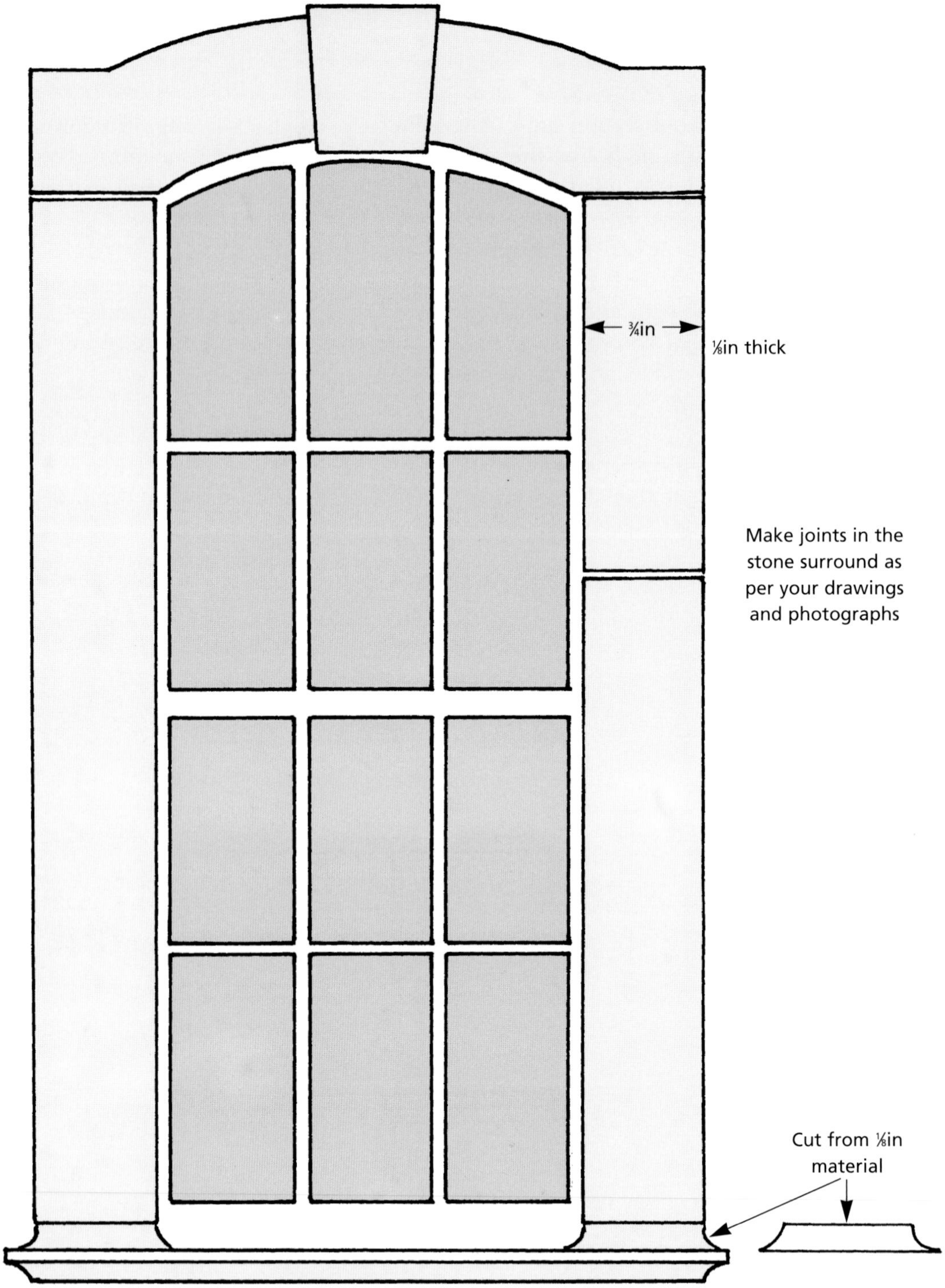

← ⅜in →

⅛in thick

Make joints in the
stone surround as
per your drawings
and photographs

Cut from ⅛in
material

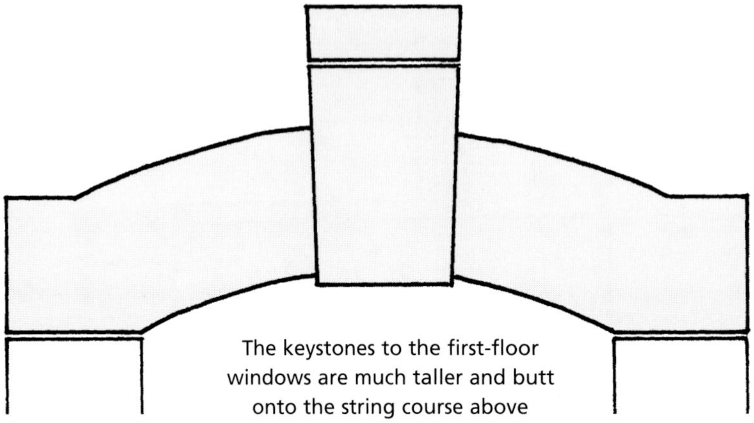

The keystones to the first-floor
windows are much taller and butt
onto the string course above

Ladythorne House
Sketch of front door

OUTSIDE AND INSIDE

The exterior of a house can give off many clues as to what is out of sight behind the walls. For instance, a town house of three bays with the front door to one side will have the hall and stairs on that side, rather than central. Look at the windows above the door: while they may be exactly the same size and shape as the others, they may not be draped in the same way. The curtains can tell us which windows belong to the same room. As a rule, the various landings above the hall will either have different curtains from the other windows, or none at all. If the curtains match across the width of the house, then it may be that the stairs rise from the side of the house, or are at the back. Iron bars at street level may be for security, but on a higher floor they could indicate a room intended for small children, perhaps a nursery.

Chimneys tend to be at either end of a house, but one stack may be larger than the other, or show signs of rebuilding; this points to greater use, and suggests that the kitchen is below. In some instances a chimney may be seen rising over the ridge from the back of the house, and this again may indicate the position of the kitchen, bake-house or brewhouse.

Houses with a central door may have equal numbers of windows either side of it, but one side may still be wider than the other; this again points to the kitchen being on the wider side. A quick look at the chimney stack above will confirm this.

Chimneys on Early Georgian houses were on the outside of the gable wall; this means that on the inside there will be no chimney breast, and therefore no recesses either side with shell hoods or display shelves. Even when chimney stacks began to be built on the inside, the larger kitchen stack still tended to be on the outside, and is much more conspicuous than the other.

The main reception rooms have the best and most important windows, so in a town house you should be able to tell whether these rooms are on the ground floor or the first floor, just by the size of the windows. When they were on the first floor, it was not unusual for the ground floor to be used as the place of work, the studio or offices of the owner.

In the elegant town houses of the eighteenth century it was unusual to have a special room set aside as a dining room. Instead, the smaller of the ground-floor rooms would have contained an elegant folding table, or in most cases a gate-leg table, which could be brought into use when required.

In smaller homes it was not unusual for the upper floor to have no windows, as in the case of Robert Adam's cottages at Lowther mentioned on page 9. The existence of this type of upper floor is indicated by a higher than normal area of wall between the window head and the roof gutters.

A coal hole in the pavement in front of a town house may deliver coal to a store under the road itself; but if there is no service area the coal will drop to a store at the same end of the house as the kitchen.

Lastly, do not rely on stench pipes and other drainage pipes from bathrooms and elsewhere; these are modern, and provide no indication of the original layout of a Georgian house without running water. Be aware of later modifications and don't jump to conclusions.

The semi-detached houses of the last 70 years show little variation in their basic plan, and the same was true for most Georgian town houses.

AN EXAMPLE: LORD CHOLMONDELEY'S HOUSE

The complete set of plans still exists for Lord Cholmondeley's house in Piccadilly (c.1730), but even if we had only the front elevation (opposite) to work from we would still have many clues to its interior layout.

It has the usual basement and front service area, so the kitchens and other facilities are at the bottom of the house, below the pavement level. Where is the kitchen fire or range? The evidence of the chimneys would suggest it is on the right-hand side, as that stack is a little wider than the other.

The position of the front door is unusual: it is not to one side or in the centre, but one bay in from the end. This admits of several possibilities. The hall may be two bays wide – that is, half the width of the house – with the window on the right opening onto it. This would make an elegant space with room for a fine staircase. On the other hand, there might be a reception room to either side of the door, one large and one small.

The first-floor windows are taller than the ground-floor ones, which tells us that the grandest rooms are on that floor, with bedrooms above.

CHOLMONDELEY HOUSE, 94 PICCADILLY, LONDON
(© British Architectural Library, RIBA, London)

▬▬▬

This view is of the main elevation of an 'average' (as stipulated in the Buildings Act) terraced house built for the third Earl of Cholmondeley. It is from a complete set of drawings by an unknown architect, held by the RIBA, which is a rare survival. From details like these you could build a house to any scale from 1/24 to full size.

In the roof are dormer windows. These may be for staff quarters, but in many houses they would be bedrooms for guests, the servants' quarters being at the back of the house, behind the kitchens. It was not unusual for servants to sleep in the kitchen – either in settle beds or in cupboards under the stairs – or above the stables in the mews area at the back.

FARMHOUSE OF 1788 AT EWART, NORTHUMBERLAND

In the next chapter we will look at an eighteenth-century plan and how to make use of it; for now, let us approach house building from another angle: the land agent's survey. All estates of any size had an agent, and this survey of a farmhouse on the Ewart estate was written up by the agent for his master. The agricultural revolution was in full swing and new, more modern, farms were being built; this document gives us a privileged view, through the agent's eyes, of the outcome of this exciting development.

The survey is dated 1788, and the details in it tell us that the house was built in the then fashionable Gothic Revival style. All the front windows are wider than they are high, and the inclusion of mullions – which were out of fashion by this time – harks back to a 'Jacobethan' style much used in the Borders region and in areas where the 'great rebuild' came late. The farmhouse still exists, but no longer looks quite as it did at the time of the agricultural revolution. In addition to the land agent's written survey there is also a simple sketch plan in the Northumberland Record Office. All the basic dimensions would hold true no matter what architectural style was chosen, so now, armed with this information, you can have a major say in the outcome.

The house was large, but remember that these dimensions include walls of up to 2ft (61cm) thick, and we will be using only ⅜in (10mm) material – so work from internal measurements at all times. (If you particularly want to preserve the deep window embrasures typical of this kind of house, a double-skinned construction might be the answer.) The agent notes the dimensions of the east room, kitchen, passage and parlour, which gives the main measurements needed to reconstruct the ground floor of the front of the house:

The Dementions of the Farmhouse and Conviences [sic] att Ewart

East Room Lenth 15 feet By 16 feet Hight 8 feet 4in
Fier Place in Dot. [i.e. in the same] 4 feet High By
   3ft 10in
Closet on South Side 5 feet 4in By 1 foot 9in Depth
Three Shelvs in Dot.
Beed Closet in Dot 5 feet 1in on the North Sid.
Window in Dot. Hight 4 feet 10in By 5 feet 11in
Midile Menien [mullion] 7 inches
The Pan[e]s 1 foot By 9in
Door 6 feet 3in By 3 feet 1in

The Kichen 18 feet in Lenth by 16 feet
Fierplace in Dot 8 feet 4in Brea[d]th By 2ft 10in
   in Depth.
the window in Dot Hight 5 feet 5in By 7 feet,
The Side Windows Hight 4 feet 8in by 2 feet 8in
Pan[e]s in Froont Window 13in By 11in
Side Dot 12in By 8in
Plain Door in Dot 5 feet 11in By 2 feet 11in
Moulded Door in Dot. 5 feet 11½in,
The Passag 16 feet By 7ft 10in

Parlor 16 feet By 16 feet
West window 4 feet 8in By 2 feet 9in
South Dot 4 feet By 5 feet 9in,
The Menien and Panes the Same as Roome Window
The Fier place 4 feet Squair
The Door in Dot. 6 feet By 3 feet,
Height of yᵉ room 8[ft] 4[in]

Of the two doors to the kitchen, the plain one would have been to the 'east room' and the moulded one to the entrance hall.

FARMHOUSE OF 1788 AT EWART, NORTHUMBERLAND

An example of a house reconstructed from a detailed written description.

Original text of the land agent's survey (by courtesy of Northumberland Record Office, ref. ZBU B5/7/23). In addition to the passages transcribed on pages 58 and 60, there is a final paragraph detailing yards and outbuildings

The Dimentions of the Farmhouse and Convences att Ewart
East Room glenth 15 feet By 16 feet Hight 8 feet 4 in Fier Place in Dot. 4 feet By 8..10
Closet on South Side 5 feet 4 in By 1 foot 9 in Depth Three Shelves in Dot. Beed Closet in Dot
5 feet 1 in on the North Sid. Window in Dot Hight 4 feet 10 in By 5 feet 11 in Midile Menien
7 Inches The Pans 1 foot By 9 in Door 6 feet 8 in By 3 feet 1 in .– – – – – – – 'Mullion

The Kichen 18 feet in Lenth by 16 feet Fierplace in Dot 3 feet 4 in Breath By 2..10
in Depth. the window in Dot Hight 5 feet 6 in By 7 feet, The Side Windows Hight 4 feet 8 in
by 2 feet 8 in Pans in Froont Window 13 in By 11 in Side Dot 12 in By 8 in Plain Door
in Dot 5 feet 11 in By 2 feet 11 in Moulded Door in Dot. 6 feet 11½ in The Passag 16 feet By 9 ft 3 in

Parlor 16 feet By 16 feet West window 4 feet 8 in By 2 feet 9 in South Dot 4 feet
By 6 feet 9 in, The Menien and Panes the Same as Roome Window The Fier place
4 feet Squair The Door in Dot. 6 feet By 3 feet, Hight of y. room 8/4

Celler and Pantery Lenth 15 feet 10 in By 11 feet.. 9 in Hight 6 feet 8 inches
window 4 feet By 3 feet Door 6 feet 2 in By 3 feet; Back Kichen Lenth 14 feet By 11.. 8
Window 4 feet By 3 feet Door 6 feet 1 in By 3 feet 2 in, North Enterence 8 feet By 11 feet 8 in
Milchhouse 16 feet By 11 feet 8 in, Door 6 feet 2 in By 3 feet 2 in Window in Dot. 4 By 3 –
Hight to Celeing 6 feet 6 in; The whole Down Stairs, Hight of Front Wall 17 feet 2 inches

East Room Upstairs Lenth 16 feet By 16 feet 9 in East window 5 feet By 3 fe
South Dot 4 feet 10 in By 5 feet 10 in The Fier Place 3 feet 2 in By 3 feet Broad Door 6 fe
By 3 feet. Hight of Dot 4 feet 7 in. The Breck on North Sid of Fier Place 5 feet 7 in

Room Over Kichen Lenth 16 feet By 12 feet Fier Place Breath 3 feet 5 in
By 8 feet 2 in Window in Passag over the Kichen window Hight 4 feet 11 in By 5 feet 11 in
Door in Dot 6 feet 1 in By 3 feet Window on Landing of Staire 4 feet 11 in By 3 feet

Room Over Parlor Lenth 16 feet By 16 feet 1 in West window 4 feet 11 in
By 3 feet 2 in South Dot. Hight. 4 feet 11 in By 5 feet 10 in Fier Place Breath 3 feet 5 in
By 3 feet 2 in Closet in Dot 4 feet 11 in With Three Shelves & A Small Closet Above
Closet Door 5 feet 8 in By 2 feet 8 in Room Dot. 6 feet By 3 feet, The Gable and
Side walls is 2 feet Thick The Petitions is 4½ Inches Each, The Joistes and floor 7¼
Hight of North wall 7½ feet from the Door Sole, The Lenth of the House 64 feet By 20

The Lenth of East Stables 64 feet By 20 feet, The Hight of walls 7 feet 8 in
The Hight of Doors 6 feet 2½ By 3 feet 2 in Pricepe Roofe in these Stables, West Stable
Lenth 32 feet 2 in Hight of walls in Dot. 10 feet 8 in, Lenth of the Granery Above west
Hemmel 21 feet 9 in By 17 feet, Betwen the Pillers 8 feet 8 in, Lenth of The foor Barns
177 feet By 20 feet Lenth of Henn house 17 feet By 18 feet, Stackgarth 222 feet from the
Barns Westward and 194 North and South, The Cortyeard 215 feet East and west By
165 feet North and South, Hemmel 73 feet in Lenth By 19 feet, The Pillers 8 feet 8 in Apart
The Pillers 1 foot 10 in Squaere, from Pavement to Sprienger 3 feet 7 in & from the Pavement
to the Under Part of the Arches 6 feet 7 in, Lenth of Byers 103 feet 9 in By 18 feet 6 in.
The Dove Cot Lenth 18 feet 2 in By 18 feet, Hay Yeard Extend from Hemmel Eastward
88 feet 8 in from North to South 80 feet

The north wall was much lower than the front wall, because an outshot or lean-to at the back of the house enclosed the cellar-cum-pantry, back kitchen, north entrance and 'milchhouse' or dairy. These rooms can be included in your house or left off, depending on the space you have available.

> Celler and Pantery Lenth 15 feet 10in By 11 feet 8in
>
> Hight 6 feet 8 inches
>
> Window 4 feet By 3 feet
>
> Door 6 feet 2in By 3 feet;
>
> Back Kichen Lenth 14 feet By 11 feet 8in
>
> Window 4 feet By 3 feet
>
> Door 6 feet 1in By 3 feet 2in,
>
> North Enterence 8 feet By 11 feet 8in,
>
> Milchhouse 16 feet By 11 feet 8in,
>
> Door 6 feet 2in By 3 feet 2in
>
> Window in Dot. 4 fet By 3 feet
>
> Hight to Celeing 6 feet 6in;
>
> The whole Down Stairs,
>
> Hight of Front Wall 17 feet 2½ in[c]hes

Now we move upstairs and view the arrangements there; there is an east room, a room over the kitchen and a room over the parlour:

> East Room Upstairs Lenth 16 feet By 16 feet 1in
>
> East window 5 feet by 3 feet
>
> South Dot 4 feet 10in By 5 feet 10in
>
> The Fier Place 3 feet 2in By 3 feet Broad
>
> Door 6 feet By 3 feet.
>
> Hight of Dot [i.e. of room] 7 feet 7in,
>
> The Brick on North Sid of Fier Place 5 feet 7in

> Room Over Kichen Lenth 16 feet By 12 feet
>
> Fier Place Brea[d]th 3 feet 5in By 3 feet 2in
>
> Window in Passag over the Kichen window
> Hight 4 feet 11in By 5 feet 11in
>
> Door in Dot 6 feet 1in By 3 feet
>
> Window on Landing of Staire 4 feet 11in By 3 feet

> Room Over Parlor Lenth 16 feet By 16 feet 1in
>
> West window 4 feet 11in By 3 feet 2in
>
> South Dot. Hight. 4 feet 11in By 5 feet 10in
>
> Fier Place Brea[d]th 3 feet 5in By 3 feet 2in
>
> Closet in Dot 4 feet 11in With Three Shelves &
> a Small Closet Above
>
> Closet Door 5 feet 8in By 2 feet 8in
>
> Room Dot. 6 feet By 3 feet,
>
> The Gable and Side walls is 2 feet Thick.
>
> The Petitions is 4½ inches Each,

> The Joistes and floor 7¾
>
> Hight of North wall 7½ feet from the Door Sole,
>
> The Linth of the House 64 feet By 20ft

The room over the kitchen has no windows of its own, being served by the stair landing and a passage to the 'east room upstairs'. In a situation like this there may have been a row of small lights above the door, or a small window in the wall onto the passage. There would not have been a glass door, as these are extremely rare in Georgian houses. To have no windows in a bedroom may seem strange to us, but in industrial and rural dwellings of the period it was not at all unusual, since you worked all the hours of daylight and slept in the dark. Ventilation, the view and health considerations were low on the list of priorities in such homes. Many of the cottages in the newly built carpet-manufacturing village of Lowther, Cumbria, designed by Robert Adam in 1766, had no windows to the first floor: good taste thought it essential that the new village had elegant circuses, crescents, squares and open spaces, but a window in a bedroom was not important. (It may be of interest to note that Sir James Lowther, who had the village built, was married to Lady Mary Stuart, the daughter of Lord Bute who built Bute Town in Glamorgan, South Wales, which has similar houses; but we digress.)

Working from internal dimensions, as previously mentioned, a reasonable plan and elevations can be drawn; but before we get down to that, let us look at the 'small print', as it were, to find out what is interesting about this house.

We have already looked at the bedroom with no windows, but most important is the position of the kitchen in the centre of the house – the very heart of the home. It is the largest and most important room, with the parlour and east room set either side of it. In most rural homes this was the room where everything happened, and even at such a late date, and in a new and fashionable house, the fireplace is the traditional huge open type, 8ft 4in wide and 2ft 10in deep (2.54 x 0.81m). The height is not recorded, but we can be sure that there was no fancy modern range here but an open fire in an inglenook. The importance of this room was further stressed by placing a bay window here, rather than in the parlour as we would expect; this was a rare element in a Georgian house. While we miniaturists tend to favour the elegant town house with

Farmhouse of 1788

Elevation and plans based on the land agent's dimensions, showing traditional mullioned windows. If you do not have space to include the back kitchen and other facilities, the main block could stand alone. Dimensions are for 1/12 scale

17¾in

2in

Front elevation

Roof line
(Gothic pitch)

Back kitchen
etc.

7½in

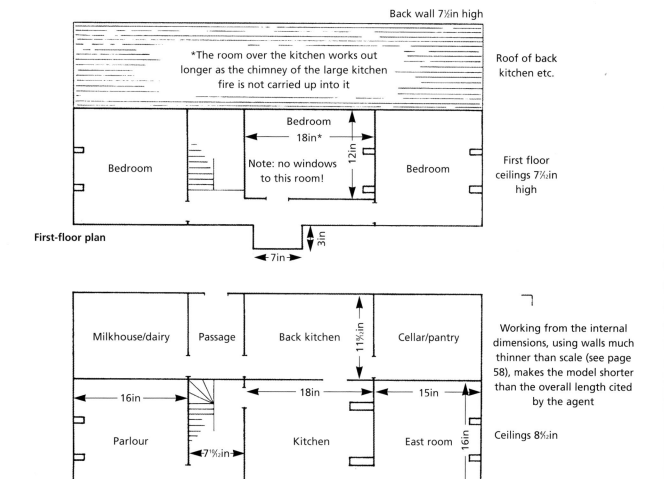

Back wall 7½in high

*The room over the kitchen works out longer as the chimney of the large kitchen fire is not carried up into it

Roof of back
kitchen etc.

Bedroom
18in*

12in

Note: no windows
to this room!

Bedroom

Bedroom

First floor
ceilings 7½in
high

First-floor plan

3in

7in

Milkhouse/dairy

Passage

Back kitchen

Cellar/pantry

11½in

16in

7½in

Parlour

18in

15in

16in

Kitchen

East room

Working from the internal dimensions, using walls much thinner than scale (see page 58), makes the model shorter than the overall length cited by the agent

Ceilings 8½in

Ground-floor plan

Farmhouse of 1788

Alternative elevation in a classical style, with the door moved to the central bay

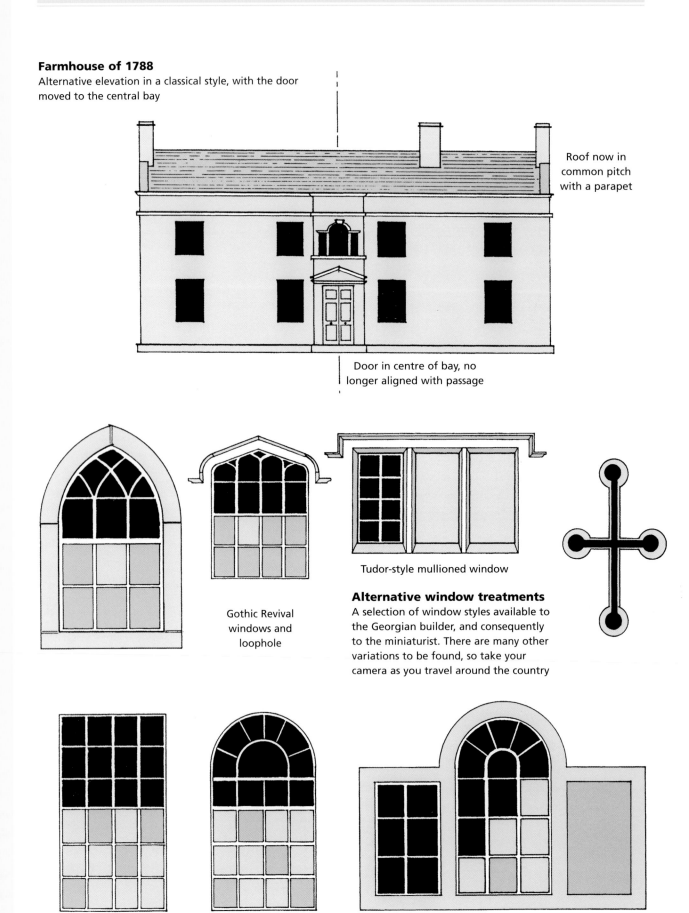

Roof now in common pitch with a parapet

Door in centre of bay, no longer aligned with passage

Gothic Revival windows and loophole

Tudor-style mullioned window

Alternative window treatments

A selection of window styles available to the Georgian builder, and consequently to the miniaturist. There are many other variations to be found, so take your camera as you travel around the country

Classical windows

Venetian window

its kitchen tucked away in the basement, far more Georgians lived in the country than in the city. What may be traditional in the dolls' house world was not true of the real thing – so do be adventurous and dare to be different.

The land agent has given us a basic house with Gothic Revival details on the outside, but if you want to reconstruct this building the choice of style is yours; my drawings include just a few suggestions on what would have been available to you in the eighteenth century in terms of window and roof treatments.

MUSEUMS OF BUILDING

Great Britain and Ireland have some outstanding museums devoted to depicting life in reconstructions of period houses. The buildings are true to period and they are furnished in true period style, so a visit would solve many of the problems you may encounter regarding details in your model. But they have even more to offer, because all the houses on site were genuine period homes and had to be taken down, moved, then rebuilt in the grounds of the museum. Prior to this work, detailed drawings had to be made and numerous photographs taken so that each house could be reconstructed correctly. This, of course, is exactly what you are trying to do, but in miniature. The photographs and plans on the next three pages are reproduced

by courtesy of the Museum of Welsh Life at St Fagans, Cardiff; when material of this standard is available, a true replica can be made to any scale.

PENPARCAU TOLLHOUSE

The Penparcau tollhouse of 1772 is an example of a type of structure which stood guard by many a country road or bridge, a relic of a time when landowners charged a toll for use of the private road or turnpike over their land. A one-roomed house, it is quite elegant from the outside, but must have presented quite a problem when it came to furnishing it, since it was not only a home to the gatekeeper and his wife but the ticket office as well.

PENPARCAU TOLLHOUSE 1772

With the advent of the private or turnpike roads for which landowners charged a toll, tollhouses and gates were required. This system only lasted for a short time, as its unpopularity resulted in riots nationwide, but the cottages still exist in many places. This example has been rebuilt at the Museum of Welsh Life, St Fagans, Cardiff, and additional drawings and photographs are available from the Museum. (Photograph on this page: Brian Long.)

Penparcau tollhouse

Side elevation from the north-east (© The National Museum of Wales)

Penparcau tollhouse

Signboard (© The National Museum of Wales). The board lists the tolls to be paid and the exemptions. You may wish to draw up your own set of tolls to fix to the wall of your miniature

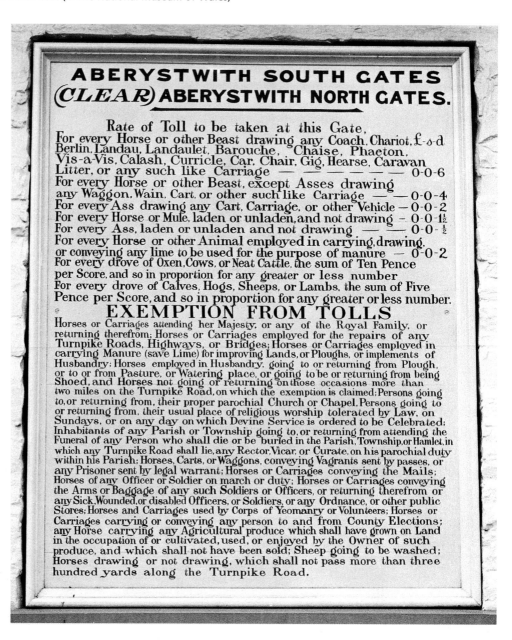

ABERYSTWITH SOUTH GATES (CLEAR) ABERYSTWITH NORTH GATES.

Rate of Toll to be taken at this Gate,

For every Horse or other Beast drawing any Coach, Chariot, £-s-d Berlin, Landau, Landaulet, Barouche, Chaise, Phaeton, Vis-a-Vis, Calash, Curricle, Car, Chair, Gig, Hearse, Caravan Litter, or any such like Carriage ——— ——— ——— 0-0-6

For every Horse or other Beast, except Asses drawing any Waggon, Wain, Cart, or other such like Carriage ——— 0-0-4

For every Ass drawing any Cart, Carriage, or other Vehicle – 0-0-2

For every Horse or Mule, laden or unladen, and not drawing – 0-0-1½

For every Ass, laden or unladen and not drawing ——— 0-0-½

For every Horse or other Animal employed in carrying, drawing, or conveying any lime to be used for the purpose of manure — 0-0-2

For every drove of Oxen, Cows, or Neat Cattle, the sum of Ten Pence per Score, and so in proportion for any greater or less number

For every drove of Calves, Hogs, Sheeps, or Lambs, the sum of Five Pence per Score, and so in proportion for any greater or less number.

EXEMPTION FROM TOLLS

Horses or Carriages attending her Majesty, or any of the Royal Family, or returning therefrom; Horses or Carriages employed for the repairs of any Turnpike Roads, Highways, or Bridges; Horses or Carriages employed in carrying Manure (save Lime) for improving Lands, or Ploughs, or implements of Husbandry; Horses employed in Husbandry, going to or returning from Plough, or to or from Pasture, or Watering place, or going to be or returning from being Shoed, and Horses not going or returning on those occasions more than two miles on the Turnpike Road, on which the exemption is claimed; Persons going to, or returning from, their proper parochial Church or Chapel, Persons going to or returning from, their usual place of religious worship tolerated by Law, on Sundays, or on any day on which Devine Service is ordered to be Celebrated; Inhabitants of any Parish or Township going to, or returning from attending the Funeral of any Person who shall die or be buried in the Parish, Township, or Hamlet, in which any Turnpike Road shall lie, any Rector, Vicar, or Curate, on his parochial duty within his Parish; Horses, Carts, or Waggons, conveying Vagrants sent by passes, or any Prisoner sent by legal warrant; Horses or Carriages conveying the Mails; Horses of any Officer or Soldier on march or duty; Horses or Carriages conveying the Arms or Baggage of any such Soldiers or Officers, or returning therefrom or any Sick, Wounded, or disabled Officers, or Soldiers, or any Ordnance, or other public Stores; Horses and Carriages used by Corps of Yeomanry or Volunteers; Horses or Carriages carrying or conveying any person to and from County Elections; any Horse carrying any Agricultural produce which shall have grown on Land in the occupation of or cultivated, used, or enjoyed by the Owner of such produce, and which shall not have been sold; Sheep going to be washed; Horses drawing or not drawing, which shall not pass more than three hundred yards along the Turnpike Road.

SLATE WORKER'S COTTAGE

The next set of drawings are of a slate worker's cottage, a much more rustic structure built by the quarryman himself. Again there is only one room, but this time we have photographs of the interior showing how it was divided by the furniture to make two miniature bedrooms with a half-loft above for the small children.

The photograph shows that this house has a rather rustic finish to the outside walls, but don't be put off, as this can be duplicated using blocks of balsa wood. Starting with irregular blocks of balsa, use a file or rasp to round off the outer face of each block to look like a large boulder, and glue them in a random fashion to the plywood carcass of your model. When complete, give the wall a few coats of emulsion (latex) paint to smooth it over and simulate the appearance of the limewashed original.

Detailed drawings and surveys like these are to be found in the many specialist museums of building and rural life, some of which have research rooms where you can sit in peace and study the information available. These places were established to help interested people, so don't be shy: give them a ring, knock on their door, and get good first-hand information. Though I have used two small houses to show the kind of detail available, there are larger, more 'polite' dwellings as well in museums of this kind.

LLAINFADYN COTTAGE *c.*1762

A slate worker's cottage re-erected at the Museum of Welsh Life, St Fagans, Cardiff. Additional drawings and photographs are available from the Museum.

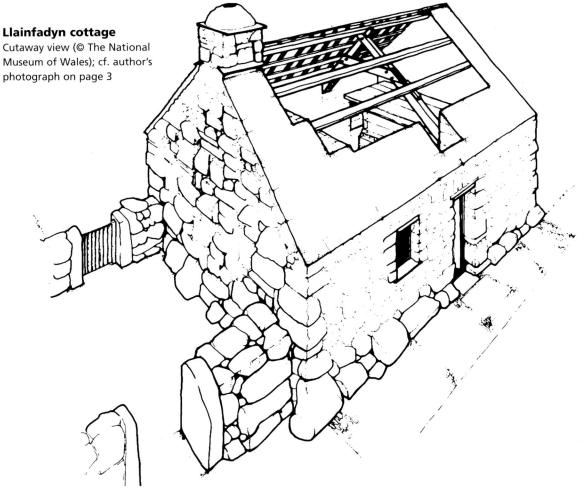

Llainfadyn cottage
Cutaway view (© The National Museum of Wales); cf. author's photograph on page 3

Llainfadyn cottage
Interior views, as re-erected at St Fagans (both photographs © The National Museum of Wales).
The dresser backs onto two box beds with a half-loft above for the use of the children

The door and fireplace. The stout rope holds a food safe overhead to keep bread, etc. out of the reach of vermin. The draught screen between table and door is made from a single slab of slate – a detail which could be reproduced in miniature using a broken slate

CHAPTER FOUR

SOME UNUSUAL HOUSES

Harbour master's house • The gatekeeper's lodges at Ewart
The Needle's Eye • Baby houses

THE HARBOUR MASTER'S HOUSE
SEATON SLUICE

On 20 March 1764 Captain Curry sailed his ship
the *Warkworth* out of the newly reformed harbour
of Seaton Sluice in Northumberland. The villagers
who had toiled over this project were in a party
mood. The cargo was Hartley coal bound for
London, and the harbour master would have had
to log the event before joining in the celebrations.

While the villagers danced on the green, he and his
family had a fine new house and office from which
to view the scene.

Legend says that Sir John Vanbrugh designed
the house after a pleasant evening at Seaton
Delaval, the hall he had built nearby for Sir John
Hussey Delaval; but it is most likely that it was
built by James Nisbet, who was employed by the
Delavals some 50 years later, around 1755. It is in
Nisbet's Gothic Revival style, even if not quite so
crisp as most of his work. Known as the Octagon,

Harbour master's house
A view of the real building from the
north-east

it would make a fine dolls' house. It has survived because a use has always been found for it. First it was the harbour master's office and home, then a customs office, then the offices from which Messrs Jopling & Co of Hartley Colliery oversaw their coal shipments. After serving as the village reading-room it was rescued, restored and converted back into a house. It is a robust building of considerable character, a weak-looking chimney being its only fault. A dolls' house modelled on this building could be furnished in a variety of ways and still be true to the house and its history. Furnish it as the harbour master would, as the village reading-room, or as it is today – the choice is yours.

THE HARBOUR MASTER'S HOUSE SEATON SLUICE NORTHUMBERLAND c.1720

The probable architect of this small house, James Nisbet, came from the Scottish borders and would have had first-hand experience of the traditional outside staircase or 'fore stair' common in Fife fishing towns. This may be why the harbour master's house has one. The original juts straight forward and would take up a lot of space, so in my drawings I have swept it round the side of the tower to make it much more compact.

The 'wing' of the house has been drawn with the usual dolls' house type of door, hinged at the right-hand or gable end, but the tower is not quite so easy. Here the entrance is via the gable end, with the fireplace incorporated in the door. This door consists of two panels, hinged together like a screen so you can open one or both. An alternative, much used today, is to secure each piece by magnets so that the whole wall or door can be removed – the choice is yours.

Harbour master's house
Elevation of the model, with outside staircase repositioned for compactness

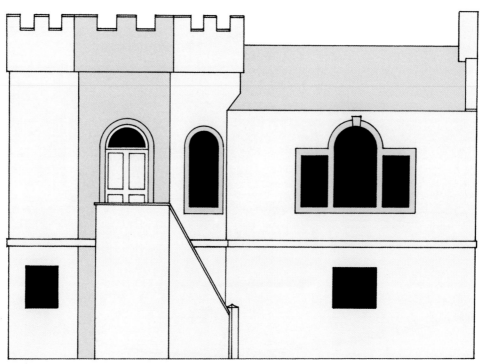

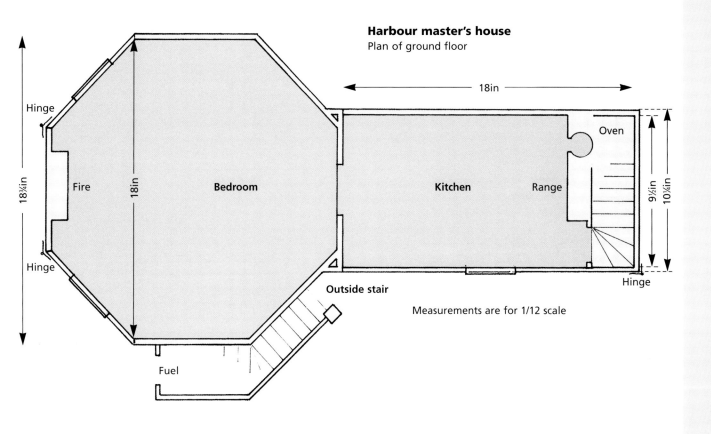

Harbour master's house
Plan of ground floor

Hinge

18¾in

Fire

18in

Bedroom

18in

Kitchen

Range

Oven

9½in

10¾in

Hinge

Hinge

Outside stair

Hinge

Fuel

Measurements are for 1/12 scale

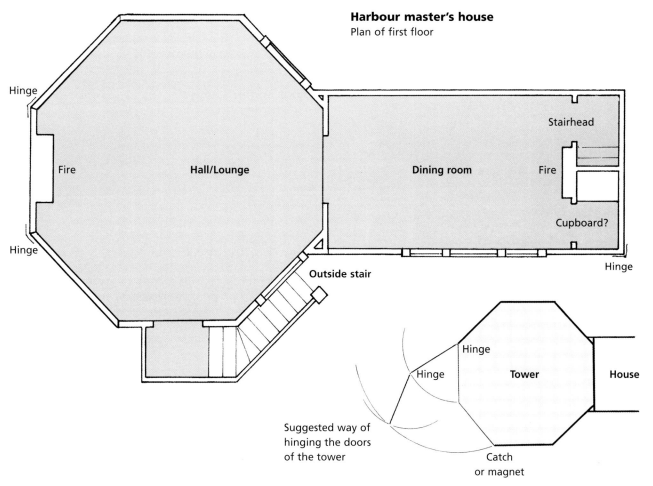

Harbour master's house
Plan of first floor

Hinge

Fire

Hall/Lounge

Dining room

Fire

Stairhead

Cupboard?

Hinge

Hinge

Hinge

Outside stair

Suggested way of
hinging the doors
of the tower

Hinge

Hinge

Tower

House

Catch
or magnet

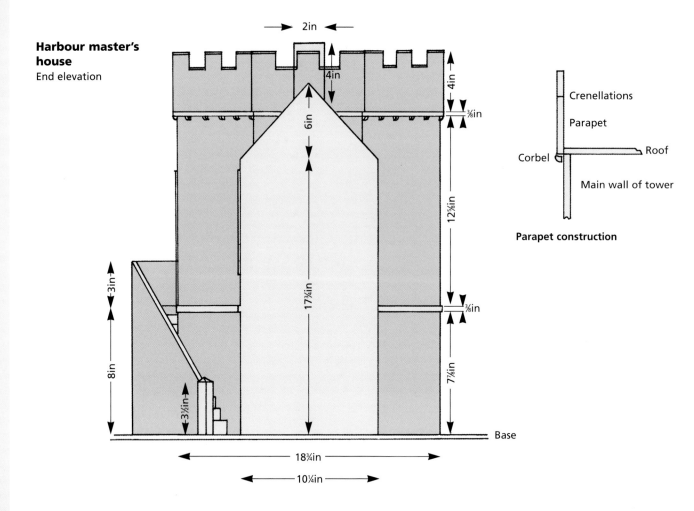

Harbour master's house
End elevation

2in

4in

6in

4in

⅜in

3in

17¾in

12⅝in

8in

3½in

⅜in

7⅞in

Base

18¾in

10¼in

Parapet construction

Crenellations

Parapet

Corbel

Roof

Main wall of tower

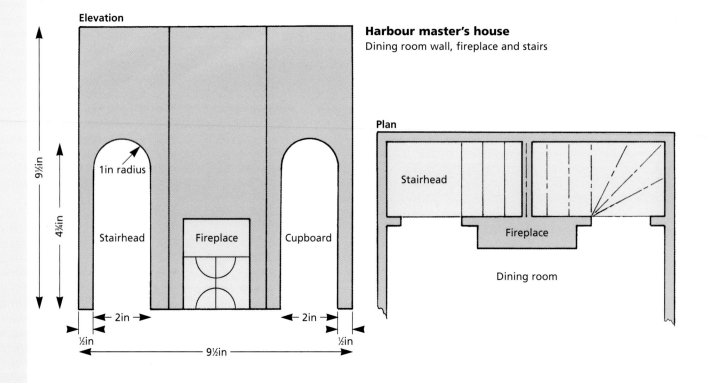

Elevation

Harbour master's house
Dining room wall, fireplace and stairs

9½in

4¾in

1in radius

Stairhead

Fireplace

Cupboard

2in

2in

½in

½in

9½in

Plan

Stairhead

Fireplace

Dining room

Plan

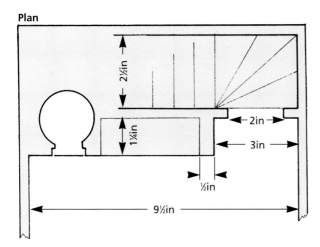

2½in

1¼in

2in

3in

½in

9½in

Elevation

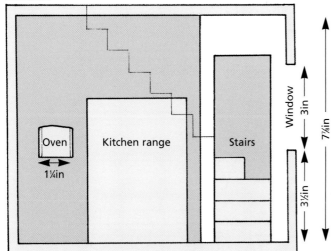

Oven

Kitchen range

Stairs

Window

1¼in

3in

3½in

7⅞in

Harbour master's house
Kitchen range and stairs

Harbour master's house
Diagram showing stairs and cupboard above

Dining room

Cupboard

Washbasin

Stairs

Kitchen

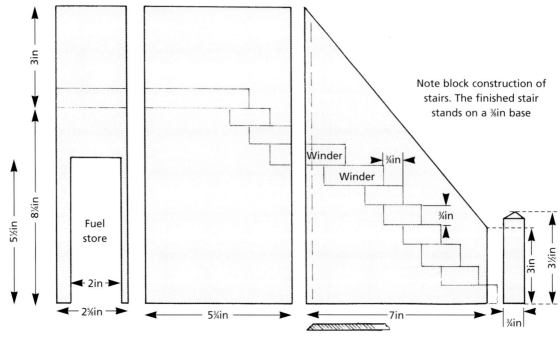

Note block construction of stairs. The finished stair stands on a ⅜in base

Harbour master's house
Outside stairs

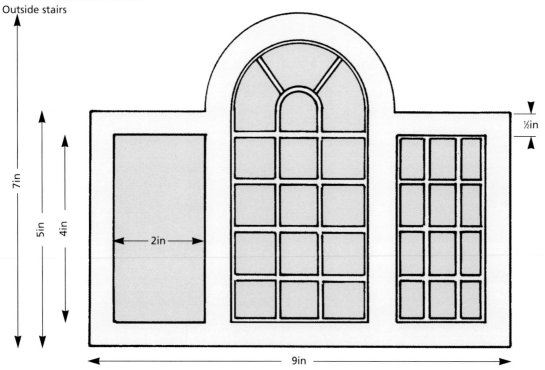

Harbour master's house
Windows

The windows are shown half-size for 1/12 scale; note that only the first-floor ones have bold, decorative frames. The ground-floor ones are simple in the extreme, and the one below the

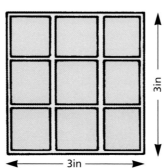

Venetian window looks as if it was once a door. The two square windows on the ground floor are identical, and there is only one Venetian window, but I have shown two arched windows in the tower which are the same as the central portion of the Venetian window. The door can be bought ready-made

THE GATEKEEPER'S LODGES AT EWART, NORTHUMBERLAND

At the beginning of our period it was usual for the labouring classes to live, out of sight and out of mind, in primitive one-roomed hovels which they may have built themselves, and often had to share with a cow or a pig. Yes, this was an age of elegance – but only for the wealthier members of the community. These simple dwellings lend themselves to adaptation as room boxes. So do the more substantial houses which came after them, since the first improvement in housing for the 'lower classes' was in the quality of the fabric, without any increase in the number of rooms or other offices. The walls were more soundly built, thatch tended to be replaced by tiles, and windows, doors and fire grates became fixtures in most cottages. So, while the tenant's lifestyle continued much as before, he

THE GATEKEEPER'S LODGES AT EWART, NORTHUMBERLAND
c.1785

This drawing by the author is based on the original eighteenth-century finished drawing, titled 'for yᵉ Lodge', in the Butler manuscripts in the Northumberland Record Office. The left-hand lodge is shown furnished; the right-hand one was for lumber, not for living in. The small doorway in the right-hand curtain wall is a sham, added to give that all-important symmetry so much thought of by the Georgians. Fine-looking lodges like these are to be found throughout Britain, and there could be as many as six to each 'large' house.

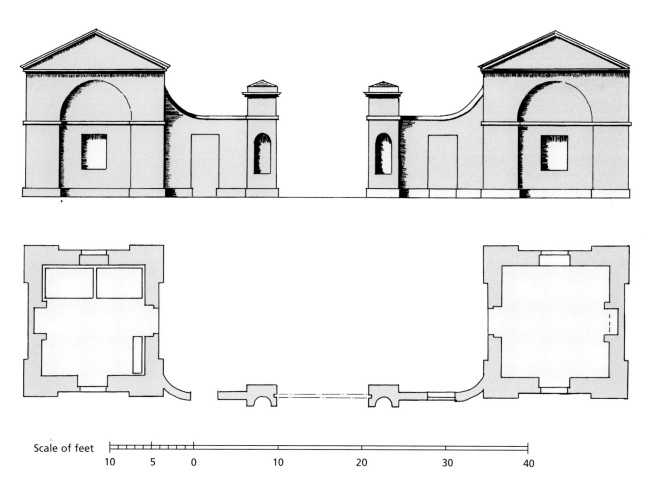

Scale of feet

10   5   0   10   20   30   40

The gatekeeper's lodges at Ewart, Northumberland
Elevation and plan

enjoyed greater security from the elements, and no longer had to carry his doors and windows on his cart at the hiring fairs. It was not until the last quarter of the nineteenth century that landowners, in any quantity, provided houses with more than one room.

The working drawings of a pair of lodges at Ewart in Northumberland, built for Horace St Paul about 1785, show this approach in practice. His lordship required the entrance to his estate to be in the latest architectural style, so as to indicate to all who might pass that this was the home of a gentleman of some taste and standing. Symmetry demanded that two lodges be built, though only one of them was to be occupied. The owner's musings on the style to be chosen are evident on the original rough drawing, in which the west lodge is shown in a classical style, while the east one has Gothic Revival detail superimposed on it. Much thought was given to the finish, with ashlar detailing and roughcast walls, yet the interior – and its occupants, the gatekeeper and his family – were given little consideration. The height of the pavilion is sufficient to allow an upper floor to be incorporated – a windowless one, if need be – but it was evidently decided that one room was plenty. The fireplace in the east lodge was deleted from the plans, since this building was not intended to be lived in.

Despite the fine exterior, the internal arrangements of the west lodge as drawn are the same as in any labourer's cottage of the time. Most important are the two beds – specifically box beds, built in such a way that a small loft area was formed above them for children or lumber. These beds are

THE GATEKEEPER'S LODGES, EWART, NORTHUMBERLAND

The Lodges at Ewart were typical of many built throughout Britain; each is of one room and measures '17ft from out to out [i.e. externally] every way', or 13ft square internally.

The west lodge was intended as the gatekeeper's residence; a note on the original drawing indicates 'this East Lodge to serve for different Uses for the Gatekeeper inhabiting y[e] west lodge & may be built without a fireplace.'

Although there is only one room, the surviving annotated plan shows several changes of mind with respect to its internal arrangements; two box beds are shown, and a space of '6. feet for his Shelves and Dresser' behind the door.

Externally the view to be presented to the world at large was one of classical symmetry, though the quatrefoil opening and arched window surround sketched on the east lodge show that the then fashionable Gothic Revival style was being considered as an alternative.

Depending on the scale chosen, models of simple structures like these can be made to sit on a mantel shelf or even act as a pelmet above a window. The intervening walls and gates can be adjusted in size to suit the intended location.

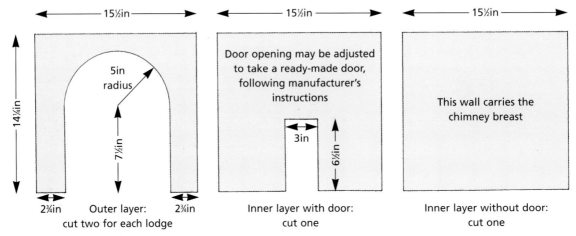

The gatekeeper's lodges, Ewart
Parts for side walls (all ⅜in thick)

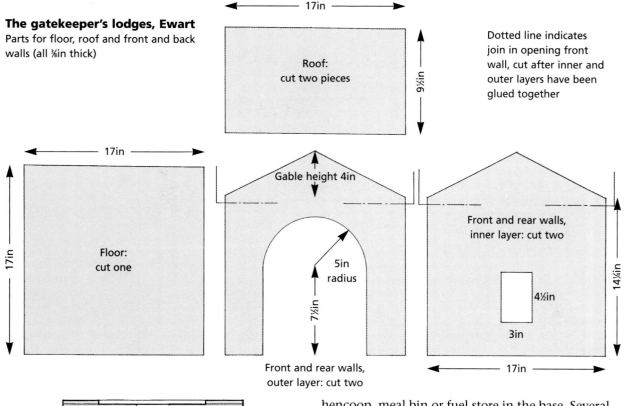

The gatekeeper's lodges, Ewart
Parts for floor, roof and front and back walls (all ⅜in thick)

17in

Roof:
cut two pieces

9½in

Dotted line indicates join in opening front wall, cut after inner and outer layers have been glued together

17in

Floor:
cut one

17in

Gable height 4in

5in radius

7½in

Front and rear walls, outer layer: cut two

Front and rear walls, inner layer: cut two

14¼in

4½in

3in

17in

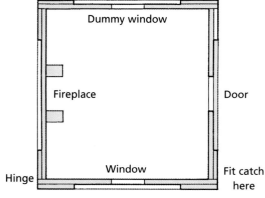

Dummy window

Fireplace

Door

Hinge

Window

Fit catch here

Ground plan of west lodge
showing wall thicknesses, position of chimney breast and hinging arrangements

to be found throughout Great Britain and Ireland, in mainland Europe and even as far as Iceland. They have various names – box bed, cupboard bed, closed bed, canopy bed, wall bed – but all denote basically the same thing. Photographs and details of how to make some of the many regional variations are given in Chapter 11.

Next in order of importance was the dresser. Here again there are many variations, from the well-known Welsh dresser to the Dutch, Irish, Highland and Lowland dressers. Like the box beds, they can be either built in or free-standing. Some have refinements ranging from spoon racks to a

hencoop, meal bin or fuel store in the base. Several varieties are illustrated in Chapter 9.

To make the lodges at 1/12 scale, as with all the houses in this book, I recommend using ⅜in (9mm) plywood. Start by cutting the bases for the gate-houses, 17in (432mm) square, followed by the walls. Each wall consists of two layers of ply, the outer one having an arch cut in it. Cut the holes for the door and for the back and front windows, remembering that the dummy back window in the west lodge is to be blocked by fixing a small piece of very thin ply on the inside.

Glue the two parts of each wall together and, when set, fix the back and two sides to the base. To allow access to the interior, the front has to be cut in two, the upper, pedimented part being glued and nailed to the box shape formed by the other walls. (The joint is positioned where it will be concealed by the shadow of the cornice.) The roof can now be fitted, and the square part of the front attached with hinges at the left-hand side for the left or west lodge, and the right-hand side for the east lodge.

The intervening walls can be made shorter or longer than the original, depending on the space in which you intend to display the model. Horace St Paul evidently toyed with many different ideas when working on his drawings, which show a curved wall next to the west lodge, and a straight

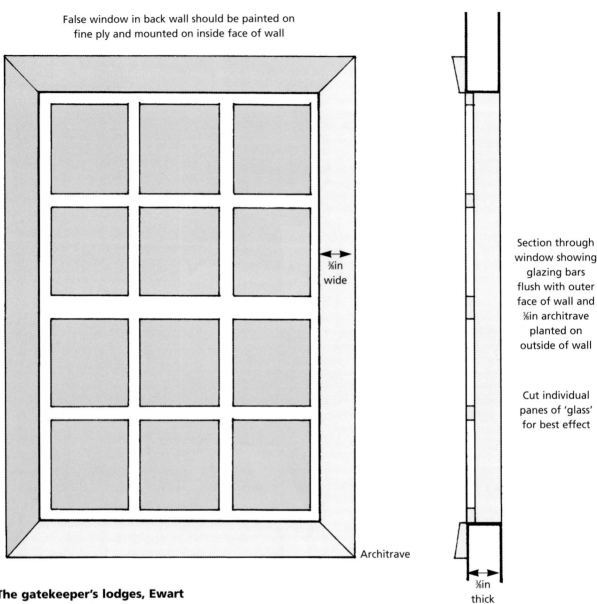

False window in back wall should be painted on fine ply and mounted on inside face of wall

⅜in wide

Section through window showing glazing bars flush with outer face of wall and ⅜in architrave planted on outside of wall

Cut individual panes of 'glass' for best effect

Architrave

⅜in thick

The gatekeeper's lodges, Ewart
Window at 1/12 scale

wall on the other side as an alternative. The straight wall rising to the lodge is quite simple to make, but a curved one is a decided challenge. The curved section can be made from wood cut partly through at intervals of, say, ½in (13mm), then bent into shape; or from strips of wood about ½ x ⅜in (13 x 10mm) stood on end like a wooden fence (see lower drawing on page 78). Any gaps will need to be filled and sanded to give a smooth curve, and the surface could even be papered over before painting. Sheets of MDF (medium-density fibreboard) with grooves cut in it to assist bending are available from do-it-yourself stores.

The width of the gateway itself is important, and this should be 10⅜in (263mm) in 1/12 scale.

The gates used can be professionally produced wrought-iron ones, or solid wooden ones.

The pillars are formed as a tall box with a pyramidal top. The arched recess in the front is not the problem it may seem at first. It is best to make this before fitting the sides and back of the pillar. Cut the hole and clean all edges, then cut a piece from fine card or very thin ply as shown in the drawing and gently fold it so that the wider, lower, part fits into the straight-sided part of the arched hole. Glue and hold until set, then cut the base and top as shown and glue these in place. (If you have the skill, you might prefer to make a domed top to the recess, either by carving it from the solid or by cutting and bending a piece of thin plywood.)

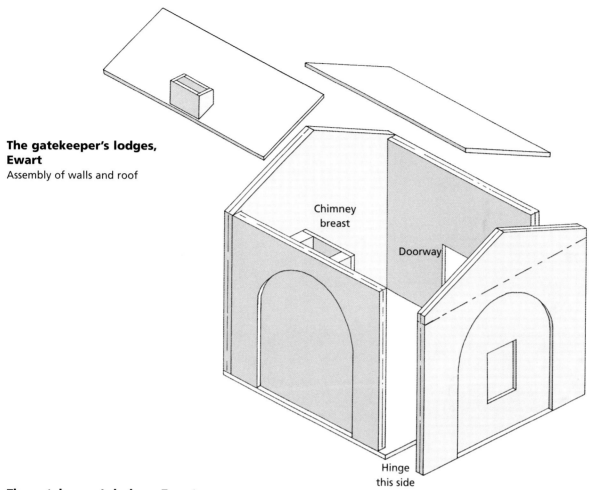

The gatekeeper's lodges, Ewart

Assembly of walls and roof

Chimney breast

Doorway

Hinge this side

The gatekeeper's lodges, Ewart

Plan and elevation of gateposts and flanking walls

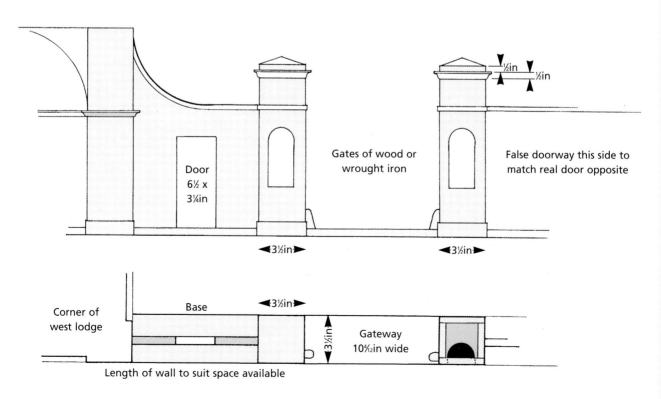

Door 6½ x 3¼in

½in
½in

Gates of wood or wrought iron

False doorway this side to match real door opposite

◄3½in►

◄3½in►

Corner of west lodge

Base

◄3½in►

3½in

Gateway 10½in wide

Length of wall to suit space available

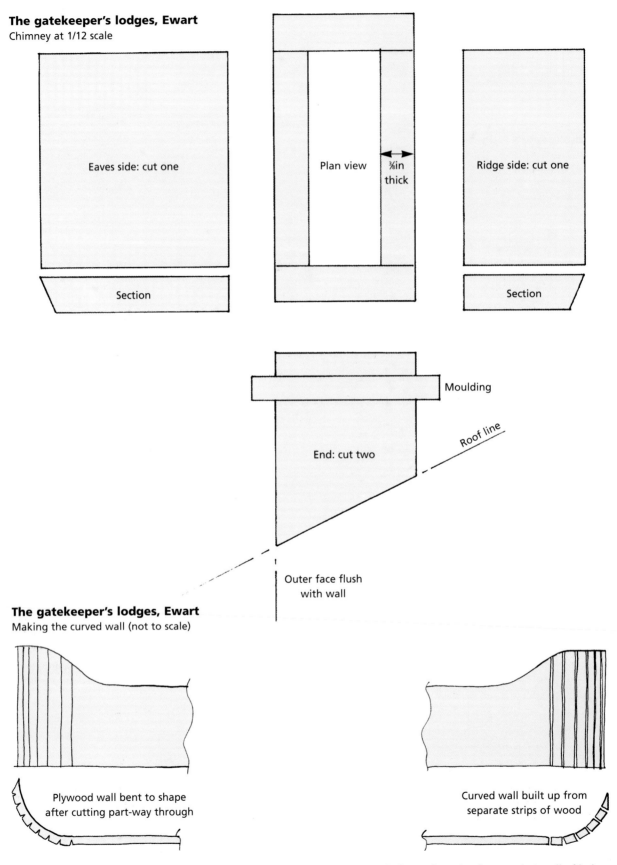

The gatekeeper's lodges, Ewart
Chimney at 1/12 scale

Eaves side: cut one

Section

Plan view

⅜in thick

Ridge side: cut one

Section

Moulding

End: cut two

Roof line

Outer face flush with wall

The gatekeeper's lodges, Ewart
Making the curved wall (not to scale)

Plywood wall bent to shape after cutting part-way through

Curved wall built up from separate strips of wood

Ends are shaped to butt against wall of lodge

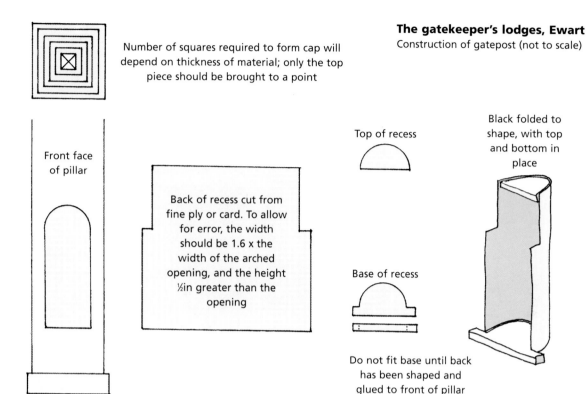

Number of squares required to form cap will depend on thickness of material; only the top piece should be brought to a point

Front face of pillar

Back of recess cut from fine ply or card. To allow for error, the width should be 1.6 x the width of the arched opening, and the height ½in greater than the opening

Top of recess

Base of recess

Black folded to shape, with top and bottom in place

Do not fit base until back has been shaped and glued to front of pillar

The tops of the original pillars were made by placing very thin layers of stone in reducing sizes one on top of the other. The model can be built up in the same way from diminishing squares of any suitable-thickness material; only the top one needs to be brought to a point.

The finishing touches are given by the mouldings to the pediment and the 'belt' or string course above the windows. The pediment moulding should be at least ⅜in (10mm) high, and the same is true of that on the pillars, but the belt can be anything from ¼in (6mm) to the ½in (13mm) indicated on the original drawing.

The coping on the wall leading to the gates is a simple, plain section at least ½in wide by ⅛in thick (13 x 3mm). It can be made from one strip of wood, but you may prefer to construct it, as the original mason would have done, by using individual coping stones in lengths of, say, 1–2½in (25–64mm).

The base of the pillars and arches is formed from strips of wood 1in x ⅟₁₆in (25 x 1.5 mm). It is important to remember that wherever there is a hinge, all ends of mouldings will need to be cut away at a 45° angle to allow the door to open (see detail at right).

The gatekeeper's lodges, Ewart
Detail (not to scale) of moulding around base of arches, made with 1in x 1/16in material

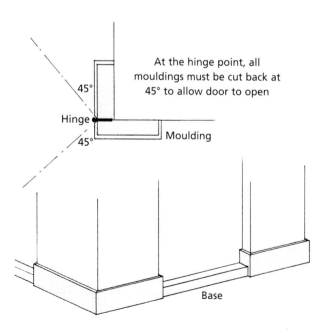

45°

At the hinge point, all mouldings must be cut back at 45° to allow door to open

Hinge

45°

Moulding

Base

THE NEEDLE'S EYE

One of the strangest gatehouses, and potentially one of the most fascinating dolls' houses, stands on the York to Pontefract Road in West Yorkshire, at one of the entrances to the Nostell Priory estate. It was built by Cosmo Wallace to plans drawn by Robert Adam in 1776. Its name, 'The Needle's Eye', is derived from the Biblical phrase about the rich man entering the Kingdom of Heaven – and we all know which side of the gate he wanted to be!

The form it takes is a pyramid pierced by an arch; it contains two one-roomed apartments, one either side of the carriageway. These rooms are only 7ft by 12ft 6in (2.13 x 3.81m), so that one must have had the beds in it while the other was used as the kitchen and living area. Above the arch is a void or loft with no apparent access, which is simply a means of reducing the weight over the

THE NEEDLE'S EYE, NOSTELL PRIORY, WEST YORKSHIRE

(© National Trust Photographic Library/John Hammond; by courtesy of Lord St Oswald)

This gatekeeper's lodge by Robert Adam, dated 1776, would make an imposing model but must have been an uncomfortable home. Adam gives all the dimensions, and his plans and elevations, still kept at Nostell Priory, help make this an interesting project. Original plans and other documents survive in many archives, so do look for them; there is a special interest in modelling a house with a documented history, or one designed by a famous architect.

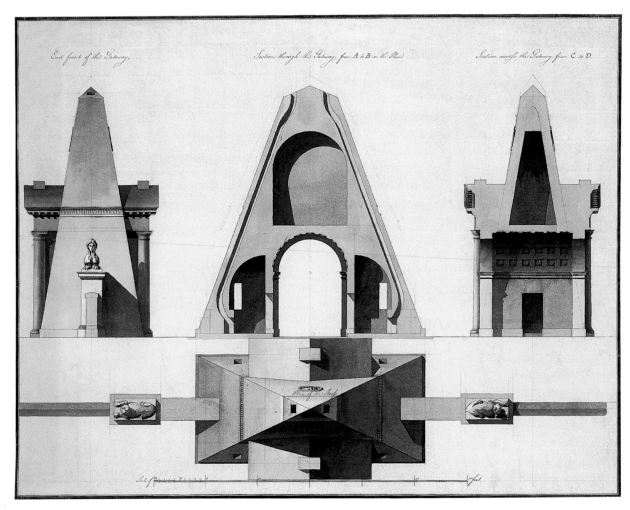

End elevation, long section, cross section, plan view

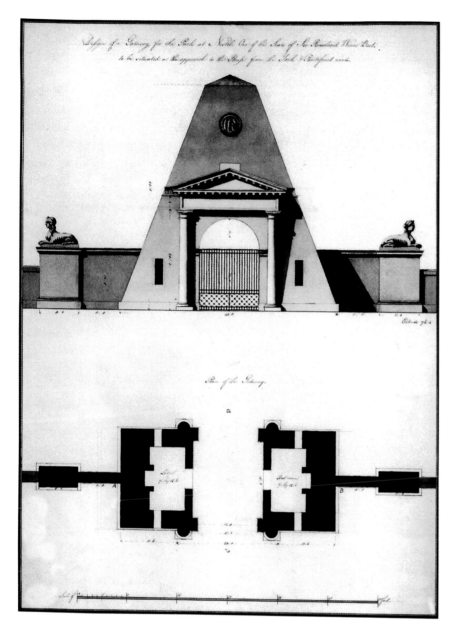

Front elevation and ground plan

arch. At 1/12 scale, without the flanking walls, this would make a model 44in wide by 26½in deep (1118 x 673mm) and 46in (1168mm) high, which might be ideal for under the stairs, or for the gap left after taking out some defunct fireplace or kitchen range. When space is at a premium, any suitable scale can be used.

TOY HOUSES

When we speak of a 'Georgian dolls' house', we usually mean a model of a real Georgian house; but there are numerous fine examples of actual dolls' houses of the Georgian period, ranging from children's toys to architectural works of art. Many of these are well documented and, with care, it would be no great problem to replicate the one of your choice.

Most of the finer ones were the playthings of wealthy, cultured ladies who made a study of fashion as well as the domestic arts and sciences. These houses were furnished and equipped with miniatures made by the best of craftsmen to the highest standards. The proud owners would use them to amuse and impress visitors and any guests who came to stay. Other specimens were not quite so fine, and were used as an aid to teaching young ladies how to manage a busy household. Few were

Travelling baby house c.1740
(photograph © Cassell & Co.)

The travelling baby house was built as a portable toy for children; it originally had brass side handles, but now has a simple handle on the top. It is of simple box construction, and only the front makes it look like a house. The original is made of mahogany with mother-of-pearl inlay and brass finials, and you could make a replica in the same way, following the detailed drawings. The dimensions given are roughly those of the original, but it could be built to any scale, even as a miniature to furnish an existing dolls' house.

intended for children to play with, and it was not until the 1850s that dolls' houses became common in the nurseries of large houses. Until then they were regarded as 'adult toys', and even the few 'baby houses' which were made for children were fitted with locks to keep unsupervised children at bay. It was Victorian manufacturers who first saw the potential for marketing dolls' houses commercially. Unlike the Georgian examples, which were invariably one-offs, runs of hundreds or thousands of one model began to be made.

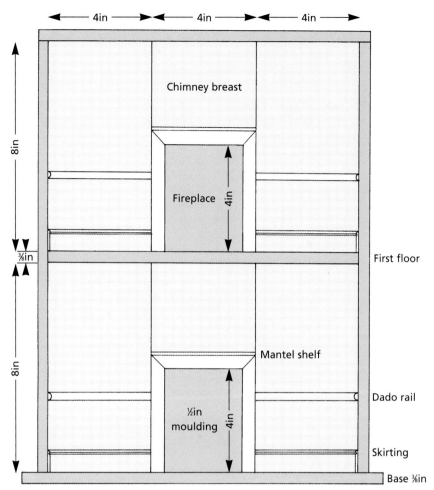

Travelling baby house

Elevation of interior and ground-floor plan

All parts made from ⅜in (9mm) sheet material (the original, being solid timber, is thicker)

4in

4in

4in

8in

⅜in

8in

Chimney breast

Fireplace

4in

First floor

Mantel shelf

½in moulding

4in

Dado rail

Skirting

Base ⅜in

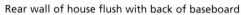

Rear wall of house flush with back of baseboard

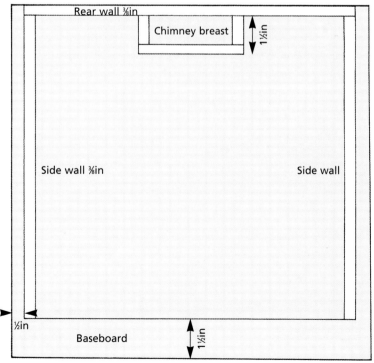

Rear wall ⅜in

Chimney breast

1½in

Side wall ⅜in

Side wall

½in

Baseboard

1½in

Well-known examples of Georgian dolls' houses representing identifiable houses include that belonging to Sarah, the daughter of Christopher Lethieullier, who married Matthew Fetherstonhaugh in 1747. The architectural details are breathtaking. In the pediment are the arms of her father, rather than her husband, which proves she had the house prior to her marriage. Little used, the house has not been altered since its arrival at Uppark, her husband's seat, and presents to us a fine Queen Anne exterior and an interior that gives a view of life in a fine house of around 1702–14 – the very house into which Sarah herself was born some years later.

Royalty were not immune to the dolls' house bug: it is recorded that Frederick, Prince of Wales, who died in 1751, amused himself by making baby houses while living at Kew. A house of the most basic design and construction was played with by the children of George III while on their holidays at Weymouth, which serves to show how the highest in the land enjoyed simple pleasures. This toy

Travelling baby house
Dimensions of front wall

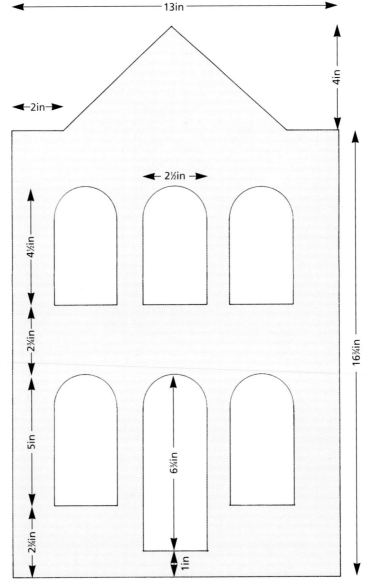

All arches 1¼in radius. Fit to the house using two offset hinges

was only of fleeting interest to the royal princesses and was passed down to the children of Sir George Grey, who was Flag Captain on the royal yacht *Princess Augusta*, a position he took up in 1801. Even the windows on this house are simply painted direct onto the wooden front, not cut out or glazed – a feature not uncommon in toys of this type. This detail illustrates the distinct difference between the simple toy houses and the better-quality replicas used to educate young ladies, let alone the superior houses which were the playthings of wealthy adults.

Most of these model houses are well documented, and many are on public display, so that you can make more than a passable replica; with modern paints and techniques you could even give it a 'genuine' distressed look. Even if you don't want a full-sized toy, you could produce an authentic version at 1/12 scale to help furnish your chosen dolls' house.

Travelling baby house
Front wall complete with mouldings and finials

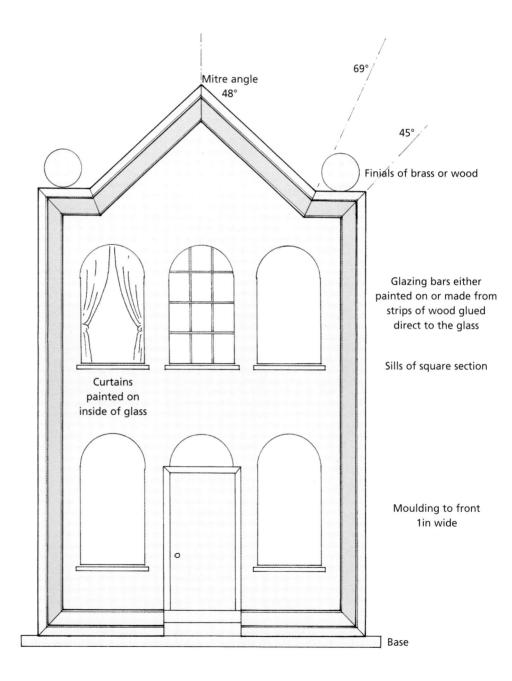

Mitre angle 48°

69°

45°

Finials of brass or wood

Glazing bars either painted on or made from strips of wood glued direct to the glass

Sills of square section

Curtains painted on inside of glass

Moulding to front 1in wide

Base

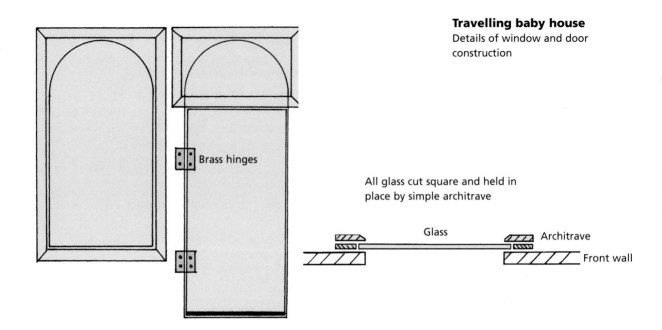

Travelling baby house
Details of window and door construction

Brass hinges

All glass cut square and held in place by simple architrave

Glass

Architrave

Front wall

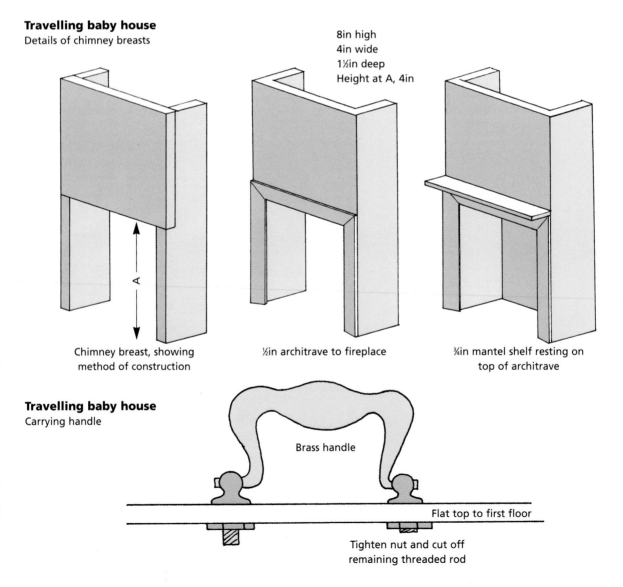

Travelling baby house
Details of chimney breasts

8in high
4in wide
1½in deep
Height at A, 4in

A

Chimney breast, showing method of construction

½in architrave to fireplace

¾in mantel shelf resting on top of architrave

Travelling baby house
Carrying handle

Brass handle

Flat top to first floor

Tighten nut and cut off remaining threaded rod

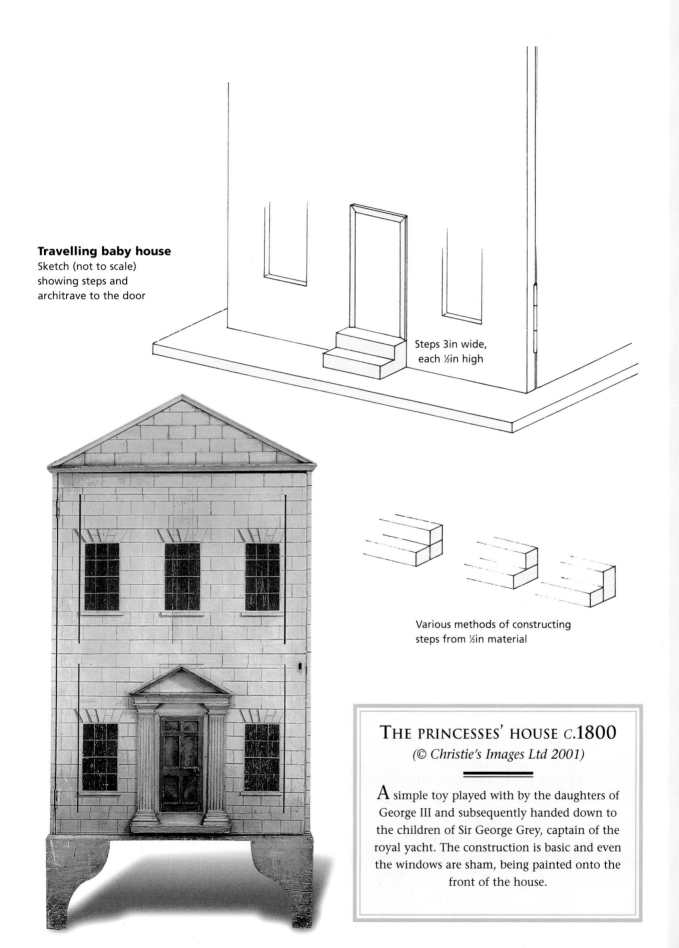

Travelling baby house
Sketch (not to scale) showing steps and architrave to the door

Steps 3in wide, each ½in high

Various methods of constructing steps from ½in material

THE PRINCESSES' HOUSE c.1800
(© Christie's Images Ltd 2001)

A simple toy played with by the daughters of George III and subsequently handed down to the children of Sir George Grey, captain of the royal yacht. The construction is basic and even the windows are sham, being painted onto the front of the house.

CHAPTER FIVE

USING INFORMATION FROM WRITTEN SOURCES

Inventories • Period literature • Dates and signatures • Fire marks

THE INVENTORY

As a source for the history of a house, an inventory can be invaluable. Surviving inventories are of varying degrees of usefulness, and are irregularly distributed. The most common source is in association with wills (these are known as probate inventories), whilst others list goods lost or forfeited by householders. The most detailed ones itemize the contents of a house room by room, giving us a remarkably clear indication of how a home was equipped and the kind of life its occupants followed. Others are less helpful for our purposes, with household goods being considered of little merit. Just such an inventory was attached to the will of Clement Reed of Elsdon, Northumberland, in 1582. The place in question is Old Town Farm ('Hoold Town') in Redesdale, Northumberland, the site of a deserted village; 'Trowen' is Troughend Farm in the same area.

> AN ENVITORI of the gudys of Clement Red prased be [i.e. appraised by] Jhon Red of Trowen and Roger Red of Hoold Town.
>
> Fyrst vj oxson pris iiij pound
> Item vj ky [cows] pris iiij pound
> Item iiij Stotys [castrated oxen, steers or heifers, according to the *Oxford English Dictionary*] pris xl^s
> Item iiij ky pris iiij mark
> Item iiij yong nout [2-year-old horned oxen] pris xxxvj^s viij^d
> Item inseth gerg x^s

Inseth or *insight gear* was the customary term for household furniture and fittings, which in this case amounts to only 10 shillings, or three-quarters the value of a cow (1 mark = £⅔ or 13s. 4d.). The wealth of a gentleman was in his stock and, as in many farms today, it was a struggle for the housewife to prise cash from the estate to make the house more comfortable.

In 1764 a poor simple Northumbrian pitman fell foul of Sir John Hussey Delaval, and to clear debts of £8 he had to forfeit the contents of his one-roomed cottage:

> . . . the several Goods and Chattells . . . which are now in the Dwelling House of me the said James Spence . . . in Hartley . . .
>
> Two Close Beds and Bedding
> One open Bed and Bedding
> One Dresser and Cupboard
> Seven Pewter Dishes
> Six Delf [Delft] Dishes
> twelve Delf Plates
> One Oak Cupboard
> One Chest
> Two Chairs
> One Table One small Ditto
> Two large Boiling Pots One small Ditto
> One Water Shool [local term for a scoop or ladle]
> One Milk Can
> One Spinning Wheel
> One Frying Pan
> One Girdle [griddle]
> One Pair of Teamses [sieves]

One Box Iron and Heaters [a hollow smoothing iron heated by a 'mouse' or 'slug' placed inside]

Six Wood Trenchers

Three White Delf Basons

One Looking Glass

One Pair of Barrs

One Wood Bowl

One Chimney Crook and three Wood Staves

INSIDE OF A PITMAN'S COTTAGE

after a drawing by Frederick William Fairholt, FSA, 1850–1

———

This Cumbrian interior is furnished in much the same way as that of James Spence, who lost his home to his landlord in 1764. When using inventories such as his, try making sketches of the goods mentioned; a visual reference is very helpful in making and furnishing an accurate miniature.

The six wooden trenchers would suggest a family of father, mother and four children, the parents using the two chairs while the children sat on the edge of the open bed. The surrender of the 'Barrs' from the fireplace and the 'Chimney Crook' also tells us a lot about the accommodation provided for eighteenth-century labourers. This unfortunate man was grossly misused, as his property should have been worth at least £10, to judge by the value put on the goods of Mary Brown of Bywell in the same county.

Saturday, 16 November 1771 was a wet, windy day on Peel Fell, just as it had been for the past week. On Sunday the infant North Tyne was raging over the heather, sweeping all before it: crops, sheep and people all fell victim to its anger. Downstream at Bywell, Mary Brown's house was almost under water, as the river in its rage plucked away all her worldly goods. Later that day, the bridge at Newcastle, which had carried royalty and the heads of reivers, was falling; it was washed out beyond the Black Middings rocks to the North Sea, along with a washtub and a spinning wheel from Bywell.

To the Right Worshipful John Erasmus Blackett Esq.ʳ Mayor of Newcastle upon Tyne, This VIEW of the RUINS of the BRIDGE of that TOWN, as they appeared after the Fall thereof in November 1771, Is most respectfully Inscribed, by his very obliged and most devoted faithful humble Servant, John Brand. October 27.ᵗʰ 1772

THE RUINS OF THE BRIDGE AT NEWCASTLE
AFTER THE GREAT FLOOD OF 1771
from Brand's History of Newcastle upon Tyne *(Newcastle, 1789)*

The caption reads:

To the Right Worshipful John Erasmus Blackett Esq.ʳ Mayor of Newcastle upon Tyne, This VIEW of the RUINS of the BRIDGE of that TOWN, as they appeared after the Fall thereof in November 1771, Is most respectfully Inscribed, by his very obliged and most devoted faithful humble Servant, John Brand. October 27ᵗʰ 1772

As miniaturists we owe a lot to the eighteenth-century flood that demolished the ancient bridge over the Tyne, and washed away the contents of many a home along its banks. The surviving lists of lost goods and chattels give us an insight into eighteenth-century living conditions and show how people from various walks of life furnished their homes. Most of the homes inventoried in this chapter stood on the banks of the Tyne, and indeed one was washed away with the bridge.

Mary Brown must have had a marvellously unimpaired memory, as the inventory she compiled is a complete list of all the furniture and fittings of a middle-class lady:

A Calculation of the Goods Lost in the Late great Flood.
belonging to Mary Brown [o]f Bywell.

	£. s. d.		£. s. d.
1 A Cubbert	1. 0. 0	2 Pair of Bars	0. 5. 0
1 A Dresser and Shelves	0. 15. 0	1 Crook	0. 1. 6
1 Case of Drawers	1. 1. 0	1 pair of Tongues [tongs]	0. 1. 0
3 Bed Steeds and 3 Teasters and 1 Back	1. 15. 0	1 Grait Iron	0. 1. 0
3 Blankets	0. 12. 0	2 Roast Crooks	0. 1. 0
2 Happins [covers]	0. 8. 0	2 Large Chists	0. 7. 6
1 Bed-Twilt [quilted cover]	0. 5. 0	2½ Stone of Owl	1. 1. 3
3 Lin Sheets	1. 0. 3	1 Stone of Tow	0. 0. 6
5 Linnen pillows	0. 7. 6	1 Boll of Wheat	0. 12. 0
5 pair of Harn [coarse] Sheets	1. 0. 0	2 pecks of Rye	0. 5. 6
9 Napkins	0. 15. 0	1 Churn	0. 4. 0
1 Tablecloth	0. 8. 4	5 Woodden Bools	0. 3. 4
2 Feather Bolsters	0. 4. 0	10 Trinchers	0. 2. 6
4 Feather Codds	0. 4. 0	1 Washing Tub	0. 2. 6
22 Yards of Linnen cloth	1. 16. 8	5 Woodden Dishes	0. 0. 10
4 Shifts	0. 8. 4	3 Woodden Stools	0. 1. 6
12 Caps	0. 4. 0	1 Spade and 1 Shovel	0. 3. 0
1 Table	0. 10. 6	1 Ax and 1 Risehook [slasher or billhook]	0. 2. 0
4 Small Chairs	0. 10. 0	1 Hack [a pronged tool for breaking ground]	
1 Large Chair	0. 5. 0	and 1 Limeston Hammer	0. 2. 0
10 Pewter Dishes	1. 10. 0	1 Large Beaf Tub	0. 1. 6
11 Pewter Plates	0. 9. 2	8 Harn [coarse] pillows	0. 6. 8
4 Large Delf Dishes	0. 4. 0	6 Hanks of Stocking Yern	0. 3. 8
9 Delf Plates	0. 4. 6	4 Poaks [pokes or bags]	0. 4. 0
1 Set of Shelves	0. 1. 6	1 Furm [form or bench]	0. 1. 0
2 Lint Wheels	0. 11. 0	2 Hammers	0. 8. 0
1 Nack Reel [both these items are to do			£5. 7. 7
with spinning]	0. 4. 6		
12 Spoons	0. 1. 4	besides a great maney palates, porrengers	
3 pewter Candlesticks	0. 2. 0	Sceps [scoops, bowls, pots] & things too	
1 Dº. Quart Tankard	0. 2. 6	tedious to mention perticular	– 2. 0
1 Dº. Porrenger & Mustard pot	0. 0. 10	4 Fothers of Coals	– 10. 0
2 Dº. Salt Fats [small metal containers]	0. 0. 6	2 Loads of Potatoes	– 10. 0
1 Drudging Box & pepper Box	0. 3		£6. 7. 7
1 Speet [spit] and Rack's	0. 3. 0		[sic]
1 Larg Yeatlean [cast-iron pan]	0. 2. 0		
1 Girdle and 1 Pot	0. 4. 0	[Total, including sums not itemized in the	
	17. 10. 8	inventory:]	£48. 2. 9

Mary Brown could tell us what she owned, but her list doesn't say (as probate inventories often do) from which rooms the swollen river plucked them. We are left to distribute them according to our present-day ideas of correctness.

Our next householder, a one-time hussar turned tanner, lived on a hill high above the river and, though he would have witnessed the great flood of 1771, he would have suffered only minor discomfort. His home town of Hexham was famous for its glovemakers and tanners, and the association between these two trades resulted in a higher than average population of prosperous businessmen. The inventory of household goods left by the deceased tanner John Bell, drawn up in 1801, moves through the house room by room to give an insight into his mode of life. There is a mention of the then fashionable wallpaper ('painted paper'), and to maintain the style an assortment of silver plate was available.

THE INTERIOR OF A LABOURER'S COTTAGE WITH TYPICAL COUNTRY FURNITURE OF *c.*1730 AND LATER

From left to right: Highland dresser, tinderbox (on side of chimney breast), fire basket and chimney crane, oak cupboard and stool, griddle iron and adjustable pot hooks (to left of window), oak chest, small tilt-top table, table of Welsh origin, wall cupboard, box or cupboard bed (English pattern), box or cupboard bed (Fife pattern), rush chair from Lancashire. The ceiling is hung with old sailcloth against draughts and dust.

A Schedule or Inventory of the Household Goods of John Bell late of Hexham Tanner deceased taken this 23rd September 1801.

In the Kitchen.

One Oak Press	0. 7. 6
1 Open dresser	0. 5. 0
One Oak Table 1 Fur Do.	0. 5. 0
2 Chair, 2 stools	0. 2. 6
1 Spinning Wheel	0. 8. 0
1 Water skeel [scoop or ladle], Bowl Dish and Bason	0. 2. 6
1 Tin Oven, 2 Dish Covers	0. 2. 6
1 Nest Pidgeon Holes	0. 1. 0
1 Cheese Toaster, Skewer, 3 Iron Candlesticks	0. 1. 3
Frying Pan, Girdle, Gridiron Trivit, Hanging Cranks	0. 7. 6
Poker, Tongs, Coal rake, Shovle, Dust Pan	0. 1. 9
2 Brass Pans, 1 Copper Tea Kettle, 1 Sauce Pan	0. 17. 0
1 Iron Pott, 1 Frying Pan, two small pans	0. 5. 0
1 Iron Tea Kettle, 1 Tin Pan, Coffee do. 1 Rester [roaster]	0. 3. 0
4 Brass Candlesticks, 2 Basters, 2 Spits and racks	0. 8. 0
2 Pair Tongs, 1 Shovle, Hanging Spit Beef Forks, 5 skewars, Broken cranks	0. 6. 0
2 Box Irons and Heaters, 3 Trenchards 1 Ladle 1 Bill Knife [billhook or slasher]	0. 8. 0
1 Knife Box and Old Knives	0. 1. 6
1 Spoon case, 2 Dishes, 8 plates, 2 Tea Pots 2 Basons, 3 Bottles	0. 1. 6
4 Brushes 1 Crook	0. 1. 6
8 Dishes, 5 Plates Delft, 3 Boats, 3 Bakers 5 Bottles, 1 p[air] Wool Cards, 7 Phial Bottles 3 Flasks	0. 5. 0
Pot and oven	1. 0. 0

In the Parlour

1 Mahogany Dining Table	1. 16. 0
1 Do. Turnover Do.	1. 1. 0
1 Oak Table	0. 2. 6
4 Chairs	1. 0. 0
1 Looking glass	3. 3. 0
1 Clock and Case	0. 2. 0
2 Cloaths Horses, 1 Bake Board, 1 Screen	0. 13. 0
2 Window Blinds	0. 3. 0
Tongs, Poker, Fender	0. 7. 6
1 Carpet	0. 5. 0
1 Tea Chest, 1 Lanthorn, 6 cups and saucers Coffee Pot, 7 jarrs, 2 Potting Pots, 5 glasses, 16 plates 3 Dishes	0. 9. 0

Bro^t. Forward	15.13.6

20 Bottles	0. 3. 4
10 Knives and Forks	0. 7. 6
2 Tin Canisters, 1 Whitning [whitewash] Brush	0. 0. 8
Books	[no value given]

Pantry

9 Bottles, 4 Dishes, 5 Basons, 2 small Tubs 2 Dishes, 1 Jar, 3 Plates, Butter Beat, Pepper Box, Mustd. Pot, Pepper Quarns, Meal Skep, Saucers, 1 Pewter spoon	0. 7. 6
	16.12.6

Front Room upstairs

Bedstead and Hangings	6. 0. 0
1 Hair Mattress	1. 1. 0
1 Feather Bed Bolster and 5 pillows	5. 5. 0
1 Blue Quilt 12/– 1 Old Do. 3/6	0. 15. 6
3 Blankets 7/– 2 sheets 5/– 1 Bolster and 2 pillows 3/–	0. 15. 0
1 Mahogany Dining Table	0. 15. 0
1 Small Oak Table	0. 3. 6
1 Chest of Wainscot Drawers	0. 15. 0
2 Arm Chairs 12/– 5 old chairs, 3 stools 6/–	0. 18. 0
Poker, Tongs, coalrake, Fender	0. 2. 6
2 Candlesticks, 1 snuffer	0. 1. 6
1 Wardrobe	1. 5. 0

[East Closet]

3 Bolsters	0. 18. 0
1 Blue Quilt 12/– One old cotton Do. 5/–	0. 17. 6
1 Cotton Quilt	0. 8. 0
1 Double Blanket 15/– 1 Pair blankets 7/–	1. 2. 0
12 Napkins	0. 12. 0
3 Tablecloths	0. 18. 0
3 Pairs Sheets	1. 10. 0
2 Pair Do.	1. 4. 0
2 Pair Do.	0. 18. 0
3 Pair Do.	0. 12. 0
2 Bolster and 12 Pillowcases	0. 18. 0
9¾ yards Linnen cloth	0. 12. 0
6½ Tow cloth 14d	0. 7. 7
3 Yards of Canvas	0. 2. 0
28 Yards of Linnen at 1/8	2. 6. 8
40 do. at 1/4	2. 13. 4
22 do. Huckabag 1/10	2. 0. 4
2 Diaper Table Cloths	1. 4. 0
3 Blankets	0. 9. 0
Mahogany Tray	0. 6. 0
1 Chest, 5 small boxes, 4 Bottles, 1 Stool 2 Glasses	0. 10. 0
Carry forward	54.17.5

[West closet]

3 Glass Decanters, 9 glasses	0. 4. 0
1 Hand Bason, Chamber pot, 2 Punch Bowls	
18 plates	0. 3. 0
11 cups, 10 saucers, Slop and Sugar Basons	
Gill Pot	0. 1. 6
5 Boxes	0. 2. 0
Weights and Scales	0. 4. 0
2 Tea Boards	0. 5. 0
1 Looking Glass 2/-	0. 2. 0
	56.16.11

Plate

	Troy Weight				
	Oz.	Dwt.	Gr.		
1 Tankard 25¼ oz					
avoirdupoise	23	1	6	at 5/6	6. 7. 0
1 Tea Pot 15¾ oz.	14	7	1		3. 19. 0
4 Tablespoons					
10¾ oz	9	15	22		2. 14. 0
6 Teaspoons					
2 Saltspoons ¾	3	0	5		16. 6
Tea Tongs 4 oz.	3	12	22		1. 0. 0
					14.16.6

Silver Watch	2. 2. 0

Plated

1 Mustard Pot, 1 Pepper Box, 2 salts	1. 0. 0
32, Hanks of Tow Yarn	1. 12. 0
	76. 5. 5

Back Room

1 Chest of Drawers	1. 15. 0
1 Half Chest	0. 15. 0
Old Cupboard	1. 0. 0
One Oak Table	0. 12. 0
Bird Cages	0. 1. 0
Table Leaf	0. 1. 6
1 Churn, 2 Picture Frames	0. 2. 0
Temses [sieves]	0. 1. 6
1 Small Table and Box	0. 3. 0
Cloaths Baskett	0. 0. 6
Painted Paper	0. 12. 6
2 Chairs	0. 2. 6

(Closet)

Chamber pot, 2 bottles, 3 Dishes, 1 Box etc.	0. 3. 0
	81. 14. 11

High Room

1 Table 2 chairs	0. 5. 0
1 Wheel and Reel	0. 5. 0
1 Feather Bed	1. 16. 0
1 Do.	2. 0. 0
2 Happings [bedcovers]	0. 7. 0
Feathers in bags etc.	0. 10. 0
Mose [more?] Feathers	0. 15. 0
14 Pokes and 1 Sack	0. 12. 0
Cloth for Carpeting 19 yards at 14d	1. 2. 2
Carpet	1. 15. 0
4 Boxes	0. 1. 0
2 Bedsteads without Bottoms	0. 12. 0
Bars, Spade, Old Boxes, 4 Matts, China Rack	0. 3. 0
35 Bottles	0. 5. 10
Small Boxes, 1 Jar, Bird Cage	0. 1. 0
1 Beckment [container holding ¼ peck],	
1 weight, 1 tub	0. 1. 0
Basket, Old Iron, Lamb Skin	0. 1. 0
2 Stools, 2 Besoms, Spoon Case	0. 0. 6
Pewter 55 at 6d	1. 7. 6
Basket and Old Door	2. 0
Brought Forward	93. 16. 11
5 Yards of Cloth at 12s	3. 0. 0
4/1/10/Huzzar Cloak	1. 1. 0
	4. 1. 0

3 wide coats		1. 3. 0
2 a		
new kid } 3 Shail Coats		0. 5. 0
and a } 3 Waistcoats		0. 12. 0
half		
	4 Do.	0. 3. 0
	1 Do	0. 10. 6
	1 Pr. of Breeches (Nankin)	0. 3. 6
3.5.6.	1 pair of Black Do.	0. 3.
1.1.0	6 Pair (Old)	0. 5. 0
		3. 5. 6

14 Pair of Stockings at 18d	1. 1. 0
6 Shirts	2. 2. 0
5 Do.	0. 15. 0
10 Do.	1. 5. 0
2 Pair Boots, 1 pair spoons,	
2 pr. shoes. 2 pr. slippers	0. 11. 0
Books	1. 0. 0
Cash in the house	25. 0. 0

In this case we can see where the furniture and other items came from within the house, and use this information to furnish a dolls' house correctly. The kitchen comes first on the list, and in rural areas this was the main living room of the house. The parlour was for show, only used for guests and special occasions: this is where that important Georgian tea ceremony took place, using the tea chest and cups and saucers. There is no food left in the pantry (north-country mice?), but there is an assortment of containers and other items.

The main or front bedroom was large and well furnished, having two closets or built-in cupboards, while the back room had only one. Up in the roof space behind the parapet was the 'high room', so called because it was at the top of the house. This room would have run the full length of the house and was full of junk, having beds without bottoms, the master's old military uniform, sacks of feathers for quilts, and an old spade. It is not unusual to find outdoor equipment in the house; indeed, the will of a Yorkshire gardener shows that he kept three wheelbarrows in his bedroom – that is devotion to duty!

PERIOD LITERATURE

Although in the course of this book you will find a few quotes from well-known works, the importance of contemporary literature in general for information on details and customs of the time cannot be overstated.

First let us look at the published works of some who did not regard themselves as writers of any particular merit, but simply wrote down what they had observed of a country and its people while on their travels. Some kept a diary, while others wrote letters home; outstanding examples of these are Celia Fiennes (1685–1741) and César de Saussure (b. 1705).

Celia was the daughter of a Cromwellian colonel, a nonconformist and a lady of great independence in a male-dominated world. Her remarkable account of her no less remarkable travels in England is a document of immense value to the social historian, ranking with Dr Johnson's account of his travels in Scotland. A lady of her time, Celia had a liking for the new, recording it where she found it, whether in architecture or in fashion.

While Celia Fiennes visited every English county, a later writer concentrated his efforts on recording life in London and Hertfordshire. This young man was César de Saussure, who was born in France in 1705 but was brought up in Lausanne. In 1725 he left home on travels which lasted 11 years, during which time he rose to become First Secretary to the British Embassy in Constantinople, as well as seeing service with Prince Ragotzky of Hungary among others. His letters home are full of sights, objects, places and people seen, and he gives his personal opinions and reflections on manners, family life, sports and pastimes, as well as details of what passed for personal and domestic hygiene.

Unlike these, Daniel Defoe (c.1660–1731) was a professional writer – a novelist and a journalist – but, like them, he wrote of his many travels in Britain, compiling his writings into the well-known book *A Tour through the Whole Island of Great Britain*, published in parts from 1724 to 1726. This collection of notes on his many business trips throughout the kingdom is regarded as by far the best authority for early eighteenth-century England, Scotland and Wales. His observations were those of an experienced soldier, spy, businessman and economic journalist, and he went on, in other works, to give us equally detailed accounts of eighteenth-century life veiled in the fiction of *A Journal of the Plague Year* (1722), *Moll Flanders* (1722) and *Roxana* (1724). Even his best-known work, *Robinson Crusoe* (1719), offers a mine of material for the social historian, as well as a stirring tale of shipwreck and adventure.

More sedate authors tell in a more gentle way how people used their homes, putting a great amount of effort into setting the scene. Jane Austen paints word pictures of a house and its location, a room and its furnishings, prior to filling them with people. In *Persuasion* she tells us how the décor and layout of rooms was changing from

the old-fashioned square parlour, with a small carpet and shining floor, to which the present daughters of the house were gradually giving the proper air of confusion by a grand pianoforte and a harp, flower-stands and little tables placed in every direction. Oh! could the originals of the portraits against the wainscot . . . have seen what was going on, have been conscious of such an overthrow of all order and neatness! The portraits themselves seemed to be staring in astonishment.

The dining room at Bridge End House

This may be over-gilding the lily for a small house, as usually only large houses had a room set aside specifically for this use. If you had such a room, then traditionally it was hung with portraits. The furniture here is in the Hepplewhite style, made by Peter B. Lane and Escutcheon. The detached pediments over the doors are typical of provincial houses, but the glass chandelier, made by Glasscraft, would have been exceptional in all but the grandest of houses.

THE RECEPTION ROOM AT BRIDGE END HOUSE

The ladies' reception or withdrawing room has paintings other than portraits and ships. As was the fashion, the bulk of the furniture is set back against the wall. The torchiers and the chinoiserie occasional table are made from hot-cast bronze and marble by Tony Knott; the small table is set for tea with silver by Simply Silver. The fire basket and fender, from C. A. and B. A. Hooper, are of a type found only in superior rooms. Note the lack of fixed lighting in this room; please remember that the provision of such fittings was sparse.

Visitors to ancient monuments and fine houses will be able to confirm from their own observations that the dining room was masculine in its décor – with the ancestors watching every bite from grim portraits in heavy frames – while the withdrawing room frequented by the ladies was much brighter and more feminine, with landscapes, floral pieces, horses and other family pets filling the frames on the walls. The rooms in Bridge End House (pages 96–7) reflect this distinction.

So get to know the period literature, but don't be distracted by the plot – pay attention to the setting and think dolls' house.

DAN PEGGOTTY'S HOUSE

Charles Dickens in *David Copperfield* describes one of a group of residences once common on the shores of Britain:

> There was a black barge, or some other kind of superannuated boat, high and dry on the ground, with an iron funnel sticking out of it for a chimney . . . There was a delightful door cut in the side, and it was roofed in, and there were little windows in it; but the wonderful charm of it was, that it was a real boat which had no doubt been upon the water hundreds of times, and which had never been intended to be lived in, on dry land. . . . It was beautifully clean inside, and as tidy as possible. There was a table, and a Dutch clock, and a chest of drawers, . . .

Living in an upturned boat at Newbiggin on the Northumberland coast
(© BEAMISH The North of England Open Air Museum)

which was well stocked with china. The walls were hung with pictures 'of Scripture subjects', and 'Over the little mantelshelf was a picture of the *Sarah Jane* lugger, built at Sunderland'. There were hooks in the beams of the ceiling for the hammocks of Dan Peggotty and his nephew Ham, while at either end of the house were other, smaller, rooms with beds for the rest of the household. David's bedroom was 'in the stern of the vessel; with a little window, where the rudder used to go through'. The walls were whitewashed and the bed had a 'patchwork counterpane'. Outside was a little wooden building where the pots and kettles and last night's catch of lobsters and crabs were kept.

Hablot K. Browne ('Phiz') did the original illustrations for the book, showing on the title-page little Emily sitting on the sand outside the 'house'. In the text, which was originally published in monthly instalments, are other views: one external, and one of the large parlour.

These picturesque upturned boats seen by Dickens were at Great Yarmouth in Norfolk, but other examples are recorded at many fishing centres all round Britain. Most surviving examples are now used as storehouses or other simple sheds, and the National Trust have just such a group in their care below Lindisfarne Castle on Holy Island (see page 4); these were once used as henhouses.

Most working-class homes were built by the residents themselves, so any structure that could easily be converted must have been welcome. That such conditions were considered preferable to the houses of the period can only indicate how deplorable many of them were. Many records show that horses, dogs and pigs were housed in better buildings than the servants. Though the cottages of farm labourers and miners were little more than damp sheds, the inhabitants furnished them in much the same way as Dan Peggotty.

Inventories and period literature can all be used in your endeavour to furnish correctly the house of your choice. Even television, given the wealth of research behind period drama productions, is an invaluable aid.

DATES AND SIGNATURES

One particularly important kind of written evidence is that which is written, either in words or in symbols, on the building itself. You should always sign and date your dolls' house, if only with a felt-tipped pen on the underside of the floor. But proud

DATE STONES

House date stones indicate the date of building or conversion and the initials of the owner.

The largest of these is a marriage stone from Jersey, with the initials of the husband and wife and the date of the marriage: Nicolas de Ste-Croix and Pierre Luce would appear to have married Sara Giffard on 30 March 1739 (could she really have had two husbands?)

Granite

Granite

Limestone

Marriage stone from Portgower, Sutherland: the two shields indicate a marriage between two noble families

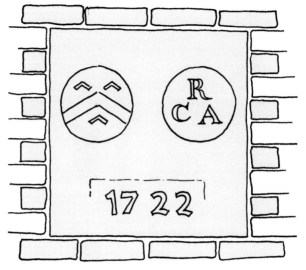

Marriage stone from West Wycombe, Buckinghamshire: a noble and a commoner

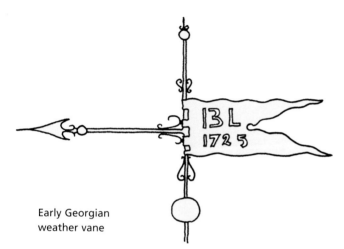

Early Georgian weather vane

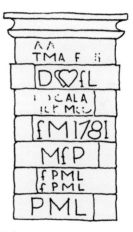

This chimney stack from Jersey appears to show a family pedigree

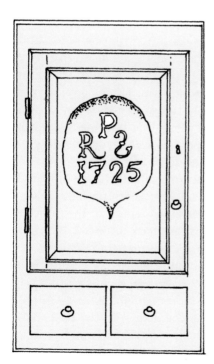

Spice cupboard from Ashes Farm, Staveley, Westmorland, with initials of Robert Philipson, 1725

Date panel from Scotton, Yorkshire, perhaps made by a monumental mason

Shawdon Hall, Northumberland, built in 1779 on the site of an earlier tower (1403) and fortalice (1541). The tympanum of the central pediment carries the arms of G. H. Pawson, c.1817

builders and owners of real houses have 'put their mark' on their homes in many different ways, and so can you.

Any building of importance today has at least one foundation stone, or a dedication stone to remind future generations just how special was the occasion of its building or opening. It is marks such as these which help us to determine the period, or even the actual date, of the building we are studying. Ordinary houses do not always have them, but it is surprising how many ways people have found of 'personalizing' their home, either when they built it or when they inherited it.

Houses of the gentry may have a coat of arms or a crest, which serves to identify the family and even the individual family member who placed it there. This enables the building (or a particular phase of it) to be dated to the period between that person's coming into their inheritance and their demise. Owners of high standing seldom put dates on their buildings; their coat of arms was their signature, and as such was perfectly understood by their peers. These arms were carved in stone and placed over the front door or in a pediment higher up. Plaster was used for arms on the inside, commonly over the fireplace or on a ceiling.

Pargeting or pargework was the art of using plaster to provide relief decoration on the exterior of a house. It was used mostly on traditional half-timbered houses, reaching its zenith in the mid-seventeenth century, but it continued well into the eighteenth century, with one house at Ashwell in Hertfordshire having the date 1762 in a gable.

Belton House in Lincolnshire has a rare painted floor in which the family crest is proudly displayed. The result is the same: a proud owner telling the world that this fine house is his home.

Your surname will almost certainly have a coat of arms associated with it, even if you do not have a personal one, and there are specialist retailers who will sell you anything from a key-ring to a three-dimensional replica of the full coat of arms. Failing this, just look up *Who's Who* in your local library, where you may find the arms described. If the archaic language used is too much for you, any book on heraldry will help you unravel it.

Lesser mortals might have a simple 'building stone' over the door with the date of completion and possibly the owner's or builder's initials. Many years after the event, these may create something of a puzzle for us. They may contain the initials of the husband and wife and even those of a second partner, as well as dates. I know of one stone that has the customary initials and date but is also decorated with a winged cherub, evidently carved by the same mason who carved the village tombstones.

Fireplaces have always been a favourite place to leave one's mark, whether a simple inscription like those found over front doors or, at times, an armorial charge. Armorial charges are also found on cast-iron firebacks; these only tell us when the fireback itself was made, but they are a nice touch in any replica. While at the fire, it is interesting to remember that chimney pots often carried the potter's name as well as the date and some small

BRIDGE END HOUSE

A view showing the portico and how it projects forward. The model was made to my plans by the Camno Workshop; to keep the weight down, the roof is made of fibre tiles by Cairn Tiles. Fire insurance marks can be helpful in dating old houses, and the example mounted above the portico is one of a series produced by Black Country Miniatures.

inscription. The lettering is not large and can only be deciphered when you are on the roof next to it. I know of some chimney stacks with strange inscriptions, but the strangest is on a chimney at Houguemont, Jersey, recording what appears to be ten lines of a family pedigree and dated 1781.

Much larger are the dates formed in the slates or tiles of a roof, usually found in rural situations. Dates picked out by using header bricks of a different colour to the body of the house are more common in artisans' dwellings, but are also found in some better-quality town houses; there are some at Holt in Norfolk.

Lead rainwater heads or hoppers are a feature of Georgian houses and there are many variations, showing anything from the date to a coat of arms. (These are discussed and illustrated in detail on pages 124–5.) The same applies to the large cisterns used in kitchens or basement areas (see pages 169–70), though many of these simply carry the monogram of the reigning monarch, in much the same way as we decorate postboxes with the initials VR, GR or ER.

Weather vanes are found on many buildings, some being quite simple while others are masterpieces of the blacksmith's art, showing the date of construction and the initials of the owner as well as the wind direction.

Built-in furniture, such as box beds or spice cupboards, was also dated, and many examples still exist in rural Britain. The spice cupboard built into the thickness of the wall might have simple shelves, but some had separate drawers for each spice.

Any of the above methods of dating may help you to determine when the house you are interested in was built, and to decide how to furnish and equip your model.

FIRE MARKS

Firefighting was much more difficult then than it is today, because of the lack of a continuous supply of water at pressure. Insurance companies took on this problem, and their distinctive metal plaques, known as 'fire marks', are still to be found on the walls of many old buildings. Usually made from copper or lead, many of them carry a date; if not, the company's period of operation can be looked up and used to help date the house. As houses are demolished, the plates tend to be removed and sold off to collectors, so the presence of a mark on a building is no guarantee that the house is of that date, or that the mark was originally placed there.

It was the Great Fire of London in 1666 that hastened the development of insurance; the Friendly Society of London was established by 1683. Each company had to be able to identify the property insured, so fire marks, which also acted as advertisements, were placed in prominent positions on houses and shops. If your house was on fire, only the company you were insured with would help you to put it out, so the mark was important as confirmation that you were a policyholder.

The foundation dates of some other companies from the Georgian period are listed here:

Hand in Hand	1696
Sun Fire Office	1710
Bristol Crown	1718
London	1720
Hibernian	1771
Liverpool	1777
Salop	1780
Dundee	1782
Newcastle	1783
Fife	1800
Globe	1803
Reading	1822
Shamrock	1823
Yorkshire	1824

Early marks were of lead, but the early 1800s favoured copper, with iron and tin being used by 1820. Replicas of some marks are available in 1/12 scale.

FIRE MARKS

A selection of the earliest marks is shown here (not to scale) for reference.

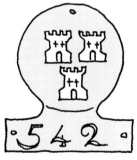

Newcastle

Hand in Hand

Sun

Bristol

CHAPTER SIX

LIGHT AND WATER

Lighting • Exterior ironwork • Sanitation • Water supply
Rainwater goods

LIGHTING

Householders in the larger conurbations were obliged by law and by various local regulations to light the area of pavement in front of their house during the hours of darkness. This was all very well, but if you had occasion to visit a friend at the other side of town the services of a linkman would be required.

Linkmen carried torches known as 'links' to light the way for late-night travellers in the dimly lit areas of towns 'linking' the lighted areas together. Most of the homes visited would have had snuffers incorporated in their front railings, to allow the linkman to extinguish his torch or link once the traveller was safely in the bosom of his friends. Trumpet-shaped snuffers are still to be found in London and Bath, with much more exotic dragons' mouths still remaining in Edinburgh.

The interiors were almost as dark and gloomy as the outside world, with rooms being greatly under-lit by the standards of the nineteenth and twentieth centuries. This was even true of 'fine' houses.

The simplest form of candle was the rush light, held in an equally simple stand. These candles had the pith from a rush for a wick. Next up the scale were tallow candles, made from rendered animal fat. These did not burn well and were every bit as smelly as the rush lights; they were either home-made or purchased in distinctive bundles with each candle joined to its fellow by the wick.

Candles were not found burning in every room, but were used sparingly, with much use of reflective surfaces to magnify the light available. Most sconces and chandeliers were only used on high days and holidays, announcing to the world the

A plain example still in situ in Bath

Three different styles from Bath

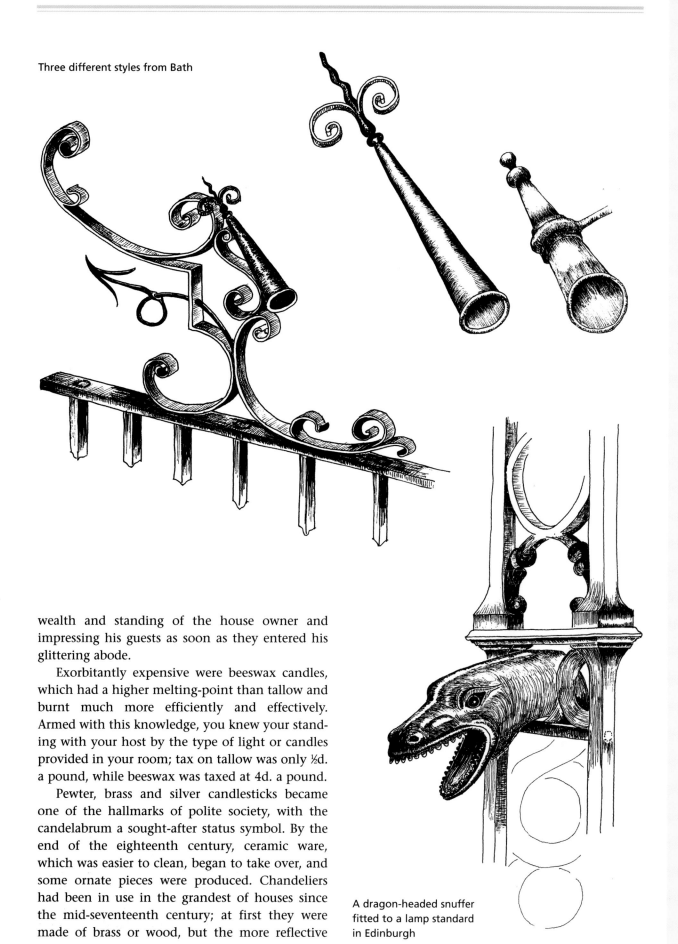

wealth and standing of the house owner and impressing his guests as soon as they entered his glittering abode.

Exorbitantly expensive were beeswax candles, which had a higher melting-point than tallow and burnt much more efficiently and effectively. Armed with this knowledge, you knew your standing with your host by the type of light or candles provided in your room; tax on tallow was only ½d. a pound, while beeswax was taxed at 4d. a pound.

Pewter, brass and silver candlesticks became one of the hallmarks of polite society, with the candelabrum a sought-after status symbol. By the end of the eighteenth century, ceramic ware, which was easier to clean, began to take over, and some ornate pieces were produced. Chandeliers had been in use in the grandest of houses since the mid-seventeenth century; at first they were made of brass or wood, but the more reflective

A dragon-headed snuffer fitted to a lamp standard in Edinburgh

glass variety, introduced around 1730, was to become the most popular.

Candles remained an essential part of the domestic scene until the advent of electricity, with most people using them to augment the expensive oil or gas lighting.

Oil lamps in the Georgian period were dirty and inefficient, and smelt even more than most candles. In 1783 G. Ami Argand, a Swiss chemist, patented the Argand or colza-oil lamp. This vegetable oil was so thick that it would not readily rise up a wick, so that the reservoir had to be positioned above, allowing the oil to flow downwards. By 1820, partly due to a temporary lapse of Argand's patent, oil lamps of this sort were fairly common in most of the better homes in Britain. While some designs were as elegant as we would expect from Georgian and Regency craftsmen, others were chandelier-like, with many branches, and could be ungainly. It was only in 1863 that a less viscous, highly refined oil was found as a substitute for colza oil, and the oil lamp as we all know it came into being.

For the most part we can forget gas lighting at this period; yet the first home to be illuminated by coal gas was that of Lord Dundonald in 1787, and the first public gaslights were ignited in 1803. Though a vast improvement on previous methods of lighting, gas was expensive; and, since the tradesmen were not regulated as they are now, it was dangerous and slow to catch on.

In short, Georgian houses were elegant yet poorly illuminated. I prefer to furnish a miniature house with the whole range of equipment: rush lights, candlesticks, candelabra, sconces, chandeliers and colza-oil lamps. These can then be lit as one would a stage set or display, using hidden electric strip lights. My own model has built-in strips of wood at the front edge of each first-floor room for this. If you wish to light your house in this way, the wires must be put in position in the loft area prior to fixing the roof on. Remember that these are not 12-volt units, but mains lighting of low wattage.

EXTERIOR IRONWORK

A lamplighter is depicted in *The Costume of Great Britain* by W. H. Pyne, published in 1805. The construction of his lamp is clear to see, with the oil reservoir and wick suspended from the top of the glass bowl or globe. The crown-like top cover has been removed and is clearly shown; it is quite decorative, and pierced to give adequate ventilation. Lamps of this kind were obligatory at the front doors of town houses of quality, and there were numerous ways of suspending them. For example, Canaletto's view of Northumberland House, London, of 1755 shows four lamps supported on obelisks, each over 12ft (3.66m) high.

In poor weather, lights might be blown out and have to be reignited. It was to overcome this

WROUGHT-IRON LAMP BRACKETS

Superior town houses were required to show a light at the front door, and this resulted in some very graceful structures.

(*Above and Right*) Two very similar arched brackets in Bath, one still fitted with a genuine lamp of the period

problem that lights were incorporated into the inside of fanlights over front doors, projecting forward over the front step.

Around 1700, the ironwork of these lamps and the area railings was generally painted blue with gilt details; later grey became fashionable (without gilding), then for most of the century generally black. At the end of the eighteenth and into the early nineteenth century, some were painted green in imitation of bronze. In the Regency period, trellis porches and balconies were a light bronze green but area railings were still black; though in Dublin at this time, area railings could be white. If you lived outside the town-centre area where a lamp was compulsory but still provided a light at the front of your house, you might be excused a percentage of your parish rates.

Making a lamp bracket is not a major undertaking; use stout wire, with strips of alloy or tin for the scrollwork. If you are not comfortable with soldering, then use Araldite or a similar adhesive, sanding back all surplus prior to painting.

An upright bracket in Dublin, with another, Edwardian, lamp hung beneath it in true Heath Robinson style

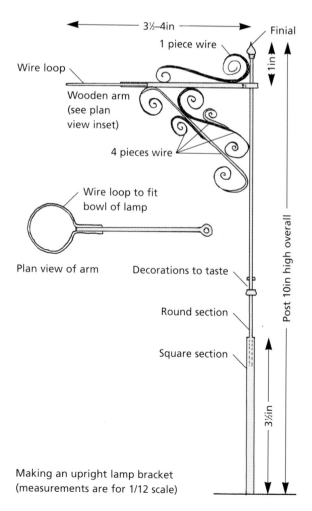

Making an upright lamp bracket
(measurements are for 1/12 scale)

A LIGHT INCORPORATED IN A FANLIGHT OVER A REGENCY FRONT DOOR

————

Another elegant solution to the same problem. Candles or oil lamps would be used. This example is from Bath, but great numbers survive in Dublin.

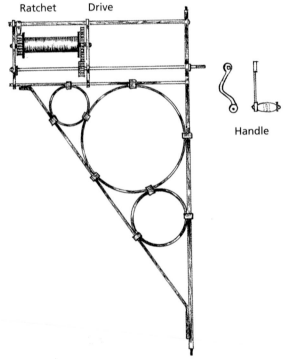

Ratchet   Drive

Handle

Snuffers are a bit more of a challenge. Dragon heads and the like are best got when your children or grandchildren are asleep. The spoils should then be butchered and the heads mounted, trophy-like, in the framework of the light. In Chapter XLVIII of *Bleak House* (1853), Dickens describes an old street of 'dismal grandeur' in which 'extinguishers for obsolete flambeaux gasp at the upstart gas'; and in Bath, London, Dublin and Edinburgh, at least, not only front area lamp brackets but snuffers as well are still to be found today.

Most front areas have railings, with a gate onto the steps which lead down to the kitchens and other offices. At least one house in Bath has no area steps, yet the owners did not want kitchen supplies passing through the front door. This was overcome by using an ingenious crane and pulley system to raise and lower supplies. The drawing and photographs on this page and the next may help you to reproduce it.

SERVICE AREA CRANE

————

This example in Bath (*above and opposite page*) is a variation on the familiar chimney crane. A crane was used when there were no steps or gate from the front street to the servants' area, so that foodstuffs, fuel, etc. did not have to be carried through the front hall.

BELLS TO SERVICE AREA

Many area railings hold remnants of bell pulls used to rouse servants from the basement, and these can easily be duplicated in miniature. They all consist of a handle attached to the railings, linked by a chain, metal rods or wires to a bell or bells in the servants' quarters. Some handles are simple, resembling a doorknob, while others are swan-necked levers; the photographs and drawings will show you how to make them.

There are two types: one mounted on the top of the railings, and the other towards the bottom. A replica of the top-mounted type can be made using a miniature brass castor; to this are glued the handle and the hook and chain. The handle can be simply a coiled piece of wire, or you can hammer it out to give a leaf shape prior to bending; fix as shown in the diagram. Drill the top rail to take the spindle of the castor, then mount the completed unit in place, painting it to match the existing scheme.

The type mounted lower down is made by using a miniature doorknob as the handle. Available on the miniatures scene are knobs with threaded rod just as in real life; remove the rod and insert the wire hook as shown in the diagram.

BELL PULLS

These simple devices were mounted on the area railings and were used to rouse servants from below stairs. The Dublin example has two, instead of the usual one. In Bath I found one with a simple knob-type handle that was lifted to operate the bell.

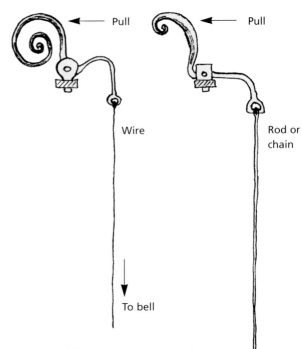

Two versions of the lever-type bell pull, from Dublin. The diameter of the ram's-horn handle is 6in in real life

Double bell pull from Dublin

Bell pull with lifting knob, Bath. Dimensions can be adjusted to suit the railings you have

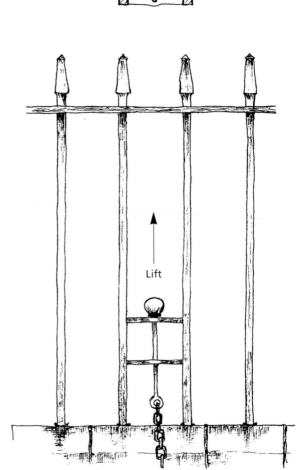

Shape of wire handle prior to bending; the part
to be curled has been beaten out flat

Making a lever-type bell pull

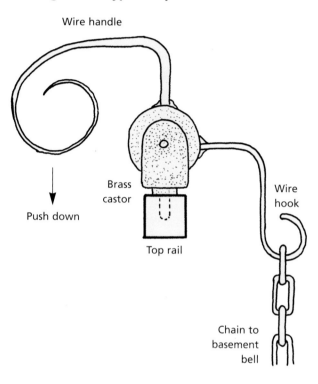

Wire handle

Push down

Brass
castor

Top rail

Wire
hook

Chain to
basement
bell

Making a knob-type bell pull

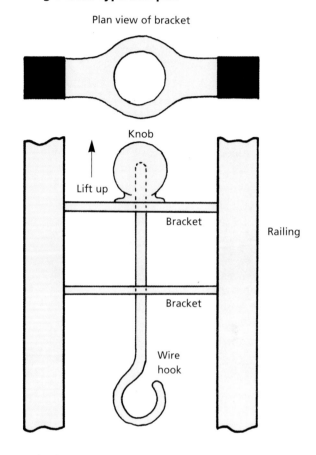

Plan view of bracket

Knob

Lift up

Bracket

Railing

Bracket

Wire
hook

Make the two brackets from ⅟₁₆in (1.5mm) hardwood, and pass the hook through these prior to gluing on the knob. Glue the completed system towards the bottom of your railings, and paint as before.

'WITH THE FAIRIES'

Privies were usually with the fairies, at the bottom of the garden, and were of the primitive earth or ash closet type. A bench with two, and at times three holes of various sizes – mum, dad and baby – was suspended over a void. A bucket or other container full of earth was close at hand, and when the bowels had been moved the offending evidence was covered with a small amount of this. The mixture was allowed to accumulate for a

period of time, after which it would be collected by 'night-soil men' and later used to fertilize crops. Evidence of this practice is seen today in the great quantity of broken china unearthed by the plough. Broken household utensils were discarded on the ash heap, then later, along with the ashes, found their way to the privy and lastly to the fields.

In more polite society, with its overriding love of symmetry, the 'necessary' building of a town house was constructed as one of a pair of visually pleasing balanced pavilions at the bottom of the back garden. In the country, these pavilions could be built one either side of the house, giving a rather grand Palladian look to an otherwise ordinary dwelling. The second structure could house a small reading room, or it might be equipped as a summer house or as a not-so-simple shed for garden tools or whatever.

In terraced houses, the emptying of the privy by the night-soil men was carried out at night, as the offending evacuations had to be brought through the house to a cart in the front street. Trade cards of the period illustrate this work in progress.

In most town houses with indoor sanitation, the main toilet was on the ground floor; but, as the principal rooms were on the first floor, one sometimes had to be squeezed into the strangest of corners. All Robert Adam's houses of the 1770s and '80s had as standard a 'water closet' in a corner off the back stairs. A 'water closet' was defined at this period as a toilet that could be flushed by water from a bucket, tank or cistern, or directly from a mains pipe. The invention of water closets is well documented, but what is in doubt is how rapidly the idea was taken up. Most areas had a poor water supply at best, and inadequate water pressure, along with the cost of such facilities, meant that most establishments continued with the earth closet. In rural areas, even this was a luxury; it is recorded that 'improvers' built earth closets against the new cottages erected for their labourers, but rather than soil such a fine building they would take a walk down a convenient hedge and use the

A NIGHT-SOIL MAN'S BUSINESS CARD
(after an original in the British Museum)

The outside privy can be seen at the bottom of the garden, the nightman having performed his duty by bringing the waste through the house into the cart in the front street. This waste was then sold on to farmers to spread on their fields.

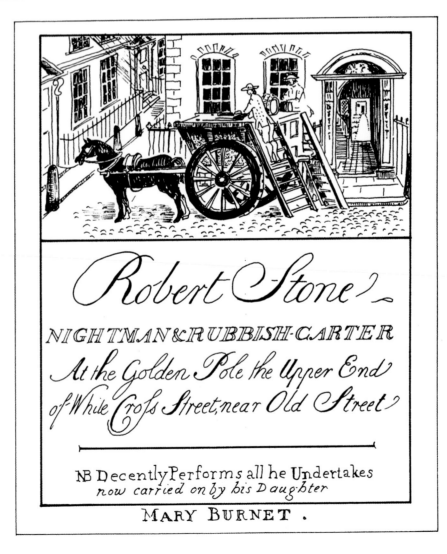

Robert Stone

NIGHTMAN & RUBBISH-CARTER

At the Golden Pole the Upper End of White Cross Street, near Old Street

NB Decently Performs all he Undertakes
now carried on by his Daughter

MARY BURNET.

building to house chickens or fuel. Many of our finest country houses had simple lean-to earth closets built against one of the main elevations; Wallington Hall in Northumberland had one of these, and it is faithfully shown in an engraving of the period.

William Kent, working at Holkham Hall in Norfolk, depicted on his plans of 1734 a simple windowless room or closet just off the hall to accommodate a basic two-holer. Later, in 1765, the Duke of Bedford installed four water closets at Woburn, at least one of them being inside the house; of special note here was the fine sewage system to carry off the results. Isaac Ware incorporated 'bog houses' in his designs for a house in 1756, but none of these were inside. While examples are to be found in yards, gardens or front areas, water closets were not usual inside Georgian houses – though George Scharf (a Bavarian artist who worked in London in the Regency period) left us a fine sketch of one in his house. So, water closets were available to the rich, but the prevailing attitude was 'not in my house!'

Horace Walpole was amused while visiting a house in 1760, and wrote: 'but of all curiosities are the conveniences in every bedchamber . . . great mahogany projections . . . with holes, with brass handles and cocks etc. . . . I could not help saying, it was the loosest family I ever saw.'

Fine decorated toilet bowls and chamber-pots are collectors' items today. Early ones were made of lead or (if you were lucky, and rich) solid marble; the pretty pottery ones arrived only at the close of the century.

Let us retreat from these inadequate appliances and the foul-smelling bog houses to the fine cabinets of Chippendale, Hepplewhite and Sheraton, all of whom designed night stands with washing bowls and commode. These were much more numerous than any of the built-in services. The humble 'jerry' has been known since the fourteenth century, and could be of metal or earthenware; it was traditionally placed on a stool or low table at the bedside, not under the bed. It had one or two handles, and a wide mouth falling to a narrow neck and on into a copious base. To reflect the refined tastes of the eighteenth century, fine glazed pots were made to replace the earlier ones which were only glazed on the inside, if at all. By 1754, transfer-printed pots were being produced in Liverpool; these became things of beauty, with

REGENCY TOILET UNDER THE STAIRS, EARLY NINETEENTH CENTURY
(after an 1842 print by George Scharf in the British Museum, Department of Prints and Drawings)

⸻

The toilet cabinet was mahogany. The walls were painted salmon colour, and other woodwork white. There was no covering on the floorboards. The cupboard at the back housed the cistern, filled as and when water pressure allowed. To the left is a washbasin, with slop cupboard below.

designs as varied as coats of arms or flowers, and by 1800 political slogans and crude verse were added to the repertoire:

> Use me well, keep me clean,
> And I'll not tell what I have seen.

Hepplewhite published drawings of pot cupboards in his *Cabinet-Maker and Upholsterer's Guide* (1794). Bidets, also built into fine cabinets, first came to light in the dressing rooms of France in 1710, but later were introduced into the bedroom, housed in improved cabinets which also contained one or two pots 'for the accidental occasions of the night'.

The 'thunderbox' or close-stool of earlier years lingered on in many houses; it could be carried anywhere in the house for night use. A fashionable variation of this known as the 'Secrets of Paris' was used toward the end of the eighteenth century. This consisted of a stack of mock books on a stool. On opening the top book a chamber-pot was revealed – and available for use, if your servants had cleaned up after the previous night's work. Instructions on how to model both of these are given below, but it is wise to buy your chamber-pot first so the dimensions can be modified if necessary to give a correct fit, or you could spend a long time looking for one just the right size.

'Thunderbox' or close-stool
(full size for 1/12 scale)

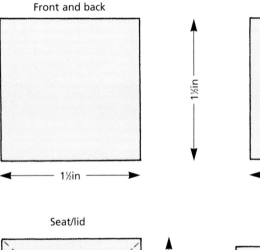

Front and back

1½in

1½in

Sides

1in

Cut two sides, a matching front and back, and one base. Glue the sides, then slot the base inside. Fit handles of your choice to the sides. The seat/lid is made to fit neatly by attaching two runners to the underside. Take care cutting and sanding the hole. Finish off by fixing skirting round the base

Seat/lid

1½in

Base

1in

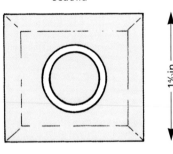

Plan view

⅔in

Handle

⅔in

1¾in

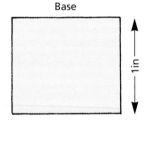

Cross section of seat and runners

Plan of runners

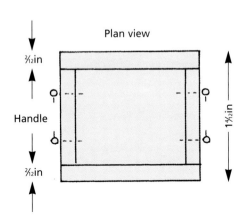

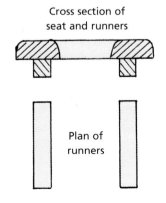

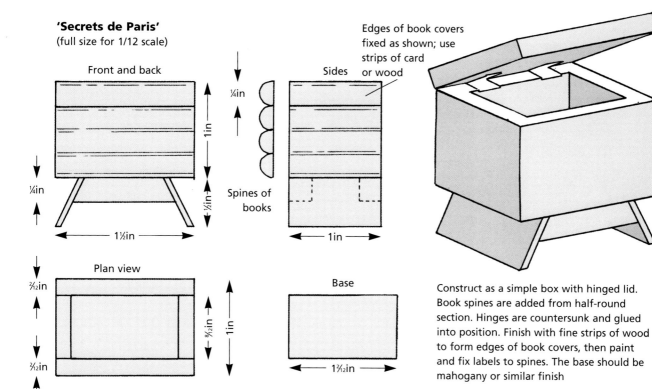

'Secrets de Paris'
(full size for 1/12 scale)

Front and back

¼in

1in

¼in

½in

1½in

Sides

Spines of books

Edges of book covers fixed as shown; use strips of card or wood

1in

Plan view

²⁄₃₂in

²⁄₃₂in

²⁄₃₂in

¾in

1in

Base

1¾in

Construct as a simple box with hinged lid. Book spines are added from half-round section. Hinges are countersunk and glued into position. Finish with fine strips of wood to form edges of book covers, then paint and fix labels to spines. The base should be mahogany or similar finish

Not always in the same room were washstands, which could be either free-standing or built in. The water containers and bowls were much smaller than the later Victorian ones with which we are familiar, and were housed in elegant pieces of furniture. A rather grand built-in unit is at 41 Gay Street, Bath, the home of the architect John Wood the younger, who no doubt used it as his 'show house' to impress clients. We will make one based on this example.

REGENCY CORNER WASHSTAND EARLY NINETEENTH CENTURY
(after an 1842 print by George Scharf in the British Museum, Department of Prints and Drawings)

These units were developed in response to an improved water supply, but still may not have had mains drains – so don't rush to fill your house with them. This particular example was fed with water from an upstairs cistern, yet the waste was collected in a pot to be emptied by servants. The detail at bottom right shows the brass tap and plug, mounted on a lead pipe.

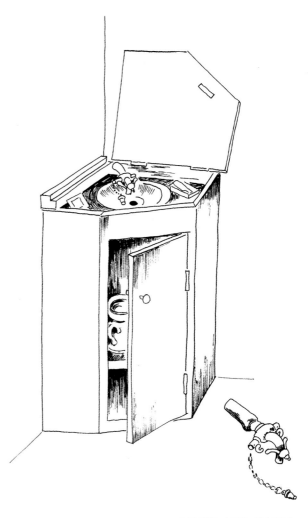

Corner toilet and washstand
(drawn full size for 1/12 scale)

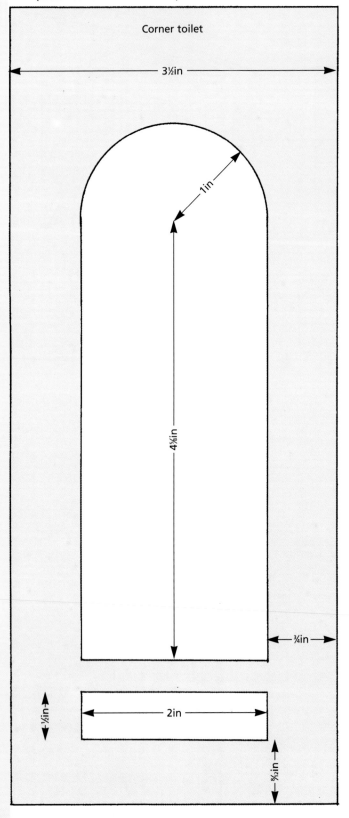

Corner toilet

3½in

1in

4⅝in

¾in

¼in

2in

⅝in

Corner washstand

3½in

1in

3½in

¾in

2¼in

Cut these front panels from ½in (0.8mm) plywood

Toilet: The bottom of the arched opening is 1½in from the floor

Washstand: The bottom of the arched opening is 2¼in from the floor, but you may wish to adjust this to match an existing dado rail or other feature. The overall height is dictated by the height of your dolls' house ceiling

MAKING A CORNER TOILET AND WASHSTAND

To build the toilet, first cut the front from fine plywood (I used ½in or 0.8mm), then with a good craft knife cut the two holes for the alcove and drawer. The overall height depends on the ceiling height of your room.

The curved back of the alcove is made of even finer plywood or card (⅙₄in or 0.4mm), measuring 3 x 7½in (76 x 190mm) in 1/12 scale. Cut two lengths of wood, ¼in (6mm) square or similar, 7½in (190mm) long, and glue these to the back of the unit as shown in the diagram opposite. These must be set back from the edges of the opening by the thickness of the plywood or card forming the back, so that the back piece can sit neatly inside without its edges being visible from the front. Leave these pieces to set, then glue in the curved back and again leave to set. The semicircular top and bottom pieces are cut from ¾₆in (5mm) material and should now be glued inside the alcove ends.

The seat can be made of better stuff, such as walnut or mahogany, with the front edge and hole given a good finish. When completed, glue this in place and finish the unit to complement your décor.

The matching washstand is of the same basic construction as the toilet, but this time the shelf holding the bowl forms the base of the recess and

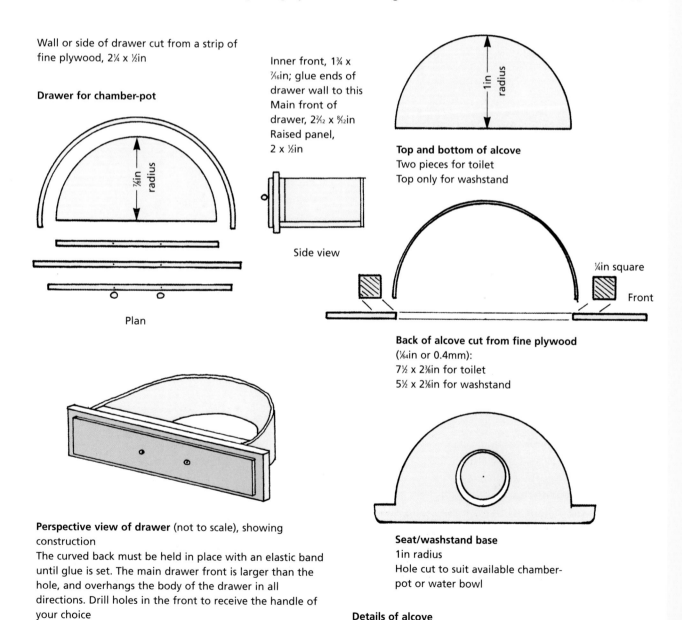

Wall or side of drawer cut from a strip of fine plywood, 2¼ x ½in

Drawer for chamber-pot

Inner front, 1¾ x ⁷⁄₁₆in; glue ends of drawer wall to this
Main front of drawer, 2½ x ⁹⁄₃₂in
Raised panel, 2 x ½in

⅞in radius

Side view

Plan

1in radius

Top and bottom of alcove
Two pieces for toilet
Top only for washstand

¼in square

Front

Back of alcove cut from fine plywood (⅙₄in or 0.4mm):
7½ x 2⅜in for toilet
5½ x 2⅜in for washstand

Perspective view of drawer (not to scale), showing construction
The curved back must be held in place with an elastic band until glue is set. The main drawer front is larger than the hole, and overhangs the body of the drawer in all directions. Drill holes in the front to receive the handle of your choice

Seat/washstand base
1in radius
Hole cut to suit available chamber-pot or water bowl

Details of alcove

MODEL OF A CORNER TOILET UNIT

To have one of these indoors was posh in the extreme, and it required a discreet servant to empty the receptacle in the drawer each day. The model is quite simple to make and install.

THE DRESSING ROOM AT BRIDGE END HOUSE

The dressing room to the Gothic Revival bedroom has a corner washstand with blue 'Bristol delft' tiles, based on one in Bath; the tiles are supplied by Terry Curran. The small oratory is as much a regional tradition as a denominational one – in this room, at least, you could be clean in body and spirit.

only one other semicircular piece is required for the top. The shelf can be plain, or have a hole in it to hold the bowl; the choice is yours.

The main differences between this and the toilet are the height of the opening, and the fact that the back of the washstand alcove is decorated with tiles. The choice of tiles is up to you – paper, plastic or the real thing – but beware the detail, as they must be Georgian tiles and not the more common Victorian ones. The originals were Bristol blue delft.

MAKING A PAIR OF MATCHING PAVILIONS

In the Georgian period it was not unusual to have matching pavilions at the bottom of the garden. One housed the privy, while the other could be put to one of many uses: the top of the list included game larder, meat safe, garden shed, summerhouse or reading-room.

Earth closets, meat safes or game stores do not require large windows, as do reading-rooms and

ELEVATION OF BRIDGE END HOUSE WITH PAVILIONS ADDED
(not to scale)

The base of the pavilions must be made to match that of the main house. The front (window) and back walls are the same size, but cut to receive the chosen window and door respectively. Dimensions are for 1/12 scale.

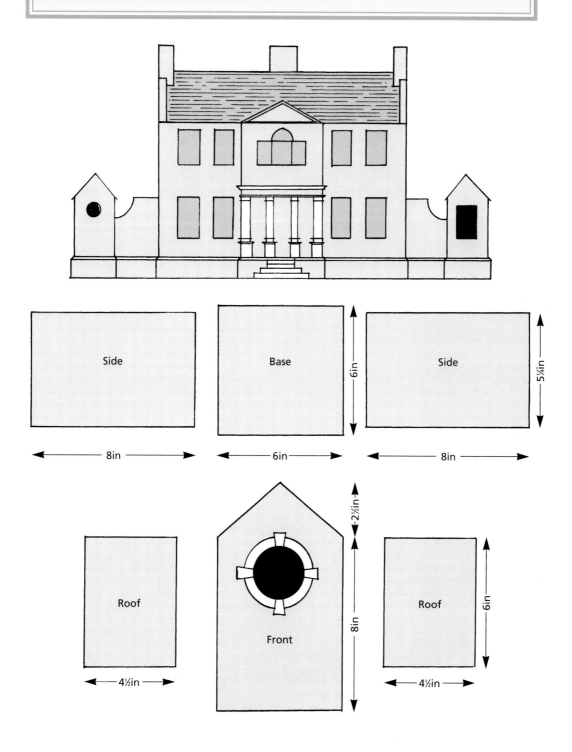

summerhouses; so if you wish to balance your privy with a building that requires a large window, you will have to stop and think. If using large windows to match the main house, the one in the privy, meat safe or game store should be a false one, blocked up on the inside. If both units are of the type that requires small windows, then a bull's-eye or similar type is ideal. The elevation drawing on page 121 shows one of each type for the sake of example, but in practice they should both match. The pavilions shown in this drawing have their opening at the back, as they would not normally open onto the street, but the choice is yours. The short length of wall linking the pavilion to the house is best kept simple; and remember that if your house stands on a plinth or base, the pavilion must have the same.

The bench you sat on was a simple box lid, hinged at the back, with holes in it, with buckets underneath to collect the waste. Remember that the front edges of the holes, not their centres, need to be in line.

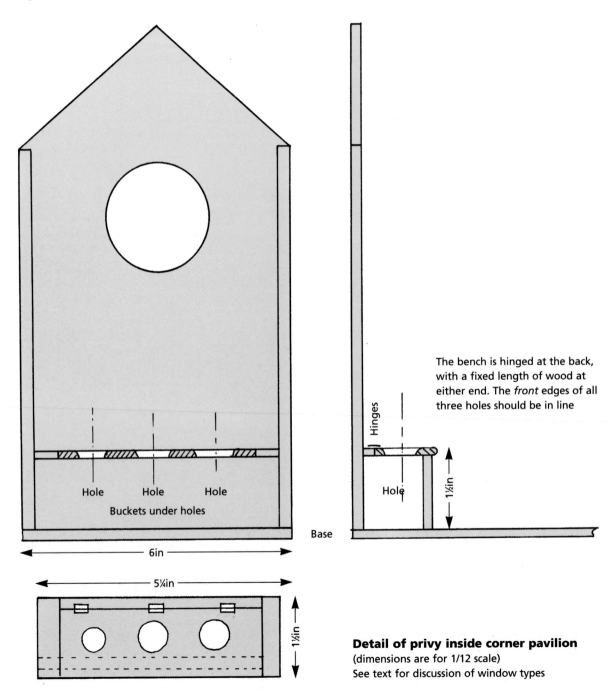

The bench is hinged at the back, with a fixed length of wood at either end. The *front* edges of all three holes should be in line

Hinges

Hole

1½in

Hole   Hole   Hole

Buckets under holes

Base

6in

5¼in

1½in

Detail of privy inside corner pavilion
(dimensions are for 1/12 scale)
See text for discussion of window types

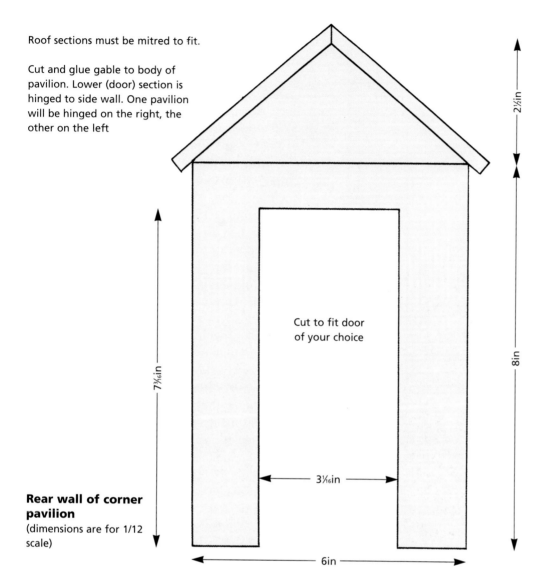

Roof sections must be mitred to fit.

Cut and glue gable to body of pavilion. Lower (door) section is hinged to side wall. One pavilion will be hinged on the right, the other on the left

Cut to fit door of your choice

2½in

8in

7⅝in

Rear wall of corner pavilion
(dimensions are for 1/12 scale)

3⅛in

6in

Summerhouses would have a small built-in table and benches, while game stores had a treelike structure with hooks to 'hang' the game on. Some also had cold marble slabs.

The drawings and ideas given here are only basic, and are intended to be treated like recipes: that is, not to be followed literally, but developed to suit your own requirements.

PRIVIES AND GARDENS

There was something about earth closets that meant that most of them were located at the bottom of the garden, with scented shrubs and flowerbeds between them and the house. No matter what fine title was bestowed on them – Temple of the Winds or Temple of Cloacina (goddess of sewers) – nor how elaborate the architecture, they were smelly places, cleaned out once a week at best. If at the bottom of the garden, they could be as simple or as architecturally grand as your pocket could withstand; but if they flanked the house, Palladian-fashion, then it was best if the style was at least sympathetic to that of the house.

The layout of gardens was formal, and subject to individual taste and size of plot. Early town gardens or yards were small, but later ones were quite large – if narrow – and this was much commented on by Continental visitors. Walkways tended to be of gravel or flagstone, and the lawn was planted with flowering shrubs: cherry, almond, laburnum, lilac and damask roses. Large glazed flower pots with myrtle, orange trees and tender flowers stood against the house and were moved to fill gaps or to give a stronger perfume as and where required. If you want to try your hand at gardening in miniature, Freida Gray's *Making Miniature Gardens* (GMC Publications, 1999) is the best introduction.

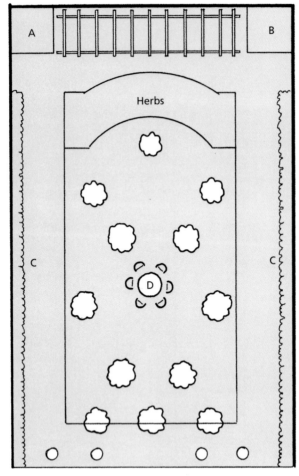

Herbs

House

A 'Conveniency', 6ft square ⎫
B Small study, 6ft square   ⎬ Linked by a pergola
                              ⎭
C Gravel walks
D Stone table and green-painted wooden chairs

A town garden of the mid-eighteenth century

WATER SUPPLY

It may surprise you to learn that the earliest water company was founded in Hull in 1420, followed by one in Bath in 1500, but most towns depended on springs until the first quarter of the nineteenth century. Wooden pipes were used as mains under the streets, while lead carried the water indoors. It was only in 1780 that iron pipes began to replace the old wooden ones. The old elm pipes persisted in most towns well into the Victorian era. Walter Rose, in his memoir *The Village Carpenter* (Cambridge University Press, 1937), describes the making of elm pumps in the 1870s or 1880s.

Throughout the eighteenth century water was supplied, if at all, only to the ground floor, from which it had to be pumped by hand to the upper floors, or carried from the buck or cistern in buckets. (A buck or butt is a barrel of 108–140 gallons (490–640 litres) capacity.) Water pumped to the upper floors was known as 'high service', and was only possible if your water company had installed iron pipes; the old wooden ones, or a combination of wood and iron, could not withstand the pressure that had to be exerted to accomplish this feat.

Every kitchen used water in a big way, yet it was in short supply in most towns, with piped water only being available on a rota system: in Soho, as late as 1760, they only had piped water for seven hours, three days a week. The day's supply for a house was held in a large lead cistern (see page 169), often located in the basement kitchen, close to the sink; alternatively, it might be found in the back yard or the front service area. Embellished with strapwork or floral work in an outdated style, and with the customary date and initials, this cistern typically held 30–50 gallons (135–230 litres) and was filled at prescribed times with water from one of the various water companies. In some fortunate households water could be raised by hand pumps to smaller cisterns in upstairs dressing rooms, but by 1820, in some areas at least, there was sufficient pressure in the supply to eliminate the need for this.

Most villages and small towns depended on the 'pant', otherwise known as the fountain or public conduit; since the population was not dense enough to cover the cost of laying pipes to each individual house, it was more economical to feed water to central points where it could be collected in buckets. Larger houses had their own well in the basement or kitchen. The Public Health Act of 1875 stipulated that no new houses should be built in rural areas unless within a 'reasonable distance' of a water supply.

RAINWATER GOODS

Rainwater gutters were of wood or lead, with a few of copper. I remember living in a house with wooden gutters as a child; these were of two sorts, either U-shaped and made from a solid piece of wood (these are still stocked by builders' merchants in

RAINWATER GOODS

Rainwater heads or hoppers were at first flamboyant, and were only for the rich. Later ones were simple inverted cones, with more elaborate ones of cast iron or lead coming in at the end of our period.

Drawings are not to scale.

Lancashire), or built up from three pieces. The downpipes were much the same, being long wooden tubes with a square section. All were painted dark green and pitched on the inside.

Rainwater heads or cistern heads were a prominent feature at this time, and were often marked with the date of building and the builder's initials. Most were made from lead, but miniatures can be made of wood, with small metal numerals glued on to make the date, then painted to look like lead. Suitable numerals are readily available from good miniaturists and clockmakers.

Ingoe West Hall,
Northumberland

Street House,
Northumberland,
c.1780

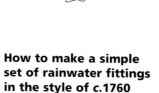

Evesham,
Hereford &
Worcester

A design in the
style of c.1800 –
why not add your
own initials?

How to make a simple set of rainwater fittings in the style of c.1760

The drawing *(right)* is not to scale, but suggested dimensions are given for 1/12 scale

Gutter: made up in box section to ⅜in or ½in square
Downpipe: made from solid wood, ¼ to ⅜in square
Rainwater head: made from a block of wood, with 1/12 scale door numbers glued on to make the date; small strips of wood form decoration
Brackets: made from ¹⁄₁₆in wood to your own pattern
Shoe: a box shape made up from ¹⁄₁₆in wood

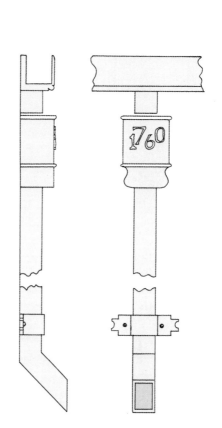

CHAPTER SEVEN

HEATING AND COOKING

Kitchens • Reception rooms • Fire screens, chimney boards and
dummy boards • Stoves • Portable heaters

KITCHEN AND COTTAGE FIREPLACES

Fire was always important in the home both for warmth and for cooking, but the receptacle it was held in has changed over the centuries. This change was quicker in some areas than others; centrally positioned hearths were still being used in some of Britain's most remote and beautiful regions as late as the turn of the twentieth century.

Most cottages or houses of the eighteenth century had large open fireplaces whose position dictated how the room was laid out; from our point of view it is a pity that this focal point was usually on the end wall, which in a dolls' house is not readily on view.

The most common arrangement was for the gable-end fireplace to be positioned slightly off-centre to allow room for a wall oven and, in the case of more humble homes and cottages, the stairs. Cottage stairs were steep and of various regional types, but all fitted into a space of 4–5ft (1.2–1.5m). The foot of the stairs was closed off by a simple door, so that when closed it looked like a cupboard.

In working-class homes the room with the fireplace was often the only one on the ground floor, while in farmhouses it was the largest ground-floor room. In both cases it was the heart of the home, not merely the abode of servants and cooks. In more elegant houses these servants worked in a kitchen tucked away at the back of the building or in the basement.

An almost universal feature was the mantel shelf, which took its name from the short curtain or 'mantle' that hung beneath it in a vain hope of controlling smoke from downdraughts. (When the fine wood or marble surrounds of the more elegant bedroom or parlour fireplaces were designed as one unit, including the shelf, they were known as 'mantelpieces'.)

With the growth of towns and cities, local sources of fuel in the form of logs became depleted and alternative sources had to be found. 'Sea coal' from the coalfields of South Wales and Tyneside filled the gap. The plague of 1665 boosted the demand even further. Physicians of the time believed that the burning of coal destroyed pestilential germs, and this unlikely curative sealed the fate of wood burning in towns as fireplaces were converted to coal-burning grates.

In rural areas, at least, cooking was on a down-hearth or open fire of hardwood logs held in place by *brandirons* or firedogs. These raised the logs above the floor, allowing a draught from below yet at the same time preventing the logs rolling forward into the kitchen. Pots and pans were hung over this fire by chains and hooks attached to a chimney crane or *sway*.

Roasting was done on a spit in front of this inferno, the spit being turned by a dog, a small boy or some variation of clockwork jack. The spit itself was supported on a pair of *andirons* or spit dogs. These were modelled on firedogs, with the addition of hooks to support the spit; better examples had a top shaped like a cresset (a metal basket) to hold a vessel full of dripping for basting the joint. (More refined historians put these forward as brackets to hold mugs of mulled ale or other such refreshment; you may accept this explanation if you prefer.)

DEVELOPMENT OF THE HOB GRATE

The progression from firebacks, brandirons and andirons to the early forms of fire basket was brought about by the change from wood to coal as fuel. Spit dogs or andirons were not only used with log fires but also with the later hobs.

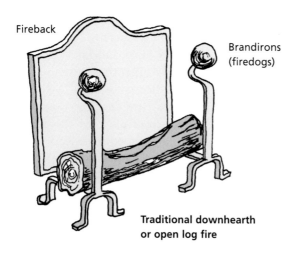

Fireback

Brandirons (firedogs)

Traditional downhearth or open log fire

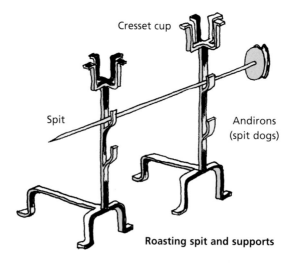

Cresset cup

Spit

Andirons (spit dogs)

Roasting spit and supports

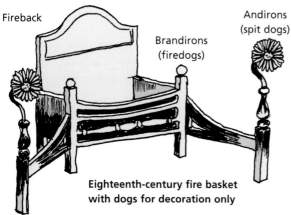

Fireback

Brandirons (firedogs)

Andirons (spit dogs)

Eighteenth-century fire basket with dogs for decoration only

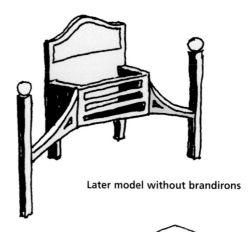

Later model without brandirons

Simple fire basket with no dogs

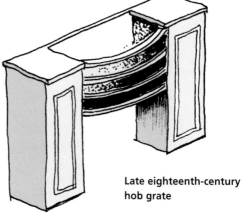

Late eighteenth-century hob grate

In large kitchens, where much larger roasts were required, the firedogs were joined together by a number of iron bars to allow more logs to be piled up, giving an even greater heat. Since the late seventeenth century, town houses at least had come to depend on coal for fuel and, as coal burns best when held in a mass, fire baskets came into being. They still incorporated firedogs as their front support, and spit dogs continued to be used as previously. This use of coal was a large step forward, and was only possible in towns on the coast or on navigable rivers; only the wealthy could afford overland haulage, so everyone else in inland districts was still burning wood or peat.

Later in the eighteenth century the basket idea developed into one of the most attractive types of fire container, for use in the better rooms of large, well-appointed houses. Though firedogs and spit dogs were no longer of use in reception rooms, at least their forms were retained, incorporated into baskets which were now designed solely to warm the room. Later models had only the spit dogs; while fine examples are still to be found, this was a short-lived fashion, replaced towards the end of the century by the hob grate. While the basket, like its kitchen cousins, was free-standing, the hob grate was fixed in such a way that it filled the fireplace. It became the accepted norm in all Georgian and Regency homes where coal was burnt.

THE DEVELOPMENT OF THE KITCHEN RANGE

As with most rooms in our dolls' houses, we tend to endow our miniature kitchens with the very best of equipment, fitting in the Agas or Raeburns of their day, while in truth most people would still have been cooking over open fires using pots and pans suspended from a chimney crane. Good examples of these warm, cosy interiors land on our doormats every Christmas in the form of illustrations on greetings cards.

The kind of range or other cooking equipment you should use in your house depends on where the house is supposed to be located. Is it from an area with a traditional fuel? Did they burn wood, peat or coal? Wood will burn easily in an open hearth with just a pair of firedogs or brandirons to support it – the traditional cottage scene. Coal has to be held in a mass for it to function well, which encouraged the development of the elevated basket.

London, for example, had no native fuel, and had imported coal from northern Britain for many years, so baskets were common there. Peat, which is intermediate between the other two fuels in its requirements, smouldered slowly in most kinds of fireplace in the upland areas of Britain. So remember that coal-producing areas would have baskets in the fireplaces of most homes, while in regions where logs were burnt the open hearth with firedogs or brandirons would persist.

From the basket for coal – modelled on, and often incorporating, firedogs – evolved the hob grate, no longer free-standing but built in. A few early ones were of brass, but later, more practical, ones were of iron. At first they were used in various rooms, since the hob allowed a kettle or pan to stand at the side, keeping the contents warm. Grates designed specifically for the kitchen only came in the late eighteenth century, so this fact dictates how your kitchen should be fitted.

At first glance, this first kitchen range looked like an extra-wide hob grate or basket. The width of the fire within the basket was adjustable by the use of cheeks or side plates which could be moved by cranking. Some had only one movable cheek, while others had two; but almost all had trivets mounted on the tops of the cheeks. A simple variation on the trivet was a shelf formed by extending the side plate upwards then bending it over to form a shelf (see the description of bakestones on page 146).

Thomas Robinson of London patented a range in 1780 with an oven at one side, but these were not the most efficient machines in the world and not many were produced. In 1783 another London ironmonger, Joseph Langmead, took the logical step of adding a boiler to the other side of the fire. Both of these ranges heated the oven and/or boiler without the use of flues, simply by contact with the fire at one side only. The flue, as we understand it, was still some time away.

Towards the end of our era (1820–40) the most scientific of kitchen appliances were being produced by the Carron Ironworks in Falkirk, Scotland. Founded in c.1760, the Carron works must have produced thousands of ranges and grates of many designs, yet only one drawing of a kitchen range of their manufacture is known to exist; it is housed in the National Archives of Scotland. This range has an oven to the left with its own fire and flue, while a wraparound boiler is

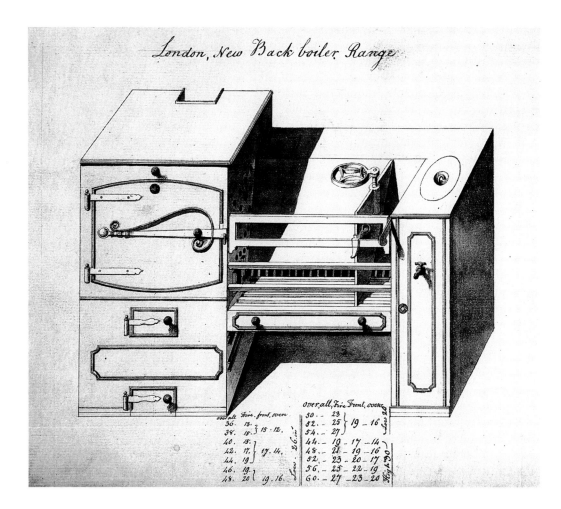

situated to the back and right-hand side of the main fire. There is also the now-standard movable cheek with a trivet mounted on it. A nice touch is the ash-box formed by a drawer under the fire, but this must have acted as a damper, tending to prevent the rise of air from the bottom.

Fourteen years after the Georgian era, in 1844, Thomas Webster published the *Encyclopedia of Domestic Economy*, illustrating a range with all these new features; but the oven continued to be of limited use and the spit was still preferred by most cooks until the end of the nineteenth century.

MODELLING A KITCHEN RANGE

Most houses would have had open fires, but most miniaturists prefer ranges. With this in mind we will build a replica of the Carron range of c.1820, with an oven at one side and a boiler at the back and other side. A chimney crane and some form of spit would still have been used. The materials required are wood, card, brass knobs and a tap. This unit can be adapted to fit most chimney breasts, but you must determine the depth of your chimney prior to starting.

The oven and boiler are made from blocks of wood, with the detail applied using card or fine plywood. The actual fire width can be adjusted to suit your chimney breast, by assembling the oven and boiler first then making the central fireplace to fit the remaining space.

The largest part of the range was the oven, which should be made out of a large block of wood, detailed by cutting card or thin ply to the shapes and sizes of the various doors and name plate. Hinges and further raised decoration should

Top made from two layers of wood or
card. Upper piece is same size as base
unit; lower one overhangs base unit
on two sides as shown by broken line

Cut out hole and
fit brass knob

1¾in*

2in

Oven door

Fire door

Decoration

Ash door (same
as fire door)

Build these up
with thin ply
or card

Fit brass tap
and decoration

Basic shape built up from three blocks of wood

MODELLING A KITCHEN RANGE

This model is based on Carron's 'London'
model of *c.*1820. Measurements are for 1/12
scale; those marked with an asterisk may be
adjusted to suit the size of the fireplace.

Ash box/drawer

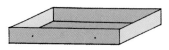

Two knobs required

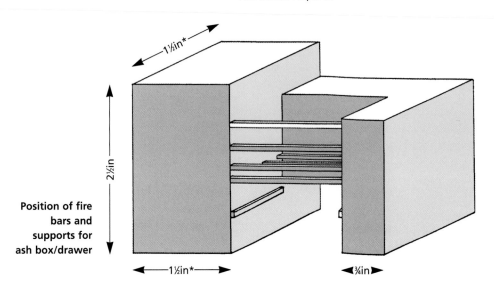

1½in*

2½in

**Position of fire
bars and
supports for
ash box/drawer**

1½in*

¾in

be applied in the same way, then the whole unit painted matt black and brass knobs fitted. The right-hand part of the boiler is much smaller but can be made in exactly the same way.

The size of the fire basket can be determined by positioning your oven and boiler at either side of the chimney breast and measuring the space left. Now complete the boiler by fitting in the part at the back of the fire. The top of this and the side boiler should be cut from one piece of card or plywood. The bars can now be positioned, being made of square-section wood or barbecue skewers. The ash box should be made like a shallow drawer with applied detail; it is held in place temporarily to mark the positions of the side supports for it to slide on. When complete, sand and clean, paint matt black and, when dry, drill holes to fit the brass knobs.

SMOKE HOODS AND CHIMNEY BREASTS

Now that you have chosen your cooking facilities, what kind of chimney breast should they be built into? As with most elements of the house, there were regional variations: besides local preferences for the use of stone or brick, some areas developed quite complicated features of their own, such as the smoke hoods of north-west England or the double flues of Ireland. The following are a few general rules:

In brick-producing areas, the chimney and the recess into which the range is built would be a straightforward structure; the top of the opening would either be a depressed brick arch, not unlike a window head, or a stout oak beam. As a simple rule, town-house ranges would be built into surrounds made entirely of brick, but in rural areas the locally found oak beam would be used.

Upland districts with stone-built houses would naturally use stone surrounds to their fires. The sides of the opening would be made of one tall

KITCHEN OR COTTAGE FIREPLACES

A selection from the many regional variations.

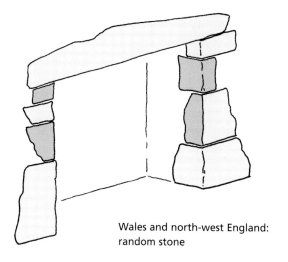

Wales and north-west England: random stone

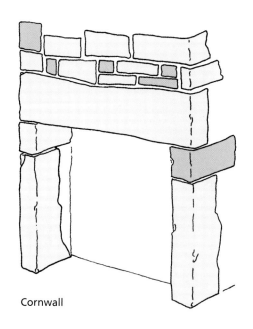

Cornwall

South-east England

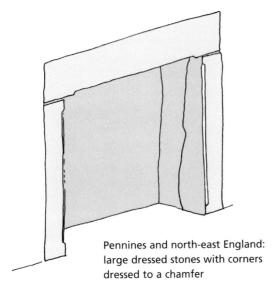

Pennines and north-east England:
large dressed stones with corners
dressed to a chamfer

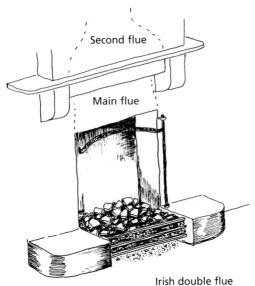

Second flue

Main flue

Irish double flue

Scottish 'hanging lum'

stone in northern Britain, while in the south-east and Wales they were built up from smaller stones; in all areas, the cross member over the opening consisted of a single large stone.

One strange survival is found occasionally in north-west England. A remnant of the much older smoke hood – a form found in big houses since the fifteenth century, from the Channel to the north of Scotland – was incorporated into a Georgian surround, resulting in the top of the fireplace projecting forward into the room.

In Ireland, towards the end of our period, there was an ingenious development, the double flue. Any smoke that escaped from the fire was drawn up a second flue, located above the fireplace but under the mantel shelf. In Scotland, a timber smoke hood or 'hanging lum' helped to direct wayward smoke towards the chimney. This was a much reduced variation of the arrangement used in Irish farmhouses.

RECEPTION ROOMS

Housed in their parks and country estates, the more aristocratic Georgians may have continued to burn wood; but most Georgian town houses used coal to heat their rooms and to cook their food. As we have seen, the shape of the old brandirons lived on, incorporated into the design of free-standing fire baskets or grates. Also at this time, steel firebacks, often assumed to have died out in the seventeenth century, were incorporated into the new grates. These basket grates could be removed in summer, prior to fixing chimney boards to prevent falls of soot and draughts.

The next big improvement was the introduction of the cast-iron hob grate around 1760; these were cheap to produce, and were made in great numbers by Carron in Scotland and Coalbrookdale in Shropshire, becoming standard issue by the end of the century. Their cast-iron fronts radiated much more heat than the old firebacks ever had. The hob could be used to keep food or drinks warm, and indeed in poorer houses this type of grate was used for cooking. So successful was the design that they were still being produced in the first quarter of the nineteenth century.

An improvement introduced in 1798 was the Rumford stove, in which the cheeks of the fire

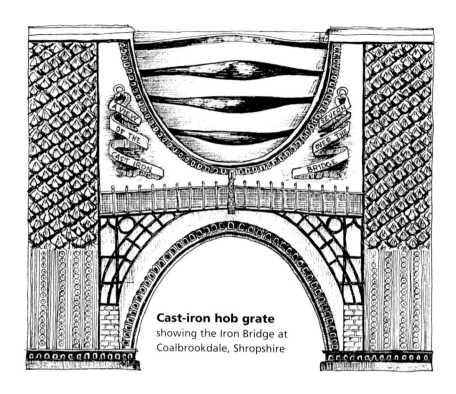

Cast-iron hob grate
showing the Iron Bridge at
Coalbrookdale, Shropshire

CHIMNEYS

Queen Anne and Early Georgian chimneys were built on the outside of
the house so that there was no chimney breast or accompanying alcoves
inside. The photographs below show a mid-Georgian house of *c*.1750, built
of brick with a large exterior chimney, and a rather nice Regency house
with two chimneys partly in and partly outside, showing that in more
rural areas change was slow. Both these houses are in areas which have
been built up in later times.

were set at angles and the fire pushed forward. The back of the fireplace also sloped forward, which had the effect of reducing the flue opening, leading to much greater efficiency.

In really fine rooms in the best of houses there were no chimney breasts, the flues being absorbed into the thickness of the wall. George Richardson's chimneypiece with Robert Adam's Roman-style cast-iron fire basket in the great hall at Kedleston Hall, Derbyshire (1775) is among the best examples of the period. Richardson was so proud of his part that he published engravings of it in his *New Collection of Chimney Pieces* in 1781.

Early Georgian fire surrounds were designed as part of the panelling of a room, with simple mouldings and no mantel shelf; though in better rooms an integrated frame or panel to receive a portrait or other work of art was positioned directly over the fireplace.

Wooden panelling in rooms was old hat by the mid-century and chimneypieces were much more important; Isaac Ware advised in 1756 that 'a principal compartment should be raised over it to receive a picture. This will be very happily terminated by a pediment. . . . it may be broken to receive a bust or a shield or other decoration.' Inigo Jones's pedimented chimneypiece at Wilton (1652) is one of only a few examples of this treatment so well thought-of by the Georgians.

CORNER FIREPLACES

Corner fireplaces can save you, as they saved the Georgians, wall space for the display of fine furniture or works of art; and they were themselves

used to display valuable pieces of china. Instead of a simple mantel shelf they had what are known as 'china steps'. Most examples are from the early part of the century, but quite a few were built later. Good places to see them include Hampton Court Palace near London, Drayton House in Northamptonshire, Mereworth Castle in Kent, and Beningbrough in North Yorkshire. Even in houses not short of space, it was fashionable to have small rooms or 'china closets' to display one's newly acquired pieces from the Orient. Later houses which were a little more pushed for space used such corner units in dressing rooms, still displaying the occupant's personal treasures.

FIRE SCREENS

The fire screen used to shield the complexion is an ancient device, with known examples from as far back as the fourteenth century. Eighteenth-century cabinetmakers developed this simple contrivance,

THE PRINT ROOM AT BRIDGE END HOUSE

The print room is decorated with prints and paper from Small Interiors; the corner fireplace, with shelves to display assorted treasures, was made by the author. The fire basket by Neil Butcher is based on Carron designs of the eighteenth century. The red oak floor, like others in the model, is supplied in sheets, ready to be cut to the room size, by House Works.

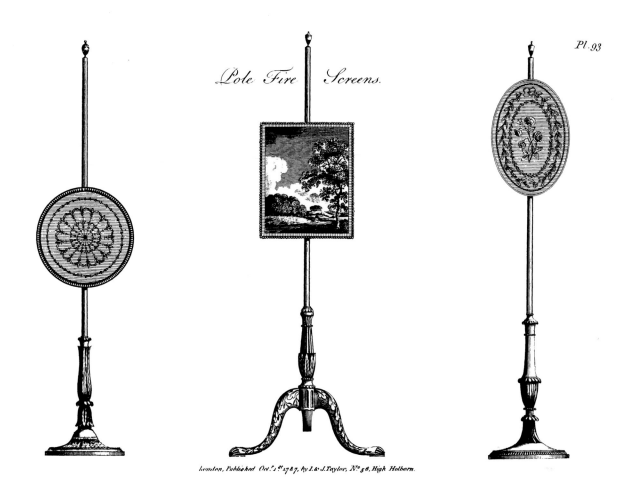

Pl.93

Pole Fire Screens.

London, Published Octr 1.st 1787, by I. & J.Taylor, N.º 56, High Holborn.

Pole fire screens, from George Hepplewhite, *The Cabinet-Maker and Upholsterer's Guide* (3rd edition, 1794) (by courtesy of Dover Publications, Inc.)

FIRE SCREENS

Many stylish and ingenious devices were created to shield delicate complexions from the heat of the fire.

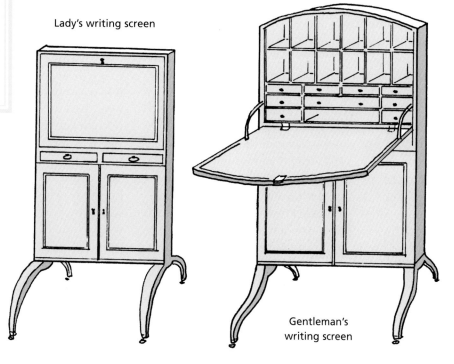

Lady's writing screen

Gentleman's writing screen

Combined desks and fire screens, after *The Prices of Cabinet Work (1797) with Tables and Designs,* published by a committee of master cabinetmakers

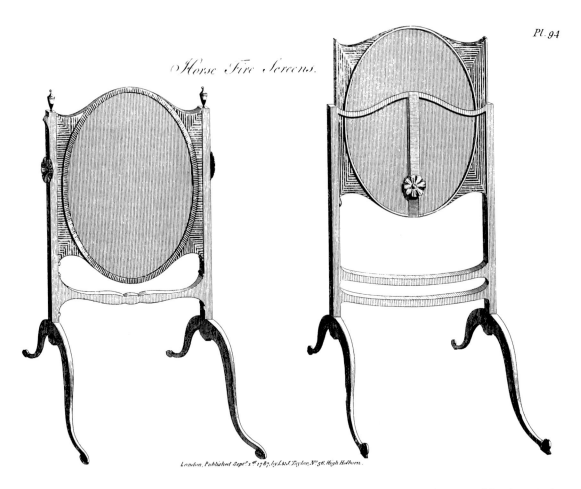

Pl. 94

Horse Fire Screens.

London, Published Sept.r 1.st 1787. by I&J Taylor, N.o 56. High Holborn.

Horse fire screens, from Hepplewhite's *Cabinet-Maker and Upholsterer's Guide* (by courtesy of Dover Publications, Inc.)

giving us the elegant pole screens and the more practical 'horse' screen in its frame supported by two legs; other varieties were incorporated into pieces of furniture.

Pole screens were amongst the most graceful of Georgian furniture, being decorated with inlay, needlework or painting, and used to protect a lady's face from the direct heat of a fire.

'Horse' fire screens were more robust; the shield was able to slide in grooves in the inner side of the uprights, and counterbalanced by weights visible on the outside. The weights were connected to the screen by a line which passed over a pulley in the top of the frame. The second design shown here has the screen suspended by a weight at the end of a ribbon which runs over a bar on one side.

Much larger screens were made for windows, so that you might enjoy the view but be protected from the sun. Understandably, many more of these survive in southern Europe.

Lastly, there were many pieces of furniture which incorporated a screen that worked just like the horse screen. Sometimes the entire piece was designed to double as a fire screen, resulting for example in a desk for writing in the cold of winter.

CHIMNEY BOARDS AND DUMMY BOARDS

It was thought for a long time that dummy boards were used in much the same way as fire screens, being positioned in front of a fierce fire to protect the occupants of the room. This is now held to be most unlikely, as their construction was such that they could not have resisted the constant heat of a fire; they served, instead, to conceal the fireplace when it was not in use. These boards were at their most popular from the mid-seventeenth century until the end of the eighteenth century, and even longer in America, where many more survive. Like the true chimney boards described below, they are of simple construction. Most are painted direct onto primed boards, while some are painted on paper then mounted onto the boards; the best

DUMMY BOARDS

These two drawings of a nurse or mother and child can be photocopied and painted (they are shown full size for 1/12 scale), or a model could be made from a postcard or any suitable period print.

Rear view of a dummy board, showing the construction

Edge bevelled at back

Ring to attach fastening hook

Brace

88°

Support

Instead of the bracket shown, feet can be fitted, with their fronts shaped to look like the toes of shoes

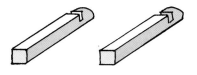

THE MURAL ROOM AT BRIDGE END HOUSE

This view of the first-floor mural room shows the chimney breast, with the fireplace closed by a chimney board decorated, like the walls, with a view of the town outside. The small figure of a girl in a red dress is a dummy board made from a postcard. The pipe box on the side of the chimney breast is made as described on page 159.

ones are on canvas mounted on boards, leading to the suggestion that they may have been cut from redundant portraits.

Among the more frequent subjects for dummy boards are seated women, either holding a baby or peeling or otherwise preparing vegetables. Figures depicting Vanity and Industry are represented by ladies standing with a mirror and comb or a broom, respectively. Military gentlemen and other household servants are also numerous. Domestic animals or household pets were not left out, but unlike their human counterparts, who were set up in believable positions, pets could be depicted on shelves or on the tops of furniture. Replica boards can be made by using postcards of period portraits or by photocopying my drawings and painting them yourself.

During the summer months – when most fires were out, and perhaps the family had moved off to fashionable resorts such as Bath, Brighton or Rome – a 'fire board' or chimney board was used to close off the fireplace. This prevented falls of soot spoiling the furnishings, or wayward crows and starlings getting into the room. It differed from a dummy board in being tailor-made to fit the fireplace exactly.

Most boards were of simple construction and design, and continued the decorative scheme of the rest of the room; like the dummy boards, they were either papered or painted direct onto the wood. Others were works of art, painted with Delft tiles or a bowl of flowers; there is even an example depicting the fire basket behind in full flame. Renowned artists were called upon to produce works for these simple pieces of furniture: the Burrell Collection in Glasgow has one painted by Jean-Baptiste Oudry (1696–1755), showing a dog standing in an alcove with its bowl. Others show the alcove with books stacked in it, or a bowl of flowers. They were usually held in place by hooks at the sides, sometimes long ones reaching back to the bars of the fire basket.

In Jane Austen's *Sense and Sensibility* (published in 1811, when their use was in decline), the eavesdropper, Miss Steele, says in her defence: 'I am sure Lucy would have just the same by me; for a year or two back, when Martha Sharpe and I had so many secrets together, she never made any bones of hiding in a closet, or behind a chimney board, on purpose to hear what we said.' The board in question must have been either a chimney board in a large fireplace, or what is more correctly known as a dummy board.

For my own Bridge End House I have made a chimney board for the fireplace in the mural room, using the bits of mural which had been cut out to make way for the doors. If you wish to make one it must be of just the right size to fit into the fireplace you have in mind. It can be made with a frame, like a picture, set on a base or plinth, or even fitted with a pair of feet.

Good examples of chimney boards are to be found at the Victoria and Albert Museum, London; Wilberforce House, Hull; Canons Ashby House, Daventry; Dyrham Park, Bristol; and many other museums and stately homes.

ENCLOSED FIRES

Today we tend to think of the fully enclosed stove as being peculiar to mainland Europe, but there was a time when they were common in the halls and lobbies of large houses in Britain as well. Robert Adam, a major shareholder in the Carron Ironworks, produced cast-iron ones for Lady Home in about 1776 for use at 20 Portman Square, London. The design incorporates an oil lamp on top, and, true to British tradition, the actual fire is open to view. A decade or so later Adam had two others made for the saloon of Kedleston Hall, but these were fully enclosed. The vents are clearly seen at the base, but the fire was serviced from the side.

The other examples shown here are from Northern Ireland. Those at Castle Coole, County Fermanagh are much more honest than the enclosed designs, with the stokeholes and vents all on the front. The maker is not known, but they were installed in 1796. In the west hall at the Argory, County Armagh is one with its flue going out under the floor (all the others have their flues at the back), with a copy of the Warwick Vase mounted on top of it. The fire door is large and the ash box is below in the base. Those from Lady Home's house, Kedleston and Castle Coole all stand against a wall in an alcove, while that at the Argory stands in the centre of the hall floor.

Knowing that such stoves were made and considered desirable in the eighteenth century, you can install similar ones, if not quite so large, in your dolls' house.

PORTABLE HEATERS

Parts of the house away from a fire could be cold and draughty, so braziers, burning charcoal, were used. Most were used as free-standing radiators, being moved to where they were most required; others were made wedge-shaped so as to fit into the fireplace of a bedroom or dressing room on a cold winter's morning. Perhaps their most important use was for cooking items that required a more delicate touch than was possible using the large kitchen fire; some were even used to prepare delicacies at the table or sideboard, which was a great leap forward in food preparation and appreciation.

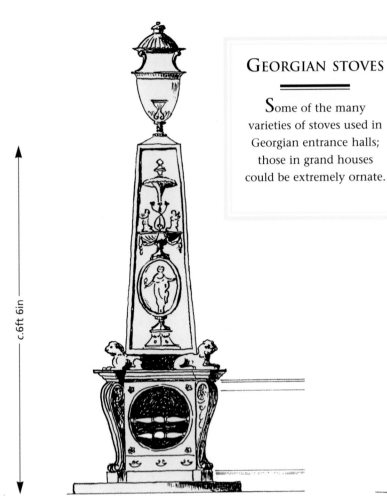

GEORGIAN STOVES

Some of the many
varieties of stoves used in
Georgian entrance halls;
those in grand houses
could be extremely ornate.

c.6ft 6in

6ft

Lady Home's House, Portman Square, London, 1776

Saloon, Kedleston Hall, Derbyshire, c.1786

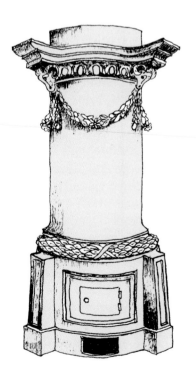

4ft

5ft

The Argory, Ulster, c.1800

Castle Coole, Ulster, 1796

A fine example of a dual-purpose brazier is to be found at Knole House, Kent, in the Spangle Bedroom, where it is flanked by a pair of obsolete brass andirons; it is wedge-shaped so as to fit into a small fireplace, but can also be used free-standing to provide extra warmth in large rooms.

Living in a world where central heating is the norm, we have forgotten how cold houses used to be. Foot warmers tended to be octagonal metal boxes with pierced sides and tops. Charcoal was placed on a copper tray at the bottom of the box, which was then carried wherever it was required, be it under the table or under the carriage seat. Understandably, few wooden examples have survived, but they were used in many homes and are easier for us miniaturists to replicate. Never large, boxes could be 4–8in (100–200mm) high and 8–12in (200–300mm) wide. For the metal type, brass 'cricket boxes', made in India for the gift trade, can be used – but look for a small one.

BRAZIERS

These simple room warmers were used to keep you warm at the back of the room, away from the fire, or in areas of the house where it was felt wasteful to light the fire. Two metal versions are shown here, the larger one from Knole in Kent; some of the smaller, box-shaped ones were made from wood. The fuel used was charcoal.

9in

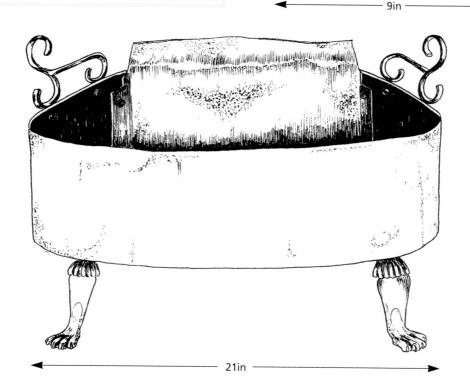

21in

CHAPTER EIGHT

KITCHENS

The Georgian kitchen • Ovens • Dressers • Kitchen accessories

THE GEORGIAN KITCHEN

By the end of the Georgian period the average kitchen had seen little change from those of the previous 300 years. The housewife had to make, amongst other things, the bread, beer, candles and soap for an enlightened household in what were still medieval conditions. The Industrial Revolution didn't come along until the end of our period, and even then only benefited a favoured few. Even after 1850, when downhearths had been definitively replaced by the more efficient coal grate, many traditional utensils remained in use.

The best of kitchens were roomy and high to allow the heat from the large open fires to rise. Windows were also high so as to let this heat escape. The light entering was important, but views out were not; this was a place of work. In some upper-and middle-class town houses (the type favoured by miniaturists) the kitchen was in the basement. In the early part of the century it would have had plain plastered walls and a stone or brick floor. By the end of the century, ideas on colour had changed – it was believed that blue walls deterred flies – yet other changes were slow. In 1780 Thomas Robinson patented a range with a side oven, but it had no flues and must have vied with King Alfred for the best burnt cakes. At the turn of the century we begin to see not only side ovens but small boilers as well.

The chimney crane, or a simple fixed metal bar, was still important, being used for the positioning of pots, pans and kettles over the flames. Oven-baked joints were still only a dream, with most households continuing to roast on a spit in front of the fire. Spits turned by a dog wheel had been common since 1600, but were finally outstripped by the weight-driven version. A weight on a line was wound around a drum, and as it descended the drum rotated, driving a chain which in turn rotated the spit. It was early in the eighteenth century that the smoke jack was introduced into large kitchens. A fan wheel was mounted horizontally in the narrowest part of the chimney, where it was rotated by the upward surge of hot air. A system of chain-driven gears turned the spit or spits. Towards the end of the century a spring-operated version, the bottle jack, was in use in smaller homes, and from 1770 these were also mounted in roasting screens or 'hasteners'. Joints were now held vertically, not horizontally as before. By 1760 hob grates with adjustable cheeks were in use, and these encouraged the use of the vertically mounted jacks, which continued well into the first decade of the twentieth century. The phrase 'done to a turn' was praise indeed for the cook operating one of these machines.

The kitchen sink was made of wood lined with lead, except in some areas where a stone trough was used; but, as we have already seen, water supplies were intermittent, with mains, where they existed, only being turned on for two hours each day, or even as little as twice a week.

The timber ceiling was supported by stout beams, and these also carried the combined weight of sides of bacon, strings of onions, bunches of herbs and a large food safe or bread wagon to keep food out of the reach of mice and rats.

While in farmhouses the kitchen was the heart of the house, in most town houses the kitchen was not the highest priority when planning a home; it was situated at the back of most large houses, and was sometimes even detached. In smaller houses, as mentioned above, it was in the basement or on the ground floor. As most dolls' houses open only at the front, these are ideal locations. Even if we cannot position the kitchen correctly, we can make it accurate in all other details; it can be one of the most interesting projects in any dolls' house.

OVENS AND BAKING

In large houses, baking was traditionally done in a side oven which had no contact with the fire but was heated by putting red hot embers into it. Early examples were simple dome-shaped brick structures in the thickness of the wall, fitted with a metal door but with no vent or flue. Improvements were on the way, however: in 1770, in Boynton Hall in Yorkshire, ovens of this traditional kind were built with the revolutionary addition of ash pits and flues.

In Ireland, while the oven was found only in better-class houses, there was a simple, practical device not used in the rest of Britain: at the side of the oven was a small table that was fixed to the wall by a hinge so that it could be raised when not in use, but was of great benefit on baking days.

MAKING BREAD, A WATERCOLOUR BY HELEN ALLINGHAM

(photograph courtesy of Spink-Leger)

It was not unusual for bread ovens to have wooden doors held in place and sealed by clay. This Edwardian servant, like most of the rural populace, is working in conditions unchanged for hundreds of years.

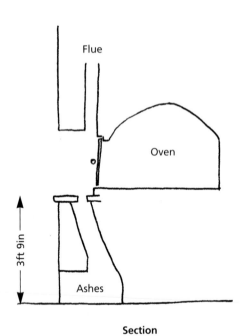

Section

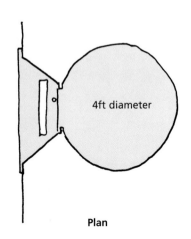

Plan

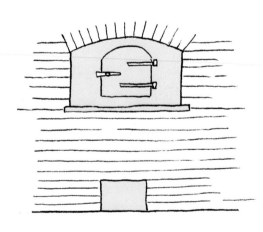

Elevation

Large oven with ash slot in threshold,
Boynton Hall, Yorkshire

144   THE AUTHENTIC GEORGIAN DOLLS' HOUSE

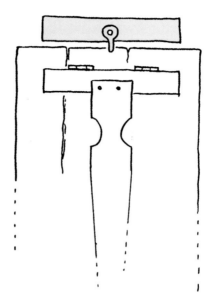

Table folded
up against
wall, with
catch to
retain it

Table hinged
at wall; leg
hinged at end
of table

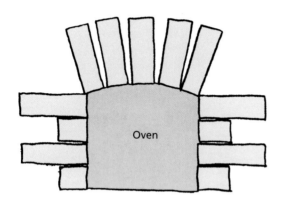

Oven

Bottom of oven same
height as top of table
(3ft)

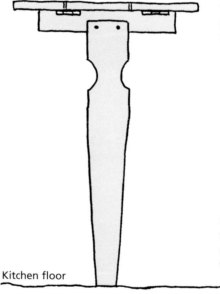

Table in
position with
leg down

Kitchen floor

Length of
table must be
at least equal
to its height

AN IRISH FOLDING TABLE

Such tables are still found in good numbers in
Ireland, though a few survive elsewhere. They
are traditionally mounted on the wall next to
the oven to receive hot food (before the advent
of heat-resistant gloves), then folded up against
the wall when not required. The model is by
the author.

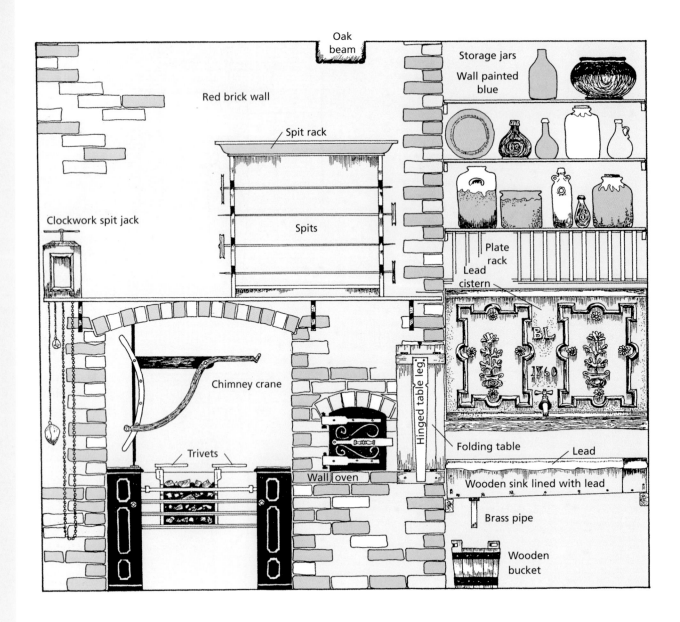

Oak beam

Red brick wall

Spit rack

Spits

Clockwork spit jack

Chimney crane

Trivets

Wall oven

Storage jars

Wall painted blue

Plate rack

Lead cistern

Hinged table leg.

Folding table

Lead

Wooden sink lined with lead

Brass pipe

Wooden bucket

BL 1760

DESIGN FOR THE KITCHEN OF BRIDGE END HOUSE

The model, in 1/12, scale is 12in long by 6 in wide and 10½in high (305 x 152 x 266mm). All details are correct for the period *c.*1760, but are drawn from various regions of Britain. Many of the individual projects illustrated in this chapter are here shown in position in my own dolls' house.

In smaller establishments baking was at first done on bakestones. These could be simple stone slabs placed over the embers of an open fire, but in rural districts from Yorkshire northwards the bakestones were incorporated in the masonry of the fireplace, forming a heated shelf. From the end of the seventeenth century, inventories begin to list 'iron bakestones', and from these simple beginnings developed the griddle or girdle which hung over Georgian kitchen fires of all types. The mid-eighteenth-century 'bachelor's oven', or tin oven, was a simple three-sided tin box which stood in front of an open fire to enable the contents to be cooked. The jack screens common in the late eighteenth and nineteenth centuries were a refinement of this system; in these, the contents were turned by a clockwork spit to ensure even cooking.

In the West Country and South Wales, cloam ovens had been produced since at least 1600; they were still being made, and presumably used, in 1937. Some are recorded as being built into the side of the fireplace, replacing the traditional brick domed oven, as in the Old Post Office at Tintagel in Cornwall. As they were found mainly in smaller houses, they were mostly used on the open hearth, being pushed into the side of the fire with hot embers piled up round their sides. The contents were slowly, if unevenly, cooked. Upland areas of northern Britain used an upturned three-legged cauldron, placing it over the items to be baked in a way similar to the cloam oven.

Cloam ovens are simple, roughly made articles which were often broken. To model one, remember what your local unglazed earthenware looks like, and choose a polymer clay to match the colour. The basic shape can be formed in a mould (made from a discarded container of suitable shape), but the finishing touches are very much up to you. The door should be made in such a way that it cannot fall in, but fits snugly in the opening.

Take pains not to over-equip your dolls' house kitchen; take regional variations into consideration as well as the date and the status of the occupants.

CLOAM OVEN

An earthenware oven from the West Country; doors were often broken and a wooden one substituted.

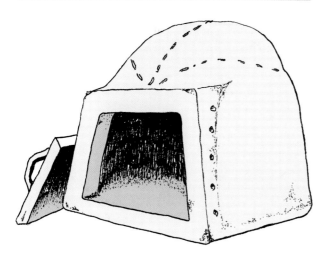

DRESSERS

Today, a dresser is essential if you want that 'country' look to your room; yet the form is of ancient origin. Many early ones were built of stone, as part of the wall, with wooden doors added to keep the contents secure. They were an important item in any house; in many inventories they are the only item prefixed by the definite article. Indeed, the contents of the dresser were an expression of the owner's status – the phrase 'She has a well-plenished dresser' implied considerable social standing at a time when most people could not hope to fill one.

Many dressers up to about 1750 did not have the familiar fixed rack of shelves above the main working surface, though they may have had shelves secured to the wall above them. Tradition says that the base was given when a couple was married, and the shelves later as an anniversary present – the origin of the 'wooden anniversary'. Be that as it may, dressers can be simple or quite sophisticated, depending on the social position of the owner and how the dresser was to be used. It shows more regional variation than any other piece of furniture. We do not just find Dutch, Irish, Welsh or Scottish dressers, nor even simply lowland or highland varieties, but variations based on much smaller zones or regions, which results in some fascinating details.

It is not possible here to illustrate anything more than a selection from this vast family of domestic furniture, but the few examples shown on the following pages do give an idea of the range that was once available. Only the more 'polite' forms are still fashionable today: the others, for the most part, have been superseded by the changing requirements of a new way of life.

One of the simplest forms was used in the kitchens of large houses; this was much like a settle, except that the 'seat' part was too high to be sat on and was used as a work surface or sideboard by day, opening up to form a bed for tired servants at night (this type is illustrated on page 192). The ornate shapes of the 'arms' of these settles may result from the tradition of storing unused spits on them. The settle type is found from northern France through Britain and Ireland, jumping the Atlantic to the New World, where it is found in Canada and the USA.

Another simple type had a large meal chest as its base, to hold a winter's supply of this basic commodity. At the back of this cavernous box was a shelf to hold various scoops, measures and bowls. On top was mounted the shelving which we now regard as usual. Not so very different was the type made to hold fuel for the kitchen, be it peat or coal; this resembled the meal-bin type in most respects.

Still in the kitchen, it was not unusual for part of the upper shelving section of the dresser to incorporate a spit rack or 'clevy'. Other varieties had small coops for hens in the base, as it was thought that the hens were more likely to lay in

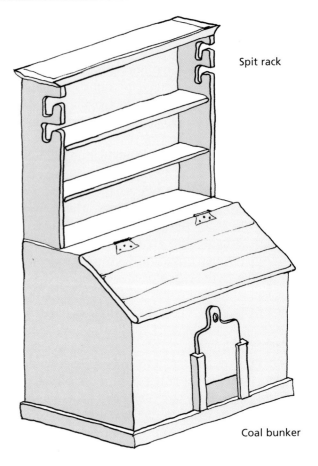

Spit rack

Coal bunker

DRESSERS

This is just a selection from the many different regional and local varieties.

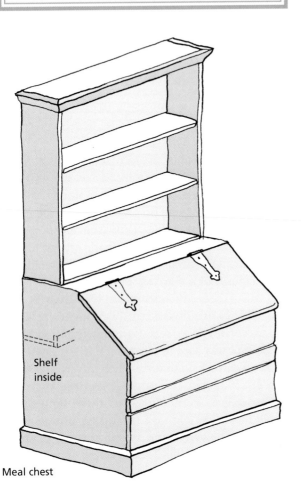

Shelf inside

Meal chest

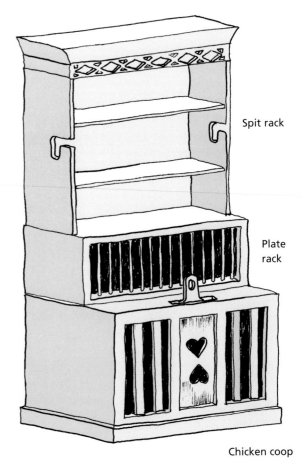

Spit rack

Plate rack

Chicken coop

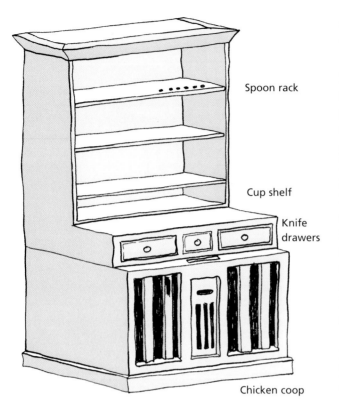

Spoon rack

Cup shelf

Knife drawers

Chicken coop

the winter if they were kept warm. Some even had two tiers of coops.

Finer examples had drawers and small cupboards as well as the now usual shelves. Some shelves had holes towards the outer edge to carry spoons; variations on this idea included wings attached to the shelves, either in pairs or singly, purely for the display of spoons. In upland areas of Britain and Ireland, where peat was the predominant fuel, the plates on the shelves were not set back on display, but were made to lean forward against a special rail to prevent the dust and haze from the peat fire from settling on their face. Cups and the numerous bowls would also be kept upside down in most kitchens of the period, for the same reason, so don't just hang things in your dolls' house as we do today – bear in mind how the Georgians lived.

A type of dresser from lowland Scotland had a high base cupboard for linen, the upper section looking like a tray overhanging at either end. At the back of this tray were cupboards and drawers.

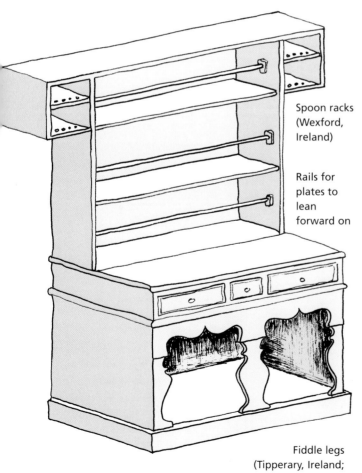

Spoon racks (Wexford, Ireland)

Rails for plates to lean forward on

Fiddle legs (Tipperary, Ireland; also mid-Wales)

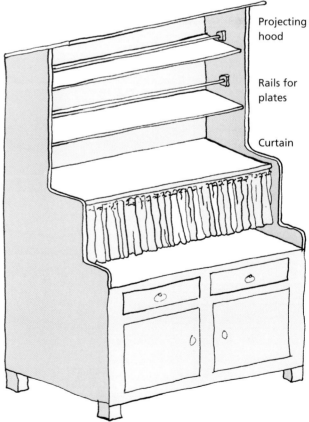

Projecting hood

Rails for plates

Curtain

Highland Scotland

**Lowland Scotland,
c.1800**

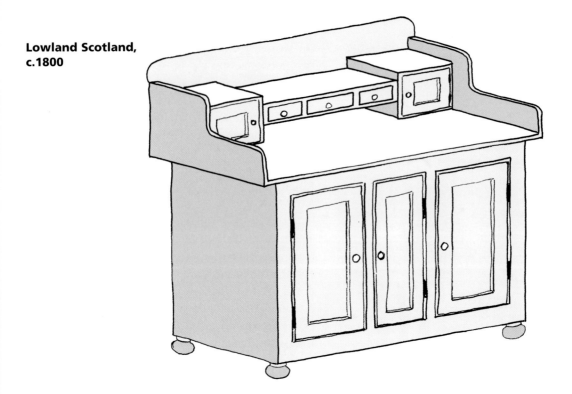

The sides of the tray were high enough to prevent small items falling off. The highland version also had these sides to the work surface, but with the addition of a short curtain hung from the lower shelf to protect the contents from the haze.

In finer parlours, towards the end of our period, classical detail was widely used as decoration. The Welsh example from around 1750 has fluted columns at either side that open to reveal tall, slim cupboards; the Cumbrian one of 1790 also

**Mid-Wales,
c.1750**

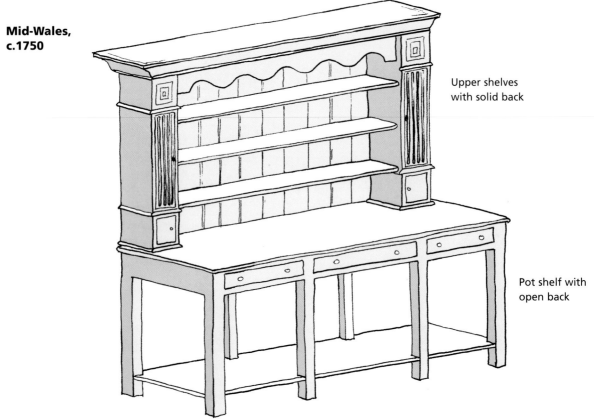

Upper shelves
with solid back

Pot shelf with
open back

**Cumberland,
c.1790**

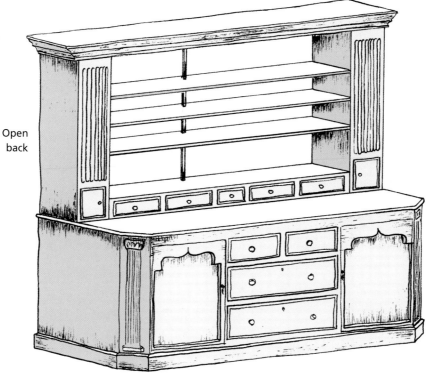

Open
back

has fluted columns, but these do not open. The Shropshire example is the most refined, having cabriole legs and much fine period detail.

Before selecting a dresser, first consider where you will put it, and how a Georgian household would have used it – not how *you* would furnish a kitchen or parlour. What was their kitchen like? What fuel did they burn? Only when you have a clear picture of how they lived and worked should you find a suitable type of dresser and install it.

**Shropshire,
c.1750**

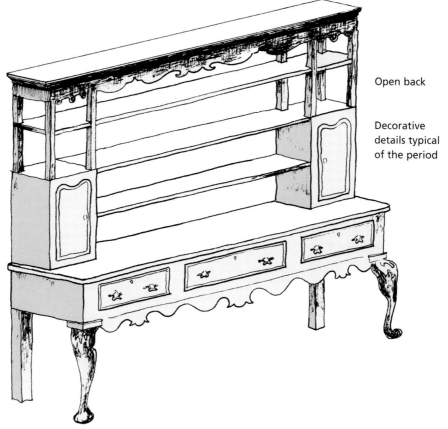

Open back

Decorative
details typical
of the period

SMALL FIRESIDE ITEMS

CURFEWS

Even as late as the beginning of the twentieth century, in deep rural areas an unprotected fire in the middle of the floor was not unusual for cottages. Trinity College, Cambridge only discarded in 1866 a charcoal brazier ordered by the Master, Richard Bentley, in 1702. It consisted of a raised platform with a gallery running around the upper edge to retain the charcoal, which was held up in the centre by a perforated dome. This brazier was not forged and would be only one of many made from the moulds, so others may still exist. Fireplaces with a chimney and, therefore, a flue against a wall were only slowly introduced into the homes of rural labourers.

Such open fires were made safe at night by covering them with a *couvre-feu* or curfew to smother the embers and perhaps retain some vestige of life to be rekindled in the morning. The earliest examples were of coarse pottery and resembled large upturned basins with handles on the top towards each end. When fires were placed against a central fireback or reredos, or in a hearth against a wall, then the shape of the curfew changed to one resembling half an upturned cup with the handle still intact. Fine examples of brass, earthenware or mass-produced tin still exist in collections. None of these were of any use if the fire was held in a basket or grate, and this fact alone should serve to remind us that the enclosed fire was, at first, for the privileged few and that even in this age of elegance an open hearth was normal in most

> ## CURFEWS
>
> These essential safety devices were not always as ornate as the examples shown here.

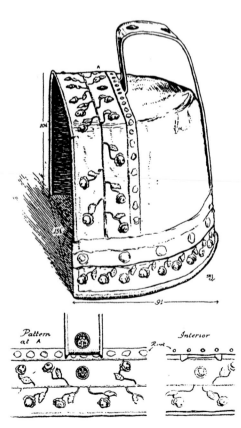

A craftsman-made metal example of the eighteenth century, drawn by S. R. Jones (© Chrysalis Books Ltd)

Eighteenth-century glazed earthenware *couvre-feu*, after a sketch by N. Hills

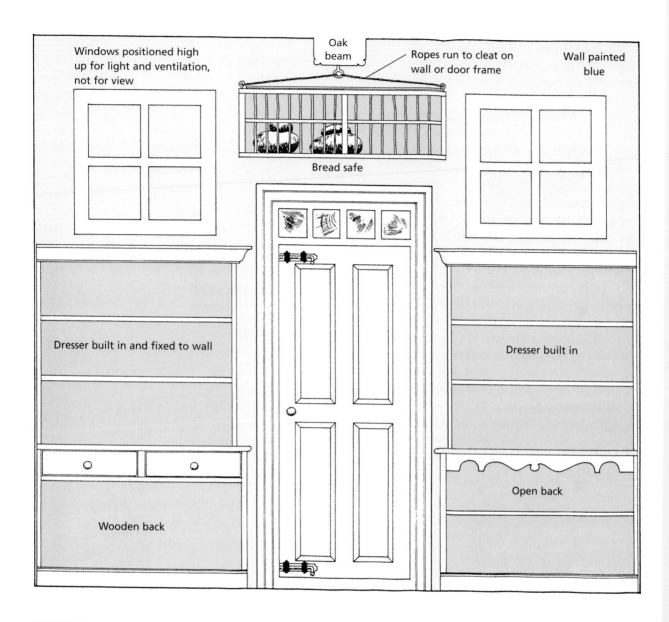

Windows positioned high up for light and ventilation, not for view

Oak beam

Ropes run to cleat on wall or door frame

Wall painted blue

Bread safe

Dresser built in and fixed to wall

Dresser built in

Wooden back

Open back

DESIGN FOR THE KITCHEN OF BRIDGE END HOUSE

The opposite wall to that shown on page 146 contains the door to the kitchen, and all furnishings are fixed to it.

households' kitchens. Curfews were to be found in all homes with open fires and, like it or not, this was most homes in the eighteenth century.

Earthenware examples can be duplicated by using polymer clay, taking into account the colour of your native unglazed earthenware. Use any suitable container as a mould to form the basic shape, then fix the handle or handles and carry out any decoration. The required decoration can be inscribed, impressed or applied. Metal curfews can be imitated by using plastic or alloy containers and painting them to resemble brass or copper. If you have a broken dolls' tea cup, as long as it still has the handle intact it can be ground back to give a good base shape. Now all you have to do is paint it to look like earthenware.

BOTTLE JACKS AND SPIT JACKS

Bottle jacks were a simple device, invented by Joseph Merlin in 1773 and refined by John Linwood of Birmingham around 1790. These clockwork devices, hung from a hinged bracket above the fire and below the mantel shelf, turned on a vertical axis and could be used for smaller joints. Many were still in use at the beginning of the twentieth century.

Some kitchens went one step further and hung a bottle jack in a semicircular screen so that the heat of the fire was reflected back onto the meat. This contraption was known as a jack screen.

More ornate variations of these were used in the dining room to keep plates warm. In outline they looked like half a large vase or urn, decorated in the style of the room and containing shelves or racks to hold plates and other items. The open side was turned towards the fire to keep the plates warm.

Local clock makers were called on to make weight-driven spit jacks from as early as 1600. Like clocks, weighted jacks had a stone weight on a line which was wound around a drum or barrel. The descent of the weight was controlled by a flywheel and gears, and the motion was transferred by a chain to a spit which was mounted horizontally in front of the fire. The simple mechanism was usually exposed to view, but some were enclosed in a wooden case.

The spits themselves were simple long steel spikes with a grooved wheel mounted at one end. More elaborate ones had movable forks to hold the joint in place, while others even had metal baskets to contain the carcass being prepared.

JACK SCREEN AND BOTTLE JACK
(not to scale)

Left: Jack screen or hastener. The jack was suspended from the frame at the top. The cooking could be inspected through the door in the back.
Centre: Bottle jack (drawn to a larger scale). The 'bottle' was held inside the frame of the hastener while the wheel revolved inside the cabinet.
Right: Interior of jack screen. Fat ran into the depression at the bottom and was used for basting the roast.

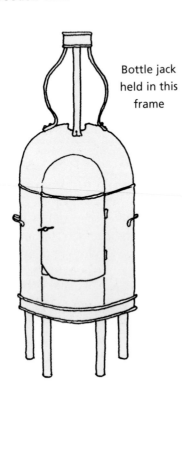

Bottle jack held in this frame

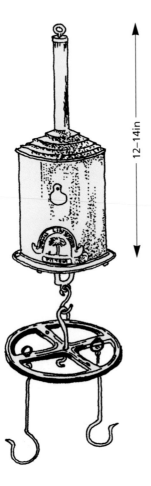

12–14in

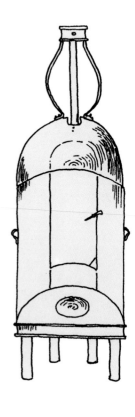

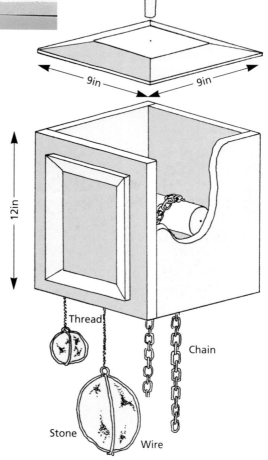

MODEL OF A KITCHEN RANGE

This model shows the spit jack with its stone weight and a drive chain connected to a spit, ready to roast a joint. Above the wall oven is a spit rack carrying more spits for use as and when required. The oven door, range and spit jack are all by Neil Butcher.

MODELLING A CLOCKWORK SPIT JACK

Construct a simple wooden box with a decorative front; the bottom of this box is open to allow the weights and drive chain to hang down. These in turn are hung over a drum formed by a short length of dowel, which is glued inside the box sideways, not back to front. The chain should be towards the fire and the weights to the side away from the fire.

As most of these jacks were mounted on the wall above the mantel shelf, holes will have to be drilled in the shelf to allow the chain and cord holding the weights to pass through. The only part

CLOCKWORK SPIT JACK

Some models had a handle to wind up the stones. Dimensions given are full size.

9in 9in

12in

Thread

Chain

Stone

Wire

of the mechanism to be seen on the outside would be the large flywheel, which can be made using fine plywood or a large drawing pin (thumbtack), such as is used to mount paper on drawing boards. Remember the wheel is not solid, and will have to be cut or drilled to remove most of the material from the centre. Mount it on top of the box as shown.

OTHER KITCHEN ACCESSORIES

Many small items which were once found in the kitchens and parlours of Britain are now rare collectors' items. This section describes how to make just a few of them. Where material sizes are given in the text, these are for 1/12 scale; dimensions on the drawings are full size.

THE KITCHEN AT BRIDGE END HOUSE

This view shows many of the small accessories described on the following pages. The kitchen block was universal; on it is a knife scouring box. Overhead hangs a bread car, used to keep food out of the reach of vermin. Next to the range, made by Neil Butcher, is a simple knife box; above the range is a clockwork spit jack designed by the author and made by Neil. The stone floor is by R. V. Burrows, and the walls are painted blue in the belief that this would deter flies.

KITCHEN KNIFE BOX

This simple wall-mounted box to hold large kitchen knives is made of ⅟₁₆in (1.5mm) wood. The back board is a simple rectangle, with the top shaped like an early Gothic window head and drilled to allow hanging. The sides should be cut out together to ensure they are exactly the same shape. The wider top ends should be shaped as shown in the diagram. The front of the box is a simple rectangle which covers the edges of the side panels. Note that the bottom edge of this panel must be bevelled so that it lines up with the back edge of the side panels and sits neatly on the back board.

> ## KITCHEN KNIFE BOX
>
> ────────────
>
> These were quite deep, as some knives were long. Dimensions given are full size.

Only when built up should the knife box be sanded to give a worn (distressed) look, then stained in a natural wood colour.

KNIFE SCOURING BOX

We all know the knife polishers found in Victorian and Edwardian kitchens, which had to be turned by some underling until their arms dropped off. Prior to this invention, and even later in poorer homes, the scouring box was put to use.

This is also made of ⅟₁₆in (1.5mm) wood. The base is shaped like a present-day chopping board, with a hole drilled in the handle end to hang it up when not in use. A rectangular enclosure is fixed to the upper surface of this board. The end nearest the handle has a semicircular notch in it to hold the collar of the knife to be cleaned. At the other end is a cover to hold sand or grit and a wet rag to clean the blades. This cover is set into the sides and bottom edge of the rectangular enclosure. The blade of the knife is supported by a shaped block of wood fixed in the bottom of the enclosed space.

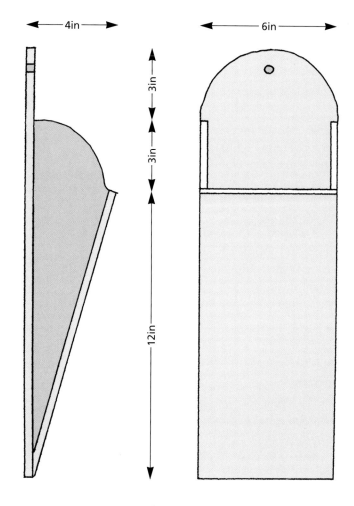

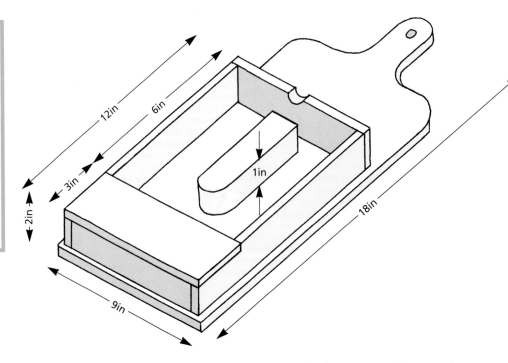

On finishing, the unit should be sanded and distressed, then stained. When the stain is dry, the central block and the edge with the groove in it should be lightly sanded to show some of the wood.

unit a more up-market look. Fine moulding can be fixed to the front edge of the drawer unit if desired. Finally, sand and stain to give your desired depth of colour.

SPOON RACK

Pewter spoons and steel knives were found in all houses, but forks were a refinement. Spoons were proudly displayed in purpose-made racks.

The large back board is simply shaped, then drilled to allow it to be hung. Three shelves of varying sizes are fixed to this, the holes in them being positioned so that the lower spoons are mounted in front of the upper ones.

The bottom of the unit is fitted with a drawer to house knives. The bottom and top of the drawer case are the same size, and the sides are fixed between them. The drawer itself is made up as a simple box and fitted with a brass knob to give the

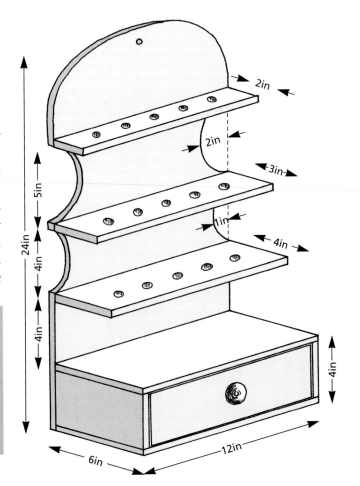

PIPE BOX

Churchwarden pipes were much used; they were burnt clean in the kitchen, so a box to hold clean ones was essential. Reflecting the shape of the pipe itself, the box was tall and slim with a tall back board dressed at the top to give a regional touch. The model can be made from ¹⁄₁₆in (1.5mm) wood.

The base of the drawer unit is fixed to the front of the backboard, then the sides of the box are positioned in the angle formed by the bottom and back boards. The base for the pipe box proper is cut to fit between the sides, immediately above the drawer opening. The shorter front section with its shaped top is then positioned so that its lower end covers the outer edge of this last piece. Sand and finish the whole unit to suit its location.

PIPE RACK

These were used in place of the above box if the pipes were to be put back into circulation immediately, which was normal in smaller households. Once again the model is made from ¹⁄₁₆in (1.5mm)

PIPE BOX

The details on the right show regional variations in the shape of the top. Dimensions given are full size.

PIPE RACK

An eighteenth-century pipe rack, used in the kitchen to hold pipes newly burnt clean. Dimensions given are full size.

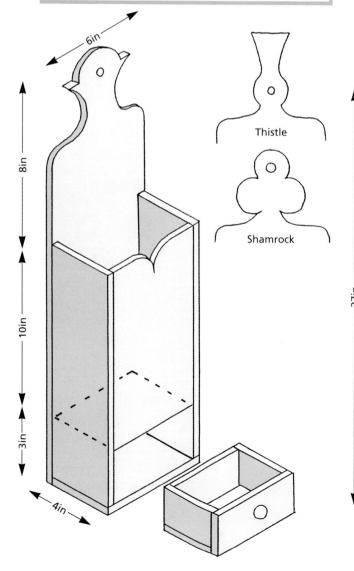

Thistle

Shamrock

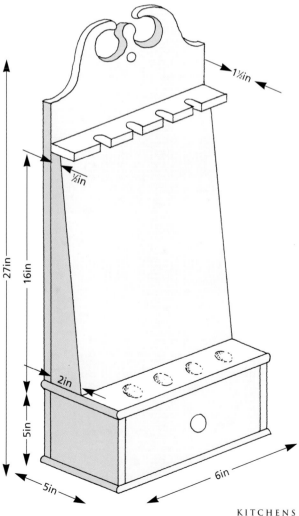

wood, apart from the sloping back which is of heavier material.

The tall back has a 'classical' head to it in the shape of a broken pediment, and this is fixed on top of the slightly wider base. The sides of the drawer box are then fixed in the resulting angle. The top of the drawer unit projects at the sides and front just like the base, but has small depressions in its upper surface to hold the bowls of the pipes. These depressions are made by just 'touching' the surface with a drill, then sanding.

The sloping back is then made from stouter material, exactly the same width as the tall back board. On top of this is fixed the upper bracket with small notches cut in it to hold the pipe stems. The drawer is a simple wooden tray with either a brass or a wooden knob.

CANDLE BOX

Candles were made at home in most houses, with bought ones only being used in wealthy houses on special occasions.

The construction is of ⅟₁₆in (1.5mm) wood, beginning with a shaped and drilled back board. The base of the box is fitted to the front lower edge of this, and the sides are set in the angles. The top of the front panel must be sanded to ensure the angle is the same as that of the sides, ensuring a good fit for the lid. The lid is made in one piece, with the back (hinged) end once again having to be sanded to ensure a neat fit against the back board. The front edge is rounded and has a simple small nail for a handle. The back edge, which receives the two brass hinges, will have to have small recesses cut out to the same depth as the closed hinge. Fix the hinges to the lid first, then mark the back board and glue or nail them to the back. Sand and finish to suit your decor.

SALT BOX

Salt was a valuable commodity and was kept close to the fire, even in the chimney recess, to keep it dry. In some areas a traditional wall cupboard was still being made and used at this time, but this simple box was more widespread.

The back board has the usual shaped head, drilled to allow it to be hung. This board is fixed onto the upper rear edge of the base, which projects slightly to either side. Fix the sides in the resulting angle. Unlike the candle box, the salt box has hinges – or even just one long hinge – of leather. These are attached to a narrow strip

CANDLE BOX

These were also mounted on the wall, but not too close to the fire! Dimensions given are full size.

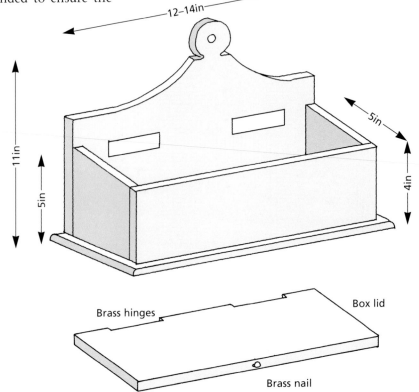

12–14in

11in

5in

5in

4in

Brass hinges

Box lid

Brass nail

of wood glued to the back and sides which, like the base, projects a little. The important thing to get right is the angles on the long edges of this strip, so that it marries neatly with the back and receives the lid comfortably. The lid is positioned and the leather hinge or hinges fixed. Because of the corrosive nature of salt, there is no metal knob to the lid, but the edge of it projects so as to allow a fingerhold.

CANDLE RESTS

Three variations of wall-hung candle rests for use in kitchens, attics and servants' quarters. All have the same basic dimensions: 14in high, 6in wide, 5 in deep.

SALT BOX

These were often mounted on the wall in the inglenook. Note the leather hinges – metal ones would corrode on contact with the salt. Dimensions given are full size.

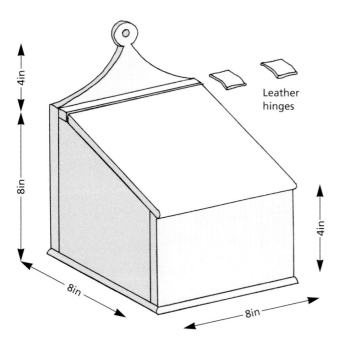

Leather hinges

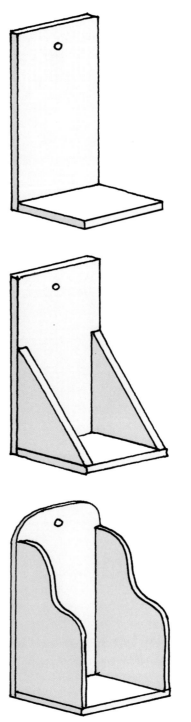

WALL-HUNG CANDLE REST

While in the best houses sconces and so forth may have been used in the reception rooms, the lower orders or servants would have used much more mundane equipment. Candle rests were simple wall-hung or free-standing brackets used to shelter the flame from draughts and, at times, to reflect the light with the help of a small piece of mirror glass attached to the back board.

Make the back first, shaping and drilling the top. Sit this on the top back edge of the base, then glue the sides in the angles. A small reflector can be made using broken glass or a small piece of metallic tape of the type used for giftwrapping. Fine glass to make a reflector is not easy to find, and you may have to use a piece thicker than the wood being used. To help overcome this, make the back of the unit out of two pieces of wood, one mounted in front of the other; in the front piece cut a hole the same shape as the glass being used, and set the mirror in this.

In coastal areas, a simple oil lamp, rather than a candle, was used. This consisted of a seashell to form the reservoir, and a wick.

POTHOOKS

All eighteenth-century kitchens used pothooks to suspend cooking pots over the fire, no matter what type of fire was in use. They were numerous in any kitchen, and some were works of art. I shall describe the basic shapes here, and leave the refinements up to you once you have mastered the technique.

POTHOOKS

Three models of varying complexity are shown here.

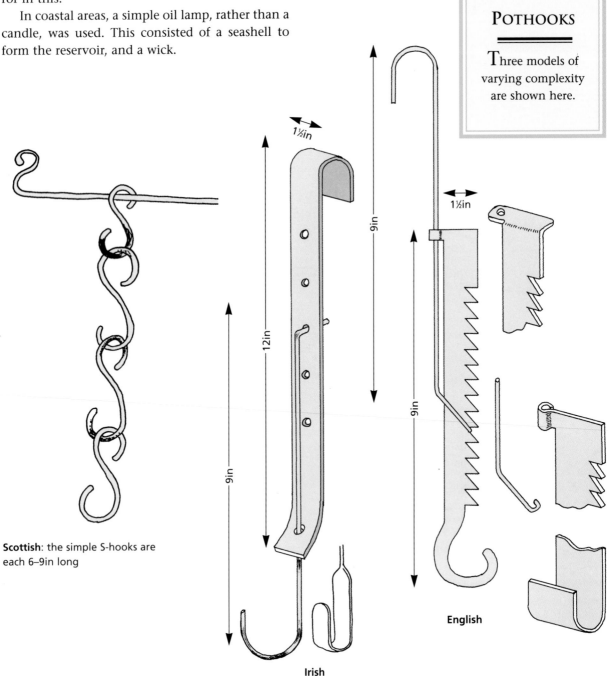

Scottish: the simple S-hooks are each 6–9in long

Irish

English

Wire and alloy cans provide the basic materials, and pliers, file, tinsnips and two hammers the tools. Why two hammers? Well, one is used as a miniature anvil.

The first example shown is the simplest, and comes from Scotland. It consists of a series of long S-hooks made by bending short lengths of wire. File down all the sharp ends and finish with matt black paint.

The next is of Irish origin and is also quite simple to make. A long strip of alloy is cut and the edges filed to make them smooth and safe. The top of this is bent over to fit onto a chimney crane, or simple metal bars across the flue. Holes are drilled at intervals along the central section, and another near the bottom. Now take a length of wire and, using your hammer and anvil, flatten one end if required, then bend up to form a hook. Pass the other end through the hole in the bottom of the alloy strip and, when through, bend the end backwards so that it will slip into any of the holes in the central section of the alloy strip. Again, make sure there are no sharp edges, then paint.

The third and most complicated version is English. Cut an alloy strip, leaving a protruding lug at one end to hold the wire support. There are two basic ways of making this. The first is to drill a hole in the end of the protrusion, then bend it over, together with the top end of the strip, so that it is at 90° to the main part. The second way is to roll the alloy protrusion round a length of wire so as to form an eye. The alloy strip must now be given a serrated edge, using snips and/or file. The lower end is cut and filed to form a large hook.

The wire used to suspend the hook is bent to fit the chimney crane or bars, and the other end passed through the eye at the head of the serrated alloy strip. This end of the wire is bent as in the diagram so as to engage the teeth and maintain the selected height over the fire for the pots and pans.

SPIT RACKS

While billiard cues are kept vertical, most spits were stored in the horizontal position. To achieve this, simple racks were made and mounted above the fireplace. In many instances the bottom of the rack rested on the mantel shelf while the top touched the ceiling. Others were finished, as here, with a moulded hood. The two sides should be cut out together to ensure they are exactly the same,

then cleaned and sanded. A fine cross member or spacer of square section should be glued towards the bottom of these, and a flat board of the same length fitted between the tops. This top hood should be finished off by applying a moulding in keeping with the status of your house. Some of these racks are stained, but most were painted with the walls.

SPIT RACK

The full-size dimensions given are only suggestions; the rack can be as high or as low as you wish.

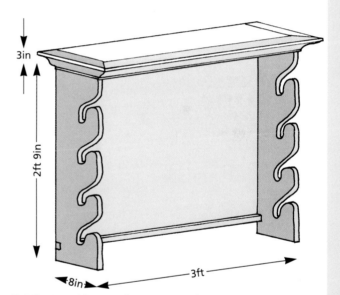

Cut the two sides together to ensure they are the same

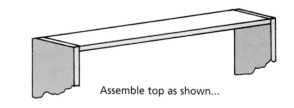

Assemble top as shown...

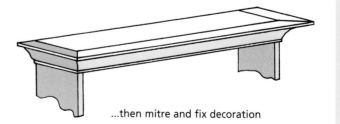

...then mitre and fix decoration

CHIMNEY CRANE

Chimney cranes, like pothooks, could be works of art or simply functional pieces of kitchen equipment; they were found in all kitchens with fires set against a wall.

They consist of three main parts, which can all be modelled from stout wire: the vertical support and hinge, the top member (the crane proper), and the brace.

The vertical support was hinged by fixing either end into holes in the masonry above and below, or into iron eyes fixed in the wall at the side of the fireplace. You must know the space available and the type of fixing suitable for your house before you begin. If you can't get into your chimney to drill holes, then use small wooden blocks with holes drilled in them and glue these in the required position. The top member or crane is turned up at the end to prevent hooks and pots slipping off.

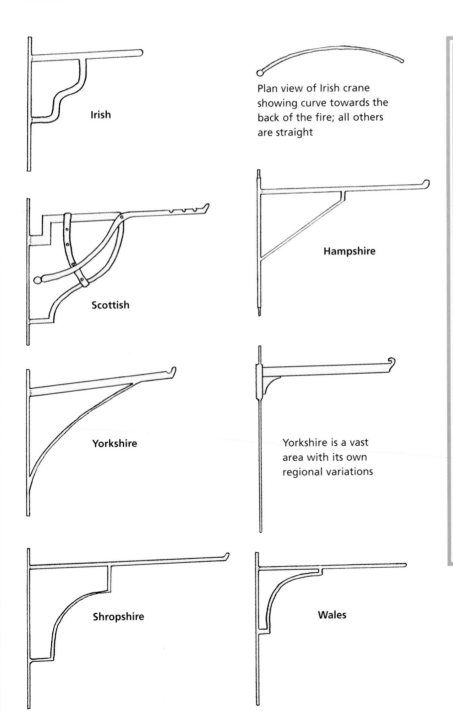

Irish

Plan view of Irish crane showing curve towards the back of the fire; all others are straight

Scottish

Hampshire

Yorkshire

Yorkshire is a vast area with its own regional variations

Shropshire

Wales

CHIMNEY CRANES

These vary in design from basic tools to works of art; they were in use from medieval times until the early twentieth century. Many were mounted over Victorian kitchen ranges but, most importantly for us, they were found in all Georgian houses.

Dimensions can be varied to suit the size of your fireplace: the finished model should extend over at least three-quarters of the fire, and the top should be low enough to clear the top of the fireplace opening when swung out into the kitchen. Average sizes would seem to be 4–5ft long and 3–4ft high when mounted over a hob or range.

If you can solder, then this method of joining should be used. Alternatively, a good-quality 'instant' glue will do the trick. The preferred construction material is metal wire, but wood may be used for some parts and, when painted black, can look just as good.

Alternative methods of pivoting the chimney crane (below)

If the uprights are square or flat in section, they will need to be rounded at the ends to allow the arm to swing in the pivot

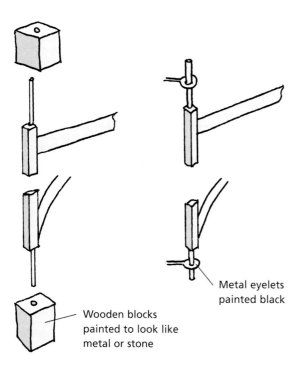

Metal eyelets painted black

Wooden blocks painted to look like metal or stone

THREE-MOTION ADJUSTABLE CRANE

Most chimney cranes were simple, but these drawings by S. R. Jones (© Chrysalis Books Ltd) show two examples of the more elaborate three-motion type. Most chimney cranes were simple fixed structures which swung in and out over the fire, while others were made so that the pothook could also be raised and lowered. On three-motion models, the boom can be extended or the pothook repositioned over the fire.

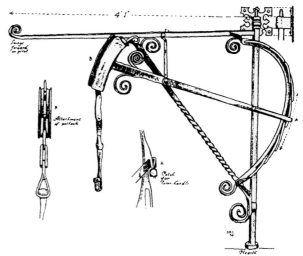

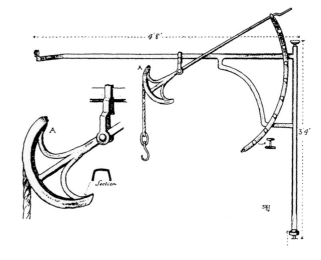

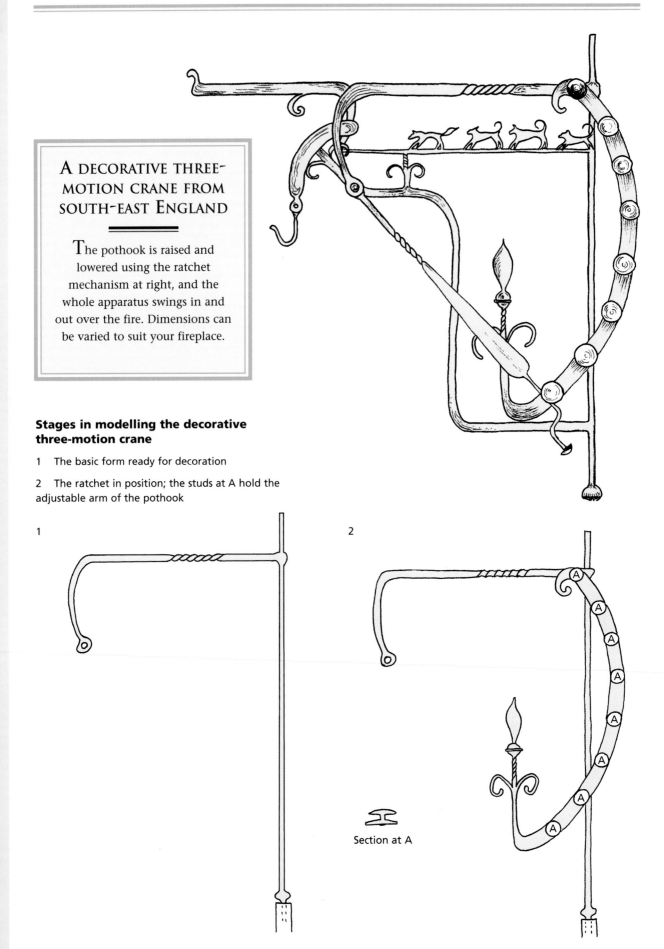

A decorative three-motion crane from south-east England

The pothook is raised and lowered using the ratchet mechanism at right, and the whole apparatus swings in and out over the fire. Dimensions can be varied to suit your fireplace.

Stages in modelling the decorative three-motion crane

1   The basic form ready for decoration

2   The ratchet in position; the studs at A hold the adjustable arm of the pothook

1

2

Section at A

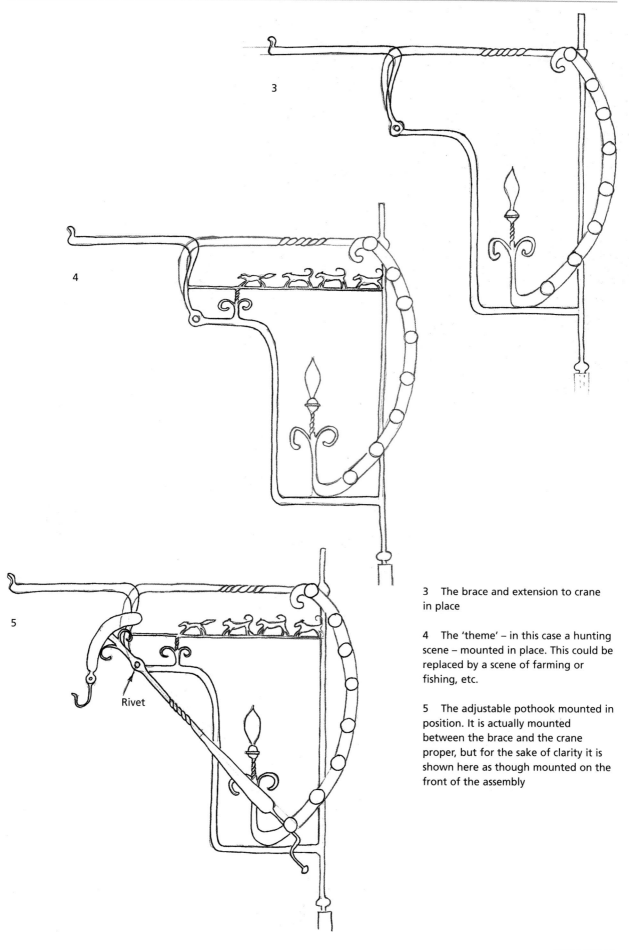

3   The brace and extension to crane in place

4   The 'theme' – in this case a hunting scene – mounted in place. This could be replaced by a scene of farming or fishing, etc.

5   The adjustable pothook mounted in position. It is actually mounted between the brace and the crane proper, but for the sake of clarity it is shown here as though mounted on the front of the assembly

Rivet

BRICK DOMED WALL OVEN

Visit any site or ruins of a castle, abbey or great hall and you will find the remains of a wall oven of some antiquity; yet for the most part they were latecomers in ordinary domestic situations.

To make a scaled-down version is not very difficult, and the materials required can easily be acquired. A plastic top from one of many containers found in the bathroom makes an ideal mould for the domed oven. (A point to remember is that the size of the completed oven will dictate the depth of your chimney breast.) The building material is miniature bricks, glue and a filler for pointing. Use half-bricks, with the good ends towards the mould, to form the dome, taking care to glue them only to each other and not to the mould; you can cover the mould with paper to help ensure this.

MODEST OVENS FOR THE GEORGIAN KITCHEN

These all have doorways 1ft 6in (46cm) wide (full-size measurement).

Plan view (with door opening at bottom) showing arch placed against mould, and half-bricks forming the base of the oven. Brick courses should be staggered so the joints do not sit directly on top of each other

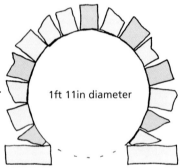

1ft 11in diameter

Oven doors

Alternative shapes all made from one piece of alloy

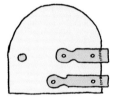

Brick arch with plastic mould (shaded) in position

Brass knob or simple window handle

Wire hooks to carry door; wall will have to be drilled for these

Alternative patterns for arched doorway

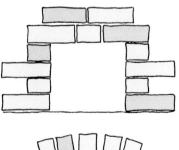

Door and hinges can be cut from one piece of alloy; hinges are shaped at ends before being bent

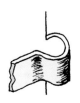

Enlarged plan and perspective views showing hinge bent over and held by small brass nails riveted at back (or glued)

Installing the oven

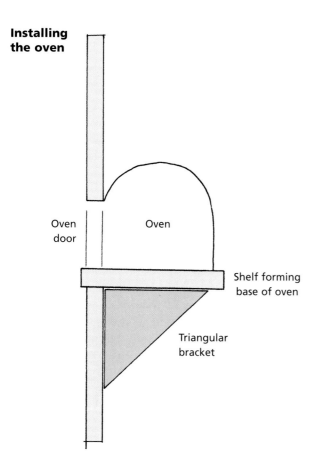

Oven door

Oven

Shelf forming base of oven

Triangular bracket

First build the arch for the doorway, following any of the variations shown on the previous page. Have a 'dry run' first. When the arch is set, place the mould up against it. Start building the dome, using half-bricks, working from the back of the arch around the sides of the dome. Remember to stagger the joints from one course of bricks to the next. When all the glue is dry, remove the mould and point up the joints on the insides.

Positioning the oven within your chimney breast requires a shelf for it to sit on; because of the weight of the bricks, this must be well supported. The diagram at left shows a triangular bracket under the shelf. If you require a brick floor to the oven, this must be fixed to the top of the shelf prior to positioning the oven. The material used can be either bricks or tiles.

LEAD WATER CISTERN

The basic shape is a simple box with an open top, with a tap fixed in the front towards the bottom. If you have some fine sheet lead, then cover the box with this; but good results can be had by painting the completed cistern with a matt finish.

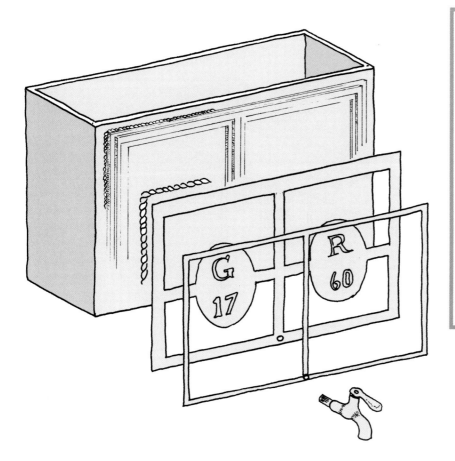

LEAD CISTERN

The basic box form is made up in wood; a thick base can be inserted to provide additional stiffness. Typical full-size dimensions might be 2ft 6in long, 1ft 9in high, 9in deep. The strapwork is cut from card or fine plywood; letters and numerals can be purchased in black metal or brass. Look out for a suitable period tap.

The 'box' can be made any size so as to fit into your kitchen design, but the example shown here is 2ft 6in long by 1ft 9in high and 9in deep (762 x 533 x 229mm). The bottom of the box can be quite thick, as this will give strength to the model and a firm point to fix the tap; but the sides should be of finer material. The strapwork decoration can be cut from card or fine ply and glued in place. This decoration looks better if built up in layers, and can be enhanced with 'cablework' by using fine string or a coarse linen thread to form an edge or border to the straps, a detail which is also found on rainwater heads. It was usual to finish the job with the date and the cipher of the monarch or the owner of the house.

When full, the weight of lead and water would have been considerable, so that stout timbers were required to support the cistern in the required position. In spite of the workmanship put into the cistern itself, the supports tended to be rough but adequate for this job. Some Georgian taps protruded 9 or 12in (230–305mm), much further than modern ones.

BREAD CAR

This simple basket-like container could be the size of a large basket or even as huge as a double bed, and was used to hoist food out of the reach of vermin.

The model can be made from cut-down newel posts to form the corners and simple square

BREAD CAR

This a small one; some are as large as a bed. The frame is of square section, drilled to take cocktail sticks. Corner posts can be made from stair newel posts. The bottom (omitted for clarity) is made of simple planking. Small hooks or eyes can be fixed in the corner posts to hang the car up. Dimensions given are full size.

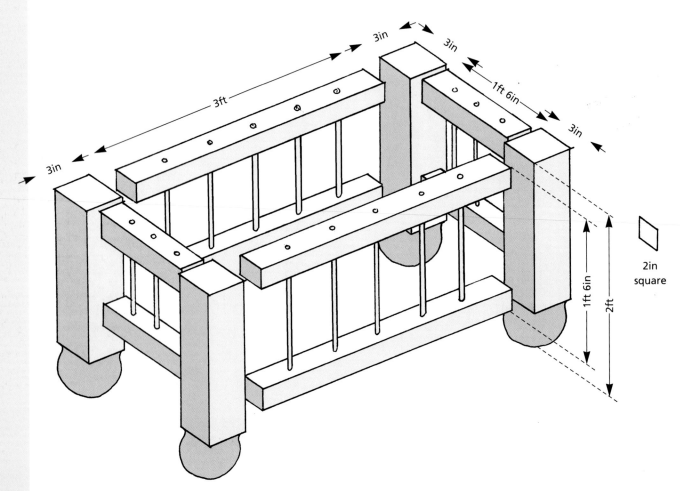

section for the frame; the sides and ends are closed with cocktail sticks. When drilling the square section to take the cocktail sticks, drill two at a time to ensure they line up when the sticks are pushed into position. The bottom of the car (not shown in the drawing for the sake of clarity) is made from simple planking, which is spaced so as to leave gaps for ventilation.

The largest examples are often of fine cabinetwork, but all are hung by rope, or rope and chain, from a beam in the kitchen.

CHOPPING BLOCKS

These were universal, and might be nothing more than a section from a tree trunk, resting directly on the ground; but most domestic ones were made from smaller sections of log, with legs as ornate as the owner wished.

The wood used for the block was one that would naturally dry white; for miniatures I have used cherry, which is traditionally used to make sticks for the blind. Legs of square section, as in the drawing, can be glued on; when set, drill through them and into the block, then insert small wooden dowels for reinforcement. If you prefer to use turned legs, drill holes in the bottom of the block to receive them; angle the holes to ensure that the legs are slightly splayed.

CHOPPING BLOCK

This fairly simple model is shown full size for 1/12 scale.

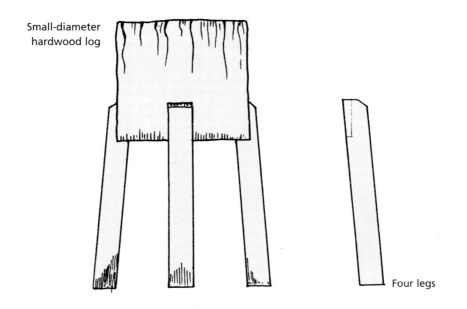

Small-diameter hardwood log

Four legs

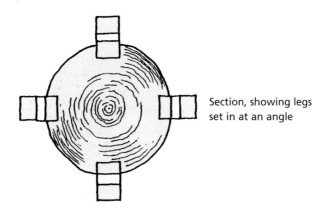

Section, showing legs set in at an angle

CHAPTER NINE

DECORATION AND FURNISHINGS

Walls • Floors • Ceilings • Colour schemes • Blinds and curtains
Protective coverings

WALL DECORATION

At the end of the seventeenth century and into the early part of the eighteenth, most walls in fine houses were covered in wainscot, usually in the form of panelling. By the middle of the century this was on its way out, and by 1774, according to Thomas Skaife, 'Wainscotting, in this fine age, is quite obsolete, . . . except in studies or offices for servants' (*Key to Civic Architecture; or The Universal British Builder* (London, 1774), p. 183).

Plasterwork came back into fashion around this time – not the traditional strapwork motifs, but in imitation of French rococo – with the best examples dating from around 1740–60.

WALLPAPER

An Italian dolls' house of the late seventeenth century, at the Museo Civico di Bassano del Grappa, has walls hung with fabrics, but the window surrounds are faced with printed paper. Although paper was used so sparingly in this example, it was soon to take over as an economic way of decorating a house. In 1740, green cut velvet cost 25s. a yard and green silk damask 12s., while flock paper was only 4s. a yard.

As early as 1715, flocks were being made in imitation of damask; many good examples still exist from the years 1730–45, at such fine houses as Hampton Court; Christchurch Mansion, Ipswich; Clandon Park, Surrey; and Temple Newsam, Leeds. Though paper was cheaper than fabric, it was thought to be a good source of revenue for Parliament, which taxed it in 1712 to help defray the costs of the Spanish wars of 1702–13. Starting off at one penny per square yard, the tax rose to 1½d. in 1714 and 1¾d. in 1797, not being repealed until 1830.

'Domino' was the most inexpensive variety of wallpaper. J.-B. M. Papillon (1698–1776) wrote the article on Domino in the great *Encyclopédie* published by Diderot and d'Alembert in 1755, where he tells us that wallpaper was not yet being made in rolls, but in small sheets. While conceding that Domino was in great demand, he derided it as

> a kind of paper on which lines, patterns and figures are printed from roughly cut wood blocks, then coloured by stencil, as is done with playing cards. This *Domino* is made especially in Rouen and in other provincial cities. It can only be of use to peasants, who buy it to ornament their overmantels. All *Dominos* are without taste, poorly drawn, even worse coloured, and stencilled with harsh colours.

As a master printer – and the son of the printmaker who invented *tapisserie de papier* (wallpaper) in 1688 – Papillon did not like to see his contemporaries making lots of money by using his father's ideas to make and mount such papers as Dominos.

It was at this time that collections of fashionable prints and engravings were being pasted on walls in a decorative way, to give us the 'print rooms' so much sought-after in the mid-century. Sets of prints and borders in 1/12 scale are available from good miniaturists' shops. In 1765–9 special lengths of 'print room' paper were produced and hung at Doddington Hall, Lincoln, but this was rare and tends to be repetitive. It was only from the end of the eighteenth century that sheets of printed paper were mounted to form lengths or rolls as we know them.

Chinese papers, in contrast to Western prints, were not pasted direct onto the wall but were hung on canvas or stout paper frames. The south-west bedroom at Saltram House in Devon is decorated with Chinese prints of many different sizes, larger landscapes and architectural views being framed by smaller scenes and figures to give all-over cover. The effect is altogether more casual than the well-organized traditional print room.

Decorative papers by Réveillon of Paris were hung in 1750 at Mocas Court, Hertfordshire, with alternating wide and slim panels of arabesques

MYRIORAMA OR 'ENDLESS LANDSCAPE'
(by courtesy of Tobar Ltd)

Towards the end of the eighteenth century, landscape papers consisting of a series of panels were being produced, each panel depicting a small section of the view and planned in such a way that they could be mounted in any order and still give a harmonious result. Matching screens were also produced using the same panels. The panels shown here are from a scale reproduction by Tobar of a set made in Leipzig; they are available by mail order from Hawkin's Bazaar (www.hawkin.com).

surrounded by delicate floral borders or frames. Once again, these are readily available on the miniatures circuit.

Early wallpapers, including flocked and printed-ink ones, had a strong vertical emphasis in their patterns, and the later pictorial papers were no exception, with the vertical being accentuated by the use of paper borders or frames.

True landscape papers were first produced in France around 1785, and the traditional vertical emphasis at last yielded to the horizontal. A series of panels were printed depicting small sections of a landscape in such a way that they could be mounted in any order and still give a perfectly harmonious design. At first these scenes were not used on walls, but to decorate portable screens. The results were admired so much that they became one of the most fashionable forms of wall decoration in the late eighteenth and early nineteenth centuries.

Today a miniature set of 24 cards is still being produced as 'the endless landscape'; this is a scale reproduction of the 24-piece 'Myriorama' (first introduced in Germany some time prior to 1790), which enables us to construct a landscape without any repetition from a series of segments measuring,

in 1/12 scale, 2 x 4⅝in (51 x 117mm). It was claimed at the time that the 24 segmental cards were capable of 1,686,553,615,927,922,354,187,744 combinations. If this is true, then you can be virtually sure your dolls' house décor will be unique!

To further the outdoor illusion, it was important to ensure that the line of the horizon came at the eye level of a standing viewer. For this purpose, the base of most landscape papers was designed to be 32–36in (81–91cm) from the floor, which was the height at which dado rails were fixed. In the best examples, everything below the landscape was

---

MURAL WALLPAPER OF c.1815
(by courtesy of Lord Camoys)

———

This pattern showing the monuments of Paris now hangs in the dining room of Stonor Park, Henley-on-Thames, Oxfordshire. The original blocks were in use for many years, so other examples may still survive.

painted to resemble stone, and was sometimes even made to represent a balustrade.

At much the same time, rooms were being decorated with wraparound landscapes, with the best examples completely surrounding the viewer and having no apparent joints, beginning or end. A superior example is in the dining room at Stonor Park, Oxfordshire; produced in 1815, it depicts 'The Monuments of Paris'. Other schemes used sections of landscape to fit the area of wall available, using rocky outcrops or trees to frame the ends. The White Hart Hotel at St Austell boasted a panoramic view of the Bay of Naples, printed around 1800 by Dufour, but don't rush to Cornwall to see it – it is now in the Victoria and Albert Museum, London.

The engravers Samuel and Nathaniel Buck, working in the early eighteenth century, produced large scenes of practically every city or town of importance in England and Wales; they also produced smaller works, much used in print rooms, showing castles, abbeys and houses of distinction. Copies of these could be used to decorate rooms with an authentic period landscape. They were produced in black and white, and can be used that way, or you may wish to paint or colour-wash them. Many ancient monuments sell copies of prints by the Buck brothers, and an outstanding book of them was published by Pavilion in 1994 under the title *A Prospect of Britain*. Part of my own collection was published as a calendar some years back.

For my own model, I was fortunate in that the brothers set up their easel just outside Bridge End House for their view of Berwick-upon-Tweed, and a photocopy of this print decorates the walls of an upstairs room in my model. I used four overlapping sheets to produce the desired result, placing the paper against the walls and marking the positions of door and windows before cutting out and pasting. The pieces from the doors may make chimney boards, and those from the windows should be used to make blinds. The lower edge of the landscape, at the point where it joins the dado rail, can be finished off by gluing on a length of gold cord of the kind used for gift-wrapping.

If you should want to reproduce the 'Domino' effect, use a suitable commercially available paper but don't cut it into small sheets like the original; mount it first, then score it when dry with a sharp, hard pencil. This not only cuts the paper, but leaves a faint line simulating the joins between the sheets.

VIEW OF BERWICK-UPON-TWEED BY SAMUEL AND NATHANIEL BUCK

(by courtesy of Berwick-on-Tweed Museum and Art Gallery)

This is the engraving which I used to paper one of the upstairs rooms in my model of Bridge End House; the view is as from the front of the real house. The Buck brothers produced many of these engravings, depicting all the major towns in Britain, so a 'local' one can be found by most British readers. The full series is published as *A Prospect of Britain*, ed. Ralph Hyde (London: Pavilion, 1994). The original measures 30¾ x 9¾in (78 x 24.7cm).

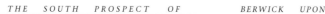

THE SOUTH PROSPECT OF BERWICK UPON TWEED.

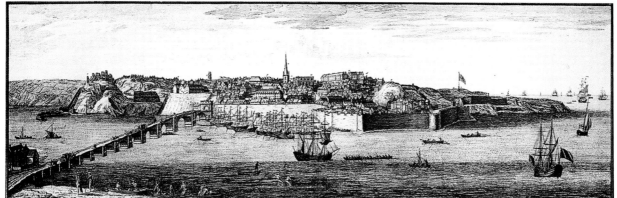

THE MURAL ROOM AT BRIDGE END HOUSE

The mural in this 'masculine' room is a view of Berwick-upon-Tweed by Samuel and Nathaniel Buck, who must have set up their easel in the road in front of the real Bridge End House. The dado is decorated to look like a low stone wall, using panels from Birchmores. The gaming table has pewter from Warwick Miniatures and churchwarden pipes by Chris Sturgess-Lief. At the back of the room is a 'Scottish' chest, on which was based the two-piece campaign chest or military trunk of the period; this was made to my drawings by Alf Larraman. The Bengal tiger, from Vienna, could have been brought back by the East India Company in a ship like the model by Newton Wood Miniatures. As befits the owner's withdrawing room, the floor is random oak.

FLOORING MATERIALS

Most parts of the country had their own favoured material for making the diaper-patterned stone floors found in kitchens and halls. Not always ideal for the purpose, they were laid to give the required colour contrast, at least when new. Slate could be a bit slippery, and the white Bath stone wore unevenly. Richer clients brought materials from further afield, even from overseas; many examples are to be found in paintings of Dutch interiors. Most other parts of the house had wooden floors made from random widths of oak or deal; uniform planking was only found in the grandest of homes. It was not unusual for the area in front of a fire to be made of large slabs of stone, even on upper floors; these were flush with the floorboards, not raised like a hearth.

There are many miniature flooring materials on the market, ranging from printed paper to the real thing; but remember what materials were in use at this period, and don't get carried away. Diaper patterns can be simulated by painting on fabric; paint the piece all over with one colour first, or you will end up with uneven edges to your squares or other shapes. When fitting wooden floors, first make a template of the area to be covered; you can then make up the floor on your work surface, rather than having to work inside the model.

FLOOR COVERINGS

Carpets, rugs and oilcloths were all to be found in the eighteenth century, but were not as numerous as you might think: even in the 'better' homes they were apt to be regarded as clutter.

On the Scottish border stands the elegant Palladian villa of Paxton, famous for its architecture and its collection of Chippendale furniture. The entrance hall of 1760 is spacious and well proportioned. It is a cube, in which all the internal walls are designed to balance each other: there is a door at every corner, even though two of them are sham and are only there to mirror the opposite walls. The floor, at first glance, looks just as you would expect in such a fine room. It is composed of a black and white diaper pattern and looks like the finest stone – but closer inspection shows it to be painted on canvas.

Floorcloths of oil on canvas were far from unusual in the eighteenth century. Many funerary hatchments in our churches have been painted onto the backs of such floorcloths – not because the cloths were redundant, but because the manufacturers of floorcloths also 'painted escutcheons trophies and all requisites for funerals', as well as coach signs, house signs and chimney boards. The trade card of one such manufacturer, Alexander Wetherstone (c.1760), begins:

Though carpets became more widespread in wealthier houses by the start of the nineteenth century, floorcloths were still an important item in most homes. After this period they moved down the social scale, being used mainly in kitchens, nurseries and other utilitarian rooms. Poorer people and the working classes even painted their own, using sailcloth as the base; and, while 'at sea', we should remember that Queen Victoria's royal yacht had cloth on its decks – painted to look like a wooden deck!

Paintings of the period show such floorcloths under dining-room and kitchen tables; and, as the more senior amongst us will remember, they finally ended up on top of the table.

Bedroom carpets were only for the very grand, and it was as late as c.1850 that they found their way into more humble homes. At first, one small rug or 'piece' was placed at the side of the bed, with another at the dressing table or washstand. The next development saw strips at either side of the bed, soon to be joined by a third one at the foot. It was just a short step from this to mitre them and sew them together to form a U-shaped runner round three sides of the bed.

It cannot be emphasized too much that floor coverings of any kind were rare in the eighteenth century, and that to include too many in a house

---

A TYPICAL BEDSIDE CARPET

The carpet is made from a runner cut and joined to fit round the foot of the bed; most of the floor would be bare planking.

Alex.ʳ Wetherstone

CARPENTER JOINER and TURNER,

at yᵉ Painted Floor Cloth & Brush in Portugal Street,

Near Lincolns Inn Back Gate.

Sells all sorts of Floor Cloths, Hair Cloths, List

Carpets, Royal & other Matting . . .

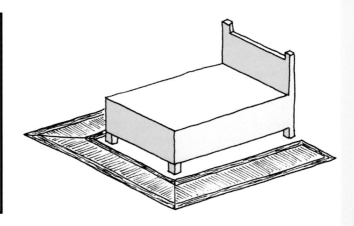

of the period would be out of character and should be avoided. The various types, in order of status or quality, were:

- **Pile carpets:** originally these were rare imports from Turkey and Persia, only being made in Britain by the Wilton factory in Wiltshire after 1751. At first these fine carpets were used as table covers.

- **Ingrain or Scotch carpets:** these were 'double-weave' carpets, woven without a pile; they were reversible, having a pattern on both sides. Centres of manufacture were Edinburgh, Hawick and Kilmarnock in Scotland, and Kendal, Kidderminster and Wilton in England. Being much more modest in price than pile carpets, they were found at the lower end of the market.

- **Floorcloths:** made of painted canvas, and eventually superseded by linoleum.

- **Haircloths:** made from hair fibre; used in hallways and at doors, then later on stairs. Most stairs were left without carpet until the late nineteenth century.

- **List carpeting:** this had a warp of woollen yarn and a weft made from lengths of rag or ribbon. Many were home-made and looked like the 'ethnic' striped rugs we use today. Known in France around 1770 as *tapis de Lizickes*, they had been established in Britain since 1730.

- **Straw mats:** early rush and straw mats were of British manufacture, but later they were imported from the Far East.

- **Crumb cloths:** oilcloths and haircloths were used under tables as crumb cloths. The governor of Massachusetts who died in 1728 left 'two old checkered canvas' to lay under a table', and workshops thrived repainting old or worn ones to bring them back to life.

- **Rugs or 'ruggs':** these were home-made, and were a kind of patchwork made of any available waste or scraps of material. Made as the dark nights of winter drew nigh, the newly completed rug was first used on the bed, then with the arrival of spring it was put on the floor.

Benjamin Franklin sent his wife a present of an English carpet while he was visiting London in 1758. This was a Wilton cut-pile, woven in widths of about 27in (69cm). He emphasized that it had to be sewn together and that there was a border for it. All this seems to indicate an early and rare example of a fitted carpet.

There are many miniature carpets and kits on the market, but don't overdo it. Try to make a U-shaped bed runner; an oilcloth or canvas can be made quite easily by painting a design onto a suitable piece of fabric.

CEILINGS

Early rooms may have had wooden ceilings, but most were of plaster. Special rooms might have ornament in low relief in the Adam style, quite different from the bold, raised ceilings of Palladian houses. Early Georgian designs included circles, squares and octagons framing painted panels and linked by delicate scrolls and sprays. After about 1780 these painted panels became less overpowering. At Kedleston in Derbyshire there are several ceilings by Robert Adam for which his original drawings still exist, showing just how rich the scheme was.

By the end of the period ceilings were plainer, but Greek motifs were predominant in cornices and in the white-painted central roses. Decorated plaster ceilings seldom occur in eighteenth-century vernacular houses or minor domestic buildings, yet a two-roomed cabin at Freshford, Co. Kilkenny, Ireland, apparently used as lodgings by plasterers working at the 'big house', has two ceilings of considerable grandeur. (Both are illustrated in James Ayres, *Building the Georgian City* (New Haven and London: Yale University Press, 1998), pp. 205 and 206; one also appears in the same author's *Shell Book of the Home in Britain* (London: Faber, 1981), p. 143.) It is pleasant to think that many a peasant host must have had such tradesmen lodged on them, and been rewarded in kind with doors, windows, floors and ceilings of superior quality.

Cornices and other motifs were as a rule made on site, but they could be purchased ready-made, either in plaster or papier mâché. Cornices were regarded as an integral part of a ceiling, and could be found in all but the smaller homes.

The ceilings in my model of Bridge End House are on the whole quite plain. The dining room has a central rose and a simple cornice at the wall head. The only other rose is on the ceiling of the portico; few rooms of the period had central hanging lights, so few roses were required. The ceiling to the hall and landing is rather fine, with pictures cut from postcards set in simple wooden frames, painted white with the rest of the ceiling. The cornice in the withdrawing room is bold – a relic of an earlier style still used in provincial schemes of the mid-to-late eighteenth century. The mural room, with its rather masculine décor, has no cornice. While most rooms in fine houses would have had a cornice, it was not unusual to go without one in vernacular or smaller houses.

THE HALL AT BRIDGE END HOUSE

The portico has been removed to show the entrance hall and stairs, and the landing with its painted ceiling. The hall light hangs by a stout metal rod, which is decorated, as was the fashion, with the same fabric as will be used for the curtains in the Venetian window. Only in the 'best' of houses would the hall floor be black and white; smaller homes used different colour contrasts, as here.

LEFT-HAND DOOR OF BRIDGE END HOUSE

This door gives access to the Gothic Revival bedroom and the dining room below. In most dolls' houses the doors are 'dead' walls, unfurnished except for curtains – yet curtains were rare at the time. The bedroom has colour-coordinated blinds, while downstairs there is nothing but an oil lamp on a bracket, of a type which came into use only in the mid-1800s. The pier tables upstairs, by Tony Knott, are here mounted (incorrectly) in front of the windows to show them off to advantage, rather than on the 'piers' between the windows.

COLOUR SCHEMES

In general, late seventeenth-century houses were dark, with dark wooden floors and dark panelled walls with raised mouldings. Bedrooms may have had tapestry or other fabric hung from a wooden cornice, falling to the dado rail; below this was a dark section of wainscotting down to the skirting board and the floor.

At the start of the Georgian period, wooden panels still lined some rooms. These could be dark and oppressive, and later it became usual to paint them in what eighteenth-century taste thought of as pale hues. Dull greens, greys and earthy colours were used at first; a little later, gilding or a second shade of the same colour was used to pick out details, but this fashion was short-lived and the plastered wall soon took over.

Plaster walls could be painted in much the same colours, but paper soon came onto the market. It was used in a few rooms only, so don't overdo it. The men's withdrawing or smoking room in Bridge End House has a dado painted to look like a low stone wall, and above it a view of the town outside. Similar murals were sometimes painted onto the plaster, as at Phippens Farm, Butcombe, Avon. If you had a collection of paintings, it was fashionable to paint the wall a dull red or terracotta. Most rooms were quite simple, even if elegant.

Many interiors of the period have survived and are treasured examples of period décor, but lesser

RIGHT-HAND
DOOR OF BRIDGE
END HOUSE

RIGHT-HAND
DOOR OF BRIDGE
END HOUSE

This is the door to the
reception rooms. Once
again there are no
curtains, but shutters to
the ground floor and
blinds, continuing the
mural, on the first floor. A
telescope lies on the left-
hand window ledge of the
mural room, and between
the windows is a simple
sconce by Warwick
Miniatures.

houses were limewashed inside, if not outside, once a year. Some homes did not even have plaster: I remember working in an old house and finding behind later layers of plaster a rough stone wall still with a good covering of limewash.

BLINDS AND CURTAINS

Some windows had simple roller blinds; these were mostly painted green, but some matched the main colour of the room, while later ones were even painted with landscapes or other designs. The list of known manufacturers of window blinds is long, starting with William Rodwell who was advertising

his services in 1727. By 1827 Nathaniel Whittock had published instructions for the making of painted window blinds. The surviving trade label of John White (c.1750) shows that he painted pictures, mended, cleaned and framed blinds for windows, at the Golden Head, Shoe Lane, Fleet Street, London.

Curtains cost a considerable amount of money; the use of billowing drapes in portraits of the time was partly intended to flatter the sitter and partly to complete a difficult composition. The curtain was actually used sparingly in ordinary houses, while the more frugal blind, with nothing lost in folds, was widely used.

Only grand houses had the kind of curtains we are familiar with today; in simpler homes the material was simply tacked to a rail at the top, and the resulting drape tied back during the day. By 1760, 'fine' festoons were in common use; these were opened by pulling on cords which raised them vertically. Only lightweight materials could be used for curtains of this type.

The next innovation was the two-part curtain; fixed at their head only, these were raised or opened by being drawn up into the top corners.

Chippendale used these in some of his schemes from at least 1767. The curtain pole with horizontally drawn curtains came into Britain from France around 1780.

Pelmets were of wood and could be painted or gilded. Some superb ones at Harewood House in North Yorkshire are carved to look like the folds in curtains; later, fabric pelmets and swags were used to hide the workings.

'A DESIGN FOR A CORNICE, FOR A VENETIAN WINDOW'

by Thomas Chippendale
(by courtesy of Dover Publications, Inc.)

———

Non-functional drapes form part of an elaborate carved pelmet in this plate from *The Gentleman and Cabinet-Maker's Director* (3rd edition, 1762).

PROTECTIVE COVERINGS

The housekeeper of the period was well aware of the detrimental effect that sunlight had on fine furnishings, and went to considerable lengths to overcome it. Shutters, blinds and later muslin sub-curtains helped to filter harmful rays, and servants were employed to turn furniture or cover it with sheets. Carpets could be protected by druggets of coarse fabric or by 'paper carpets' to prevent deterioration of the fabric or colours.

CHAPTER TEN

AND SO TO BED

Beds • Bedwarmers

The end of day was not the same for all of Georgian society. Most went to bed when it was dark and woke when it was light. In other words, farmers, labourers and most working people worked all the hours of daylight and retired only when it was too dark to work.

Most dolls' houses are modelled on the homes of people who were better off and had a social life that was not dictated by the sun; these houses had lights both inside and on the street.

The stair, if you had one, could be elegant, but was not usually carpeted – only palace-like dwellings had such comforts. The bedroom was cold and, as we have seen already, in working-class houses or servants' quarters it may not have had windows. To build up and conserve heat, beds had curtains or were of the 'box' type. As the period progressed, houses came to be better heated and beds in better rooms either lost their curtains or retained them only for decoration.

Feather beds and quilts are recorded, but most mattresses would have been filled with straw or horsehair, with woollen blankets and a patchwork quilt or other decorative coverlet. By the Regency period, the better beds would have had valances to hide the bed legs and anything kept under the bed for use at night. (Under the bed became the usual place for such things from now on.)

Early rooms were sparsely furnished, but by the Regency period essential items included a chair, a bedside cabinet with or without a mirror, a chest of drawers and a wardrobe. Even at this late date, wardrobes were still of the press type, with drawers in the lower half and the top section having shelves concealed by doors. It was only around 1830 that hanging wardrobes came into fashion, but variations were in use as early as 1780.

Washstands were elegant but meagre by later standards; the jug and bowl were much smaller than the later Victorian ones. Other small items in the bedroom may have included wig stands, and even a commode and screens.

BEDS

The majority of people, including some in superior homes, slept in box beds or in what was known as a low-post, stump or open bed, much like the ones we use today. More refined beds used by the most prosperous were symbols of their owners' status, but the best of these are far too large for most dolls' houses – indeed, some were excessively large even for the house they were intended for, being anything up to 12ft (3.66m) high and rich in the extreme.

Perhaps the best example of such a state bed is that sent to Calke Abbey, Worksop, Nottinghamshire, in 1734 by Queen Caroline as a gift on the marriage of her maid of honour Lady Caroline Manners to Sir Henry Harpur. This magnificent bed was never used – indeed it was not even taken out of its cases until 1985, as there was no bedroom in the house of sufficient height for it. The upholstery was made for George I in about 1715, and may never have been exposed to light and dust since it was made. Today the bed is displayed behind glass in a darkened room to protect the magnificent fabrics, which are densely embroidered with processions of warriors on horseback, mandarins, and ladies in bright robes; in the forests are dragons, birds, gazelles and other animals. A fascinating detail is the use of peacock feathers, tightly rolled to form knots in the trees and markings on butterflies' wings.

Much smaller versions were made in great numbers for lesser rooms or homes, but even these could be massive, with a canopy up to 9ft 6in (2.9m) high. The posts could be in the form of classical columns, or swathed in acanthus leaves, with lion's-paw feet. Hangings were of damask or velvet with tassels and fringes, completely concealing the woodwork of the canopy.

Later Georgian beds were still four-posters, but the fine woodwork of the cornice or tester was

THE GOTHIC BEDROOM AT BRIDGE END HOUSE

The Gothic Revival bedroom features a rich four-poster by Reverie Miniatures. Note the sparing use of carpet on an otherwise plain wooden floor. The small table has two wig stands on it, and under the cradle is a foot (or space) warmer made in copper by Tom Pouce. The marble-topped gilt-bronze table by Tony Knott adds to the richness of the furnishings.

generally exposed – though until about 1780 many were also draped. Bed curtains were now much lighter in colour and in material, being of floral or striped silk, and they were seldom pulled round the bed.

As houses became warmer and draught-free the great curtains were no longer required. They became less full and in most cases were used only for decoration; by 1750 they were hung only at the top of the bed, leaving the posts at the foot of the bed exposed so that they could be finely decorated.

This led to the half-tester bed, which had only two posts at the head and simple decorative curtains – a style which survived through the Regency and into the early Victorian period. The square canopies or testers used at first were replaced around 1800 by half-round or D-shaped ones, often supported by rods or chains from the ceiling.

Smaller homes or rooms sported 'tent' or 'couch' beds. Tent beds had four posts supporting the framework of the canopy, the latter usually being made of curved laths with the fabric draped over so that it looked like a tent. Couch beds – a type refined in the Regency period – took many forms, often being made like divans with head and foot boards and low, curved sides; like day couches, they were fitted with roll cushions.

Early mattress supports were of interwoven cords; stretched canvas tapes followed, only to be replaced by wooden slats about 1750.

During the early part of the nineteenth century countless wooden beds were destroyed in the attempt to eradicate bed bugs, and replaced by the new, more hygienic metal versions.

BOX BEDS

In my childhood, being a member of a large working-class family was more often than not a happy experience, which was heightened when holidays or festive seasons of the year dictated that aunts, uncles and cousins would swell the numbers. In homes that were already bursting at the seams, temporary sleeping quarters had to be found by stripping beds of their mattresses for use by the adults, while visiting babies had the warm comfort of their parents' now empty trunk, or a drawer from the proverbial tallboy or dresser. This temporary bed was an unconscious relic: a reminder of the box bed which was once universal among the working classes, with variants found in finer households.

The close bed or box bed was, as its name implies, a bed in a box, closed off from the rest of the room. The box was a simple rectangle of 6 x 4ft (1.8 x 1.2m) with doors in one side to allow access to its relative comfort and privacy. The enclosing sides and ends were some 5ft (1.5m) high, and on

Built-in box bed of 1712 from Starthouse, Boldersdale, Yorkshire, with the initials of the owners carved on the door

Cupboard bed from Kennixton Farmhouse at the Museum of Welsh Life, St Fagans, Cardiff (© The National Museum of Wales). This example is much like the Boldersdale one, except that it has a settle attached to the front of it. It also boasts sliding doors with ventilation panels above

these rested a low roof. In some cases the beds were closed by curtains rather than wooden doors, as this was thought more convenient for access to sick occupants. Both types could be free-standing and movable, the property of the tenant, as in the case of James Spence (see pages 88–9); or they could be fixed, built in as part of the house.

Later, 'open' beds were often placed in an alcove or bed-nook to give all-round protection from draughts and to prevent them intruding into valuable floor space. Sir Charles Monck had bed-nooks in all of the main bedrooms of his great Greek Revival house of Belsay Hall, Northumberland (1810–17).

These simple contrivances, once common throughout Europe, gave what little privacy was demanded by morality and decency in the confines of a one-roomed cottage.

Some box beds found in fine mansions are rather grand, but most of those used throughout northern Europe are quite simple. Tiered box beds built to sleep as many as possible in a confined space are to be found on the island of Ruskholm, Orkney. In the Lothians and Fife, wrights made fine arched box beds, their design based on Andrea Palladio's *Quattro libri dell'architettura* of 1570 and displaying a simple 'keystone' to the arch, which was supported by Corinthian pilasters. In 1683 apprentices in the Lothians region of Scotland were required to make 'ane close bed the lidds [doors] to be of raysed work, out of the timber it self, angled from point to point with one dorick entablature, to be all done in wainscott'. The attics of many cottages in the Pennines had primitive

A BED-NOOK
after a 1933 photograph of a house in North Shields, Tyne & Wear

This nook is in the eighteenth-century home of a working man, but the idea was used in great houses as late as the nineteenth century.

box beds built in them to house seasonal labourers or the ever-growing family; examples are still to be found at Sinnington Lodge, Spout House and Midcable in Yorkshire.

As late as 1825, one historian thought it 'shocking that a man, his wife and a dozen children should be obliged to live huddled together in one miserable hovel'. He mused that 'it would be delightful to observe gentlemen as attentive to the erection of cottages as of stables and kennels'. Other 'improvers' wrote recommending various arrangements of the position of the box bed to give the illusion of more than one room, but these ideas were based on the existing practice of forward-thinking individuals in cottages like that from Llainfadyn of 1762 (see pages 65–6).

English
This variety can be made with or without doors

MAKING BOX BEDS

The choice of style is up to you; Irish, English, Scottish and Welsh varieties are illustrated here. The construction is much the same for all of the many regional variations. A joiner of the time would have made a simple rectangular frame, and on this hung all the sides of the box. For the model, it is best to build the front of your choice first, as this is the most complicated part. Next

---

BOX OR CLOSE BEDS

All the front elevations on pages 187–90 are all drawn full size for 1/12 scale.

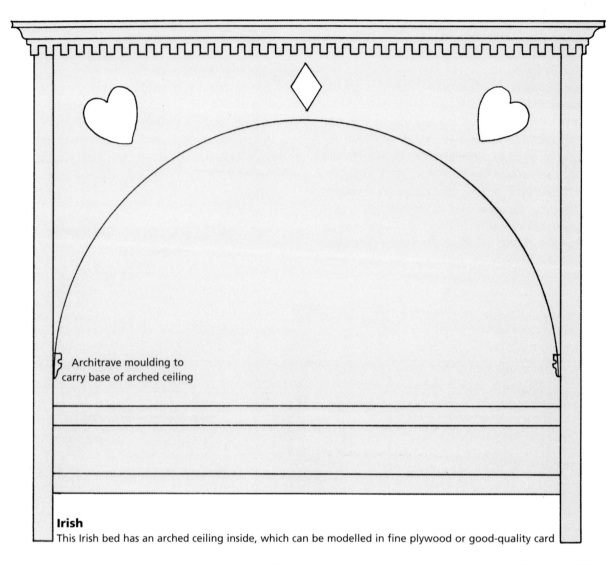

Architrave moulding to
carry base of arched ceiling

Irish
This Irish bed has an arched ceiling inside, which can be modelled in fine plywood or good-quality card

MODELS OF BOX BEDS

Box beds are found throughout northern Europe and there are many regional variations, of which only five are shown here. Top left is a pine bed characteristic of the Lothians and Fife areas of Scotland, and next to it an upland one with doors to ward off the colder winter nights. The painted one is typical of parts of Ireland, while the Welsh one from the Gower Peninsula has a low settle built onto the front of it. Lastly there is a simple English variation.

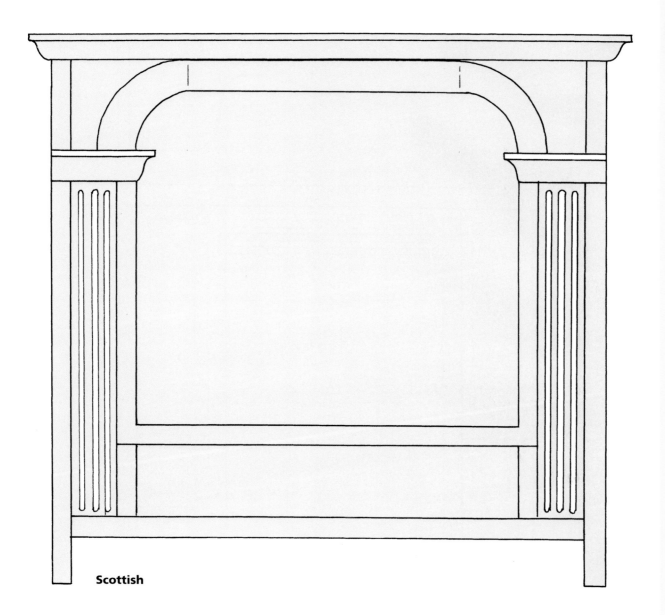

Scottish

make up the back, and when these are set, join them together at the ends with cross-pieces top and bottom; the end panels are added last. The width of the ends will determine whether you are making it a single, three-quarter or double bed; this may depend on the space you have available, or on the number of people to be housed.

The bases of the later models (after about 1750) are usually made up of laths, but I have seen them strung with stout cord as well. The best examples were of natural rich-coloured hardwoods, but some were made from cheap materials and stained in imitation of the real thing. The Scottish one shown here is of natural 'antique pine', but the Irish ones are always painted; the others have a dark finish, in natural or imitation oak, mahogany or walnut.

TRUCKLE OR TRUNDLE BEDS

The 'lowest' form of bed (in both senses of the word) was the kind known in England and Wales as the 'trundle' or 'truckle' bed; this was called a 'hurle' or 'hurley' in Scotland and a 'Shaker' bed in nineteenth-century America. These beds were almost always singles, and were used by children or guests in cottages and smaller houses; in finer establishments they were used by the maid or manservant who slept in the same room as the mistress or master, so as to be on hand when required. When not in use, the truckle was trundled underneath the four-poster, and to help with this, some were fitted with simple wheels at one end only.

Welsh

The ends of the settle (compare the photograph on page 186) are shown to either side

Plan view of box bed
(not to same scale)
suitable for use with all the preceding
drawings

Back and sides
mounted on
outside of frame

Strip of wood front and back to carry laths

Front: use regional variation of your choice

MAKING A TRUCKLE BED

The corner posts or legs can be made from pieces of
stair newel post, or from simple square section if
you wish to fit wheels. It is best to start by cutting
the ends and sides of the frame. Drill these to take
the cords, then glue the rails and posts together,
starting with the long sides; when these are dry, fit
the ends. Only in later years would a mattress have
been used, it being more usual to have layers consisting of a bag of chaff, a bag of horsehair, and a
sheepskin on top if you were lucky.

To finish off, you can stain or paint the bed to
link up with the décor it is going into.

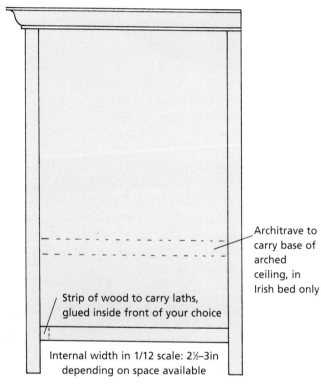

Architrave to
carry base of
arched
ceiling, in
Irish bed only

Strip of wood to carry laths,
glued inside front of your choice

Internal width in 1/12 scale: 2½–3in
depending on space available

End elevation of box bed
(to same scale as plan view)

TRUCKLE OR TRUNDLE BED

The model should be sized to fit underneath
the main bed.

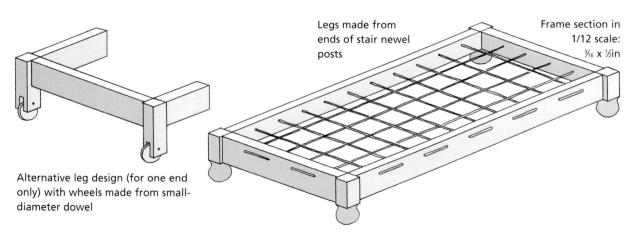

Legs made from
ends of stair newel
posts

Frame section in
1/12 scale:
³⁄₁₆ x ½in

Alternative leg design (for one end
only) with wheels made from small-
diameter dowel

SETTLE BEDS

The Irish settle was another distinctive type of bed. Like the Dutch and Welsh dressers, it was not peculiar to its country of origin; it was found in large numbers in French-speaking Canada, where it is known as a *banc-lit*. Looking like an ordinary settle by day, at night the seat was pulled forward on a

hinge to reveal a sleeping space filled with bracken to form a mattress. Earlier versions were higher, and were used not as seats but as a work surface by the housewife or kitchen servant. This type was not only found in upland cottages but in the kitchens of large houses, where scant provision was made to accommodate servants.

SETTLE BED OR
BANC-LIT

This example is Irish, and judging by its height it must have been used as a work surface rather than a seat.

Full-size dimensions:
60in long
58in high
21in front to back
Height of 'seat' 35in

ATTIC BEDS

When the wind blew fresh across the moors of northern England, all kinds of debris such as straw dust and insects fell onto the sleeping occupants of cottages and attics – a problem which was overcome by building four-posters with a sloping canopy to fit under the eaves. The posts on one side were much shorter than the other two, and the framework of the canopy carried a simple cloth roof to protect the sleepers. The mattress was of chaff, straw, wool, horsehair or feathers, and was supported on a stout canvas strung from the frame. Beds of less comfort had a simple mesh of woven cord to carry the occupant. In keeping with the late eighteenth-century date and the utilitarian nature of the bed, the decoration of the posts was of the simplest kind.

These beds in their traditional form were used by all classes of society and can be made to fit into any attic space. Once again, many were built in, but Richard Gillow of Lancaster, arguably Britain's greatest cabinetmaker, made them in good numbers for the gentry to house excess guests at shooting parties.

The best-known furniture makers of the Georgian era – Chippendale, Hepplewhite, Sheraton – all wrote and published books and have consequently given their names to 'styles'. Gillow produced hundreds of drawings but didn't publish, so his name is relatively unknown. He was the first to sign his furniture, and many pieces previously thought to be by others are now known to be his; some even have clear evidence of his (or someone's) mark having been sanded off. So don't worry about the name – just make fine miniatures based on the originals, whoever designed them.

MAKING AN ATTIC BED

Cut the sides and ends first, then drill them to take the cords. Make up the long sides first, and when these are set, insert the ends. The upper framework is light, and onto this you fix your fabric. The drapes on fine four-posters were to keep the draughts out and keep you warm in an elegant but cold room, but the function of the drapes on attic beds was twofold: to keep you warm and to prevent debris from the unceiled thatch or slate roof falling on you on windy nights.

ATTIC OR SERVANT'S BED
(not to scale)

Dimensions are given for 1/12 scale, but may need to be adjusted to fit the space available.

Base frame from ½ x ³⁄₁₆in section
Posts or legs ³⁄₁₆in square
Rope holes in base at ½in centres
Framework to carry canopy cut from ³⁄₁₆ x ¹⁄₁₆in section

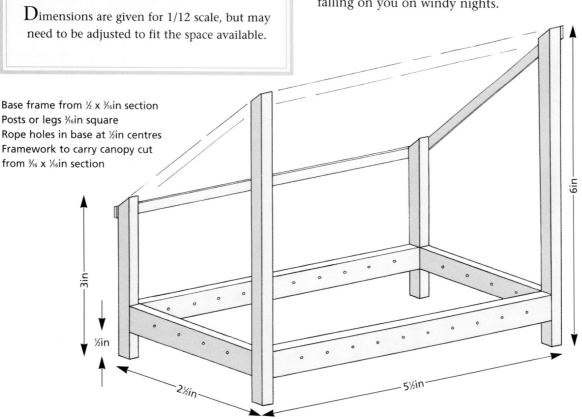

3in

½in

2½in

5½in

6in

STRINGING THE BED FRAME

The stringing of the bed is quite simple: starting at any corner, thread your cord in one direction first, either side to side or lengthways. When you have worked all the way along in this direction, don't cut the cord but pull it across the corner and start working in the opposite direction, this time weaving it over and under the strands already in place. When this is complete, fasten the cords by tying knots in the ends, giving them a dab of glue to make sure they hold.

Some examples have a wooden plug or peg pushed into the hole to wedge the cord in place. When the cords required tightening the wedge was removed, to be replaced when the task was completed. This is said to be the origin of the phrase 'sleep tight'.

The stringing of beds may have had regional variations, but it is difficult to be sure. Only in Ireland have I seen bed frames that were not drilled, but had pegs driven into the top of the frame, round which the cords were stretched. Holes drilled through the sides of the frames, as in most of my drawings, are found in many parts of Europe, but I have seen others with the holes drilled at an angle, starting in the top of the frame and ending up half-way down the inner face. Once again, the choice is yours.

> ## VARIOUS WAYS OF STRINGING A BED
>
> These techniques are suitable for all the beds illustrated on the preceding pages.

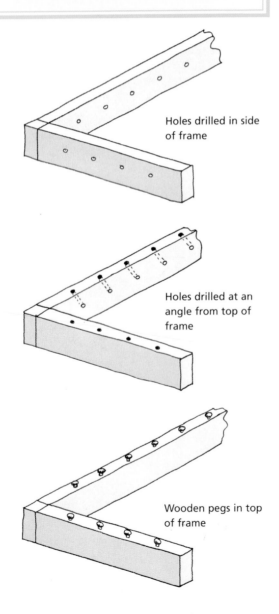

Holes drilled in side of frame

Holes drilled at an angle from top of frame

Wooden pegs in top of frame

BEDWARMERS

Warming pans hung in the kitchens of homes large and small, ready to be charged with hot ashes and put to work. They were usually made with a long, turned wooden handle and a lidded pan of iron, brass or copper. The metal was decorated by engraving or punching designs into the surface, or sometimes by piercing. Some early examples were even made from silver.

Gertrude Jekyll and Sydney R. Jones were well-known recorders of traditional domestic equipment, and in their *Old English Household Life* (London: Batsford, 1939 and various subsequent reprints) they describe a 'bed wagon' made as follows. There was an oak frame 3–4ft (90–120cm) long, consisting of four rails; an iron tray rested in the middle of this on four iron rods; on this sat a trivet which held a pan of hot ashes; over this, attached to the underside of the upper part of the frame, was a second piece of sheet iron. The bottom tray and upper iron sheet prevented any scorching of the bedclothes.

Mr Jones was an outstanding draughtsman, but for this item no drawing was produced. However, since reading this description I have found variations on this design in museums from Norfolk to Surrey.

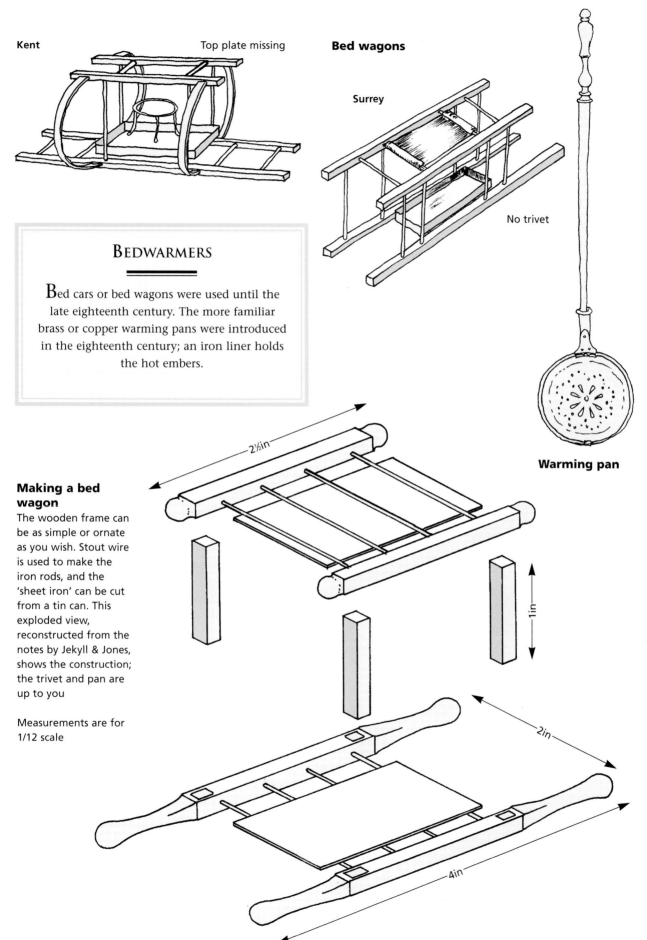

Kent   Top plate missing   **Bed wagons**

Surrey

No trivet

BEDWARMERS

Bed cars or bed wagons were used until the
late eighteenth century. The more familiar
brass or copper warming pans were introduced
in the eighteenth century; an iron liner holds
the hot embers.

Warming pan

2½in

**Making a bed
wagon**

The wooden frame can
be as simple or ornate
as you wish. Stout wire
is used to make the
iron rods, and the
'sheet iron' can be cut
from a tin can. This
exploded view,
reconstructed from the
notes by Jekyll & Jones,
shows the construction;
the trivet and pan are
up to you

1in

Measurements are for
1/12 scale

2in

4in

EPILOGUE

The Georgian World

We all live in houses of various degree, according to our taste, income or social standing; so what is new? – it has always been the same.

Today, as in no other time, we can find out how many people have homes with two toilets and a garden; where most car owners live, whether they have a garage and, if so, whether they keep their car in it. Such minutiae are only available because of regular census returns, backed up by other statistical information compiled by banks, insurance companies, tax offices, etc., which are then re-interpreted and published by the Central Office of Information (not the usual haunt of dolls' house enthusiasts, perhaps) in a kind of 'state of the nation' report. Such reliable information about our population and its social divisions cannot be had prior to 1801 when the first official census was commissioned, so for the most part we have to resort to informed guesses.

For the Georgian period we do have one such 'statistical' return, published in 1688 by Gregory King and based on the hearth taxes of 1662–8 and other data. This was revised and updated by Charles Davenant in 1771; we are not likely to get a closer look at the make-up of Georgian society than this.

The total population of England and Wales was put at 5,500,520 people, with over 5 million depending on an income of less than £100 per annum per household. Most lived in low-grade, outdated houses – and worse – so the type of Georgian house favoured by most miniaturists would have been confined to superior mortals. (Don't let this stop you looking at the homes of the 5 million whose lifestyles were much more varied than those of their 'betters', and whose homes offer a considerable variety of challenges to the miniaturist.) Native timber had been in decline for many years, and since the plague of 1665 coal fires had been regarded as the healthy option in all but the most rural areas.

The following year, 1666, saw the Great Fire of London, which gave rise to many of the building regulations of the eighteenth century. One such regulation required the newfangled sash windows (introduced *c*.1670) to be set back from the front

GEORGIAN SOCIETY IN ENGLAND AND WALES

The four main social groups, showing their relative sizes as a percentage of the population, and their share of the available income, according to King (1688) and Davenant (1771).

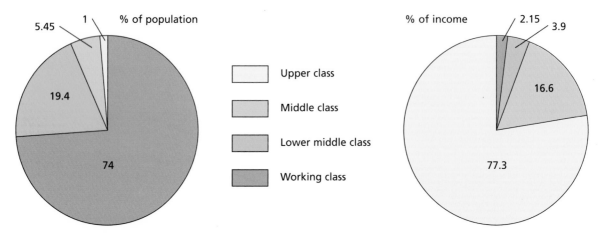

% of population

5.45   1

19.4

74

☐ Upper class

☐ Middle class

☐ Lower middle class

■ Working class

% of income   2.15   3.9

16.6

77.3

face of the house, in an effort to prevent fire spreading when burning thatch was pulled off the roof onto the pavement using the parish thatch hooks kept at the church. This act of 1724 was further strengthened in 1774 when windows had to be rebated into the wall – a regulation that still applies today. That thatch was dangerous and out-moded was not a new idea, as tiles, stone or clay had already been in use for over a century. When George I came to the throne in 1714, pantiles were fixed at a standard size of 13½in by 9½in by ½in thick (343 x 241 x 13mm). There was no such rule for other roofing materials, and many regional variations of considerable charm still persisted.

In 1715 we find interior decorators using flock papers, and by 1727 window blinds were available to match the papers – so colour co-ordination existed long before our time, but only for the few. These new, brighter interiors were by 1730 illuminated not just by rush lights and candles, but also by glass chandeliers; though the oil lamp, invented by Argand, did not come in till 1783.

The dreaded window tax was reintroduced in 1746, which has caused confusion in the minds of local historians and miniaturists ever since. Rare Turkish and Persian carpets came to Britain before 1750, but only some were used on the floors, others being spread over tables or beds. (I can remember a time when new mats or carpets were used on the bed.)

'Floor carpets' were protected by cloths with a design painted on them. In lesser homes this cloth was used in place of the carpet and became a work of art in itself; indeed, many workshops were set up to produce them. Wilton pile carpets were man-ufactured from 1751, and Benjamin Franklin sent his wife a present of a fitted one in 1758.

Curtains, if used at all, were simple. By 1760, lightweight material was hung, blind-like, and raised by pulling cords as in the present-day 'Austrian' blind; while 1770 saw two-part curtains drawn up, again by cords, to the top corners of the window. It was not until 1780 that the curtain pole allowed curtains to be drawn horizontally across the window as is the norm today – a point over-looked by many dolls' house decorators.

Hall stoves gave a warm welcome in the best of houses by about 1770. From this time on, a sales gimmick of Robert Adam was the inclusion in all his new houses of a 'water closet' of sorts – but before you rush to install one, consider how many people lived in a house built by Robert Adam, and what their social standing was.

American Independence came in 1776. The French Revolution in 1789 heralded the Napoleonic wars, with the Battle of the Nile in 1798, Trafalgar in 1805 and Waterloo in 1815. The world at large was in turmoil, yet at home life went on just the same. From 1775 your front doorway may have been decorated with details cast in Coade stone. French doors were used to gain first-floor balconies by 1780. Coal gas was being exper-imented with in 1787, with some success; yet it was only in 1803 that the first public gaslights were to glow in the dark city streets.

Remaining on the bright side, the slave trade in Britain was abolished in 1807; tax on roofing slates was removed in 1831, followed twenty years later by the window tax.

An age of elegance was over – an age which also saw the advances of the Agricultural Revolution, followed by the Industrial Revolution, and which has left us a legacy of one million, one hundred thousand period houses, united not just by the title 'Georgian' but by a unique quality of work-manship. This is indeed a rich legacy for miniatur-ists to build on.

For in the days before roads were metalled, move-ment was no part of daily life, and the home must have been so much the more important for all. For the most part they were country dwellers or lived in country towns. Indeed, a salient difference between that generation and our own is that then England was rural, with a hankering for the town; whereas now it is urban with a hankering for the country. . . .

No doubt, as we now are, we should have found it uncongenial to live in a house lit by candles, with no ease of washing, with smallpox at our elbow, and a barber-surgeon to attend without anæsthetics to our injuries. But for the needs of the time these houses are admirably and simply planned, generous in line and workmanship, without extravagance or ostenta-tion; essentially, as a house should be, habitable and adorning life. (William G, Newton, MA, FRIBA, *Wren and Early Georgian Houses* (London: Architectural Press, 1928))

FURTHER READING

Place of publication is London except where otherwise stated.

DOLLS' HOUSES

Olivia Bristol and Leslie Geddes-Brown, *Dolls' Houses* (Mitchell Beazley, 1997) ISBN 1 85732 824 8

Vivien Greene, *The Vivien Greene Dolls' House Collection* (Cassell, 1995) ISBN 0 304 34948 8

Joyce Percival, *Architecture for Dolls' Houses* (Lewes: GMC Publications, 1996) ISBN 0 946819 98 X

DECORATION

Lesley Hoskins, *The Papered Wall* (Thames & Hudson, 1994) ISBN 0 500 23695 X

Ralph Hyde, *A Prospect of Britain* (Pavilion, 1994) ISBN 1 85793 142 4

Dawn Jacobson, *Chinoiserie* (Phaidon, 1993) ISBN 0 7148 2883 1

James Macaulay, *The Gothic Revival* (Blackie, 1975) ISBN 0 216 89892 7

Charles Saumarez Smith, *Eighteenth-Century Decoration* (Weidenfeld & Nicolson, 1993) ISBN 0 297 83051 1

FURNISHING

James Ayres, *The Shell Book of the Home in Britain* (Faber & Faber, 1981) ISBN 0 571 11625 6

Annette Carruthers, *The Scottish Home* (Edinburgh: National Museums of Scotland, 1996) ISBN 0 948636 72 6

George Hepplewhite, *The Cabinet-Maker and Upholsterer's Guide*, 3rd edition (Hepplewhite, 1794; reprinted New York: Dover Publications, 1969) ISBN 0 486 22183 0

Claudia Kinmonth, *Irish Country Furniture* (New Haven, CT: Yale University Press, 1993) ISBN 0 300 05574 9

Lawrence Wright, *Clean and Decent* (Routledge & Kegan Paul, 1960)

Doreen Yarwood, *The English Home* (Batsford, 1956)

PERIOD ARCHITECTURE

James Ayres, *Building the Georgian City* (New Haven, CT and London: Yale University Press, 1998) ISBN 0 300 07548 0

Stephen Calloway, *The Elements of Style* (Mitchell Beazley, 1991) ISBN 1 85732 834 5

Dan Cruickshank, *Georgian Buildings of Britain & Ireland* (Weidenfeld & Nicolson, 1985) ISBN 0 297 78610 5

Dan Cruickshank and Neil Burton, *Life in the Georgian City* (Viking, 1990) ISBN 0 670 81266 8

Walter Ison, *The Georgian Buildings of Bath* (Faber & Faber, 1948)

N. Lloyd, *A History of English Brickwork* (Architectural Press, 1925; reprinted New York: Blom, 1972)

Robert J. Naismith, *Buildings of The Scottish Countryside* (Gollancz, 1985) ISBN 0 575 03383 5

S. Parissien, *The Georgian House* (Aurum/The Georgian Group, 1995) ISBN 1 85410 370 9

Sean Rothery, *The Buildings of Ireland* (Dublin: Lilliput, 1997) ISBN 1 874675 81 3

John Woodforde, *Georgian Houses for All* (Routledge and Kegan Paul, 1978) ISBN 0 7100 8680 6

A. J. Youngson, *The Making of Classical Edinburgh* (Edinburgh University Press, 1966) ISBN 0 7486 0446 4

An invaluable source of information, county by county, is to be found in the outstanding Penguin series founded in 1951 by Sir Nikolaus Pevsner, *Buildings of England, Scotland, Wales, Ireland.*

HISTORICAL BACKGROUND

J. Richardson, *The Local Historian's Encyclopedia* (New Barnet: Historical Publications, 1974) ISBN 0 9503656 7 X

G. M. Trevelyan, *Illustrated English Social History* (Longmans, 1949)

The Georgian Group, 37 Spital Square, London E1 6DY, publishes a series of guides on most aspects of the Georgian house.

PLACES TO VISIT

HOUSES

GREAT BRITAIN

1 Royal Crescent, Bath *c.*1767

Belle Isle, Cumbria: circular in plan *c.*1775

Belsay Hall, Northumberland: Greek Doric *c.*1806

Georgian House, Charlotte Square, Edinburgh by Robert Adam *c.*1791

Georgian House, George Street, Bristol *c.*1790

NORTHERN IRELAND

Castleward, Co. Down: textbook Palladian and Gothic *c.*1760

REPUBLIC OF IRELAND

29 Merrion Square, Dublin, begun 1762

Castletown, Co. Kildare: most important house in Ireland, *c.*1720

Newbury Hall, Co. Kildare *c.*1765

TOWNS AND VILLAGES

GREAT BRITAIN

Arundel, West Sussex

Bath, Avon: eighteenth-century spa town

Belsay, Northumberland: Greek Revival estate village *c.*1806

Berwick-upon-Tweed, Northumberland: eighteenth-century garrison town

Blaise Hamlet, Bristol: *cottage orné* estate village *c.*1811

Lowther, Cumbria: model village by Adam brothers *c.*1760

Ludlow, Shropshire

Marford, Clwyd: Gothic Revival houses *c.*1806

Milton Abbas, Dorset: model village by Lancelot Brown *c.*1786

Nuneham Courtenay; Oxfordshire: estate village *c.*1760

Scone, Tayside; model village *c.*1780

REPUBLIC OF IRELAND

Dublin: especially Merrion Square *c.*1762

Tullamore, Co. Offaly: eighteenth-century planned town centre

Tyrellspass, Co. Westmeath: eighteenth-century estate village

Westport, Co. Mayo: planned town *c.*1780

MUSEUMS

GREAT BRITAIN

Building of Bath Museum, Bath, Avon

Museum of Welsh Life, St Fagans, Cardiff

York Castle Museum

NORTHERN IRELAND

Ulster Folk Park and Transport Museum, Co. Down

REPUBLIC OF IRELAND

Irish Agricultural Museum, Wexford: furniture

INDEX

Adam, Robert 6, 9, 60, 80, 114, 139, 178, 197
Allsopp, Bruce 15
andirons 126–8
area railings 109, 110
Argand lamp 108
armorial charges 103
attic beds 193
Austen, Jane 6, 95, 139

baby houses 81–7
bachelor's (tin) oven 146
bakestones 146
balconies 14, 16, 109
banc-lit 192
Barker, Thomas 33
Bath 13, 32–3
bed-nooks 186
bed runners 177
bed wagons 194–5
bedrooms 95, 183
beds 74–5, 183–94
bedwarmers 194–5
beeswax candles 107
Bell, John 92–5
bell pulls 111–13
Belsay Hall, Northumberland 186
Beltingham, near Hexham 15
Belton House, Lincolnshire 102
bidets 116
Blaise Hamlet 16
blinds 181–2
boats, as houses 3, 4, 98–9
bottle jacks 142, 153–4
box beds 74–5, 183, 185–9, 190, 191
brandirons 126–8
braziers 139–41, 152
bread car 170–1
brick domed wall ovens 143, 168–9
brickwork 49
Bridge End House 29, 33–47, 103, 121, 180, 181
    assembly of cut parts 38–42
    dining room 32, 96
    dressing room 120
    Gothic bedroom 31, 184
    finishing off 42–5
    hall 179
    kitchen 142, 143, 146, 153, 156
    making the windows 45–6
    mural room 138, 175, 176
    portico 42, 43, 47
    print room 134
    reception room 97

Brighton Pavilion 16
Brown, Mary 89–92
Browne, Hablot K. ('Phiz') 98, 99
Buck brothers 175
building legislation 5–8, 12, 15, 196–7
building stones 102–3
bull's-eye windows 25

Calke Abbey 183
candle box 160
candle rests 161–2
candles 106–8
Capheaton Hall 9, 10
Caroline, Queen 183
carpets 15, 177–8, 182, 197
Carron Ironworks 128–9
casement windows 5, 20
cast-iron hob grates 132, 133
ceilings 5, 143, 178–9
    heights 30, 31
chamber pots 115–16
chandeliers 11, 106–7, 107–8
chicken coop dressers 148–9
chimney boards 136–9
chimney breasts 131–2
chimney cranes 126, 142, 164–7
chimneypieces 134
chimneys 9, 13, 48–9, 56, 101, 103–4, 133
china steps 134
Chinese wallpapers 173
Chippendale, Thomas 6, 115, 182, 193
Cholmondeley House 32, 56–8
chopping blocks 171
cisterns 10, 104, 124, 169–70
classical windows 62
cloam ovens 147
close-stool 116–17
Coade Stone 13
coal 56, 126, 128
coats of arms 102
colour 109, 142, 180–1
columns 5, 11, 42–3, 44
colza-oil lamp 108
common pitch 27, 28
corner fireplaces 134
corner toilet and washstand 117–20
cornices 178, 179
couch beds 184
cranes
    chimney 126, 142, 164–7
    service area 110, 111
crumb cloths 178

curfews 152–3
curtains 15, 56, 181–2, 197
    bed curtains 183–4
curved walls 75–6, 78

Dan Peggotty's house 98–9
dates 100–4
Davenant, Charles 196
decoration 9–10, 15, 172–82, 197
Defoe, Daniel 6, 95
Dickens, Charles 6, 98–9, 110
dining rooms 56, 96, 98
Domino wallpaper 172
doors 25, 26, 53, 55, 68, 69
    period styles 5, 11–12, 13, 16–18
dormer windows 23, 58
double flue 132
drainage pipes 56
drawings 48–51
dressers 75, 147–51, 153
dummy boards 136–9
Dundonald, Lord 108
Dutch bond 49

Early Georgian 6, 9–13, 18
earth closets 113–15, 123
Embleton 18
enclosed fires 14, 139, 140
English bond 49
English garden wall bond 49
Ewart, Northumberland 9
    farmhouse of 1788 58–63
    gatekeeper's lodges 73–9
exterior clues to interior 56–8

fanlights 11, 13, 24, 109, 110
farmhouse 58–63
field work 48–51
Fiennes, Celia 95
fire baskets 127, 128, 132
fire marks 104–5
fire screens 134–6
firedogs 126–8
fireplaces 2, 13, 103, 126–34
first-rate houses 15, 30–2
Flemish bond 49
Flemish garden wall bond 49
floor coverings 177–8
floorcloths 177, 178, 197
flooring materials 176–7
flush toilets 15, 114, 115, 197
folding table 143, 145
Foulston, John 16

fountain (public conduit) 124
four-poster beds 183–4
fourth-rate houses 15, 30–1
Franklin, Benjamin 178, 197
Frederick, Prince of Wales 84
furnishings 172–82
    see also carpets; curtains

Gainsborough, Thomas 6, 33
game larders 120–2, 123
Gardener's House, Lemmington 25
gardens 123–4
gas lighting 108, 197
gatekeepers' lodges 73–81
George I 5, 6, 28, 183
George III 6, 28, 84, 87
George IV 5, 6
Georgian society 196–7
Gillow, Richard 193
glazing bars 22, 23
Gothic pitch 27
Gothic Revival 16–18, 58, 62, 67
Gray, Freida 123
Great Fire of London 9, 104
Grey, Sir George 85, 87

haircloths 178
half-tester beds 184, 185
Hampton Court 21
'hanging lum' 132
Harbour master's house, Seaton Sluice 67–72
Harpur, Sir Henry 183
Hepplewhite, George 1, 6, 115, 116, 193
Herschel, Sir William 33
Hexham 92
high room 95
hinges 79
Hoare, William 33
hob grates 127, 128, 132, 133
Holkham Hall 115
Holy Island (Lindisfarne) 4, 99
hoods over doors 5, 8
hoppers 104, 125
Hoppus, Edward 21
horse fire screens 136
hunting lodges 33

ingrain carpets 178
interior, clues from exterior 56–8
inventories 88–95
Irish folding table 143, 145

ironwork, exterior 16, 108–10

jack screens 142, 146, 154
Jekyll, Gertrude 194–5
jerries 115–16
Johnson, Samuel 6, 20
Jones, Sydney R. 194–5

Kedleston Hall 134, 139, 178
Kent, William 6, 115
keystones 13, 54, 186
Kielder Castle 17
King, Gregory 196
kitchen ranges 128–31, 155
kitchens 9, 56, 60, 95, 142–71
    accessories 152–71
    see also dressers; ovens
kneelers 37
knife box 157, 158
knife scouring box 157–8
knob-type bell pulls 111–13
Knole House, Kent 141

Ladythorne House 31, 48–55
    construction of 51–5
lamp brackets 108–9
land agent's survey 58–63
landscape papers 173, 174–5
Langmead, Joseph 128
Late Georgian 6, 13–15, 19
lead water cisterns 10, 104, 124, 169–70
Lethieullier, Sarah 84
lever-type bell pulls 111, 112, 113
lighting 2, 11, 106–10, 197
limewash 65, 181
linkmen 106
Linley, Elizabeth 33
list carpeting 178
literature, period 95–9
Llainfadyn cottage 3, 65–6
Lord Cholmondeley's house 32, 56–8
Lowther, Cumbria 9, 60

Manners, Lady Caroline 183
Mansard roofs 27, 28
mantel shelf 126
marriage stones 100, 101
matching pavilions 113, 120–3
meal chest dresser 148
meat safes 120–2
modillions 5, 16
Monck, Sir Charles 186
murals 174, 175, 180
museums of building 63–6
'Myriorama' 173, 174

Nash, John 6, 13, 16
Needle's Eye, Nostell Priory 80–1
Newbiggin 99
Newcastle, bridge at 89, 90
night-soil men 113, 114

night stands 115–17
Nisbet, James 67, 68
note-taking 48–51

oil lighting 108, 197
Old Town Farm, Redesdale 88
Oudry, Jean-Baptiste 139
ovens 143–7, 168–9

'palace' façade 13
Palladianism 5, 9
Palladio, Andrea 5, 186
panelling, wooden 172, 180
panes, proportions of 22–3
pantiles 28, 197
Papillon, J.-B. M. 172
parapets 13, 16, 17, 52, 53
pargeting 102
parlour 95
pavilions, matching 113, 120–3
Paxton, Sir Joseph 177
pediment pitch 27, 28
pelmets 16, 182
Penparcau tollhouse 63–4
period literature 95–9
period styles 5–20
photographs 48
pile carpets 178
Piozzi, Hester (formerly Thrale) 33
pipe box 159
pipe rack 159–60
pitch of roof 27–8
pitman's cottage 88–9
plan of a room 1
plasterwork 172, 178–9
pole fire screens 135, 136
portable heaters 139–41
pot cupboards 115–17
pothooks 162–3
princesses' house 84–5, 87
print rooms 172–4
privies 113–24
protective coverings 182
public conduit 124
Pyne, W. H. 108

Queen Anne style 5–9, 18
quoins 43, 44, 53

rainwater goods 104, 124–5
ranges, kitchen 128–31, 155
reception rooms 30, 31, 56, 97, 98
    heating 132–4
Reed, Clement 88
Regency 6, 13, 15–20, 23, 24
Restoration style 5, 6
Richardson, George 134
roasting spits 126–8, 129, 142, 154
Robinson, Thomas 128, 142
Rodwell, William 181
Roman Cement (stucco) 13, 16
roofs 5, 13, 27–8, 48
Rose, Walter 124

rugs 178
Rumford stove 132–4
rush lights 106

salt box 160–1
Saltram House, Devon 173
sanitation 113–24
sash windows 5, 12, 20–1
Saussure, César de 95
scaling down 48, 49–51
Scharf, George 115
Scotch carpets 178
second-rate houses 15, 30–1
'Secrets of Paris' 116, 117
servants' quarters 9, 58
service area 110–13
settle beds 147, 192
sham windows 23
Shawdon Hall, Northumberland 102
shell hoods 5, 8
Sheraton, Thomas 6, 115, 193
Sheridan, Richard Brinsley 33
shooting boxes 33
shutters 12–13, 25–7
signatures 100–4
skew putts 37
slate roofs 28
slate worker's cottage 65–6
smoke hoods 131–2
snuffers 106, 107, 110
Spence, James 88–9
spice cupboards 101, 104
spit dogs 126–8
spit jacks 142, 153–6
spit racks 148, 163
spits, roasting 126–8, 129, 142, 154
spoon rack 158
St Paul, Horace 74, 75–6
stairs 45, 68, 126, 183
Standing Stone Farm, Hexham 17
stone-tiled roofs 28
Stonor Park, Oxfordshire 174, 175
stoves 14, 139, 140
straw mats 178
stretcher bond 49
stringing bed frames 194
stucco 13, 16
styles, period 5–20
summerhouses 120–2, 123
Susie's Castle, Portincaple 4
Sussex bond 49

tallow candles 106, 107
tanner's cottage 92–5
tea 2, 95
tent beds 184
terraced housing 9, 13, 15, 20, 114
thermal windows 25
third-rate houses 15, 30–1
three-motion chimney cranes 165–7

three-part windows 23
'thunderbox' 116–17
tin (bachelor's) oven 146
tollhouses 63–4
town houses 30–3
    'rates' 15, 30–1
    see also Bridge End House
toy houses 81–7
travelling baby house 82–7
truckle (trundle) beds 189, 191
true pitch 27, 28

upturned boats 3, 4, 98–9

Vanbrugh, Sir John 6, 67
Venetian windows 23–4, 46, 62, 72

wainscot 172, 180
wall ovens 168–9
Wallace, Cosmo 80
Wallington Hall 115
wallpaper 10, 15, 172–5, 180
Walpole, Horace 6, 115
wardrobes 183
Ware, Isaac 115, 134
washstands 117–20, 183
water cisterns 10, 104, 124, 169–70
water closets 15, 114, 115, 197
water supply 10, 15, 124, 142–3
weather vanes 101, 104
Webster, Thomas 129
Wetherstone, Alexander 177
White, John 181
Whittock, Nathaniel 181
William IV 6, 16
window tax 23, 27
windows 20–7, 45–6, 62, 72, 76, 196–7
    period styles 5, 12–13, 14, 16
    proportions 21–3
    researching houses 53, 54, 56, 58, 60
    town houses 30, 31
    upper floors without 9, 56, 60
withdrawing rooms 97, 98
Woburn Abbey 115
Wood, John, the elder 6, 33
Wood, John, the younger 6, 33, 117
wooden panelling 172, 180
workers' houses 3, 88–9, 92, 114–15, 126, 186–7
    gatekeepers' lodges 73–81
    slate worker's cottage 65–6
    upturned boats 3, 4, 98–9
Wren, Sir Christopher 6, 21
'wrestler' slates 28
wrought-iron lamp brackets 108–9

York, Duke of 33

GMC PUBLICATIONS

BOOKS

DOLLS' HOUSES AND MINIATURES

1/12 Scale Character Figures for the Dolls' House	James Carrington
Architecture for Dolls' Houses	Joyce Percival
The Authentic Georgian Dolls' House	Brian Long
A Beginners' Guide to the Dolls' House Hobby	Jean Nisbett
Celtic, Medieval and Tudor Wall Hangings in 1/12 Scale Needlepoint	Sandra Whitehead
The Complete Dolls' House Book	Jean Nisbett
The Dolls' House 1/24 Scale: A Complete Introduction	Jean Nisbett
Dolls' House Accessories, Fixtures and Fittings	Andrea Barham
Dolls' House Bathrooms: Lots of Little Loos	Patricia King
Dolls' House Fireplaces and Stoves	Patricia King
Dolls' House Window Treatments	Eve Harwood
Easy to Make Dolls' House Accessories	Andrea Barham
Heraldic Miniature Knights	Peter Greenhill
How to Make Your Dolls' House Special: Fresh Ideas for Decorating	Beryl Armstrong
Make Your Own Dolls' House Furniture	Maurice Harper
Making Dolls' House Furniture	Patricia King
Making Georgian Dolls' Houses	Derek Rowbottom
Making Miniature Food and Market Stalls	Angie Scarr
Making Miniature Gardens	Freida Gray
Making Miniature Oriental Rugs & Carpets	Meik & Ian McNaughton
Making Period Dolls' House Accessories	Andrea Barham
Making Tudor Dolls' Houses	Derek Rowbottom
Making Victorian Dolls' House Furniture	Patricia King
Miniature Bobbin Lace	Roz Snowden
Miniature Embroidery for the Georgian Dolls' House	Pamela Warner
Miniature Embroidery for the Victorian Dolls' House	Pamela Warner
Miniature Needlepoint Carpets	Janet Granger
More Miniature Oriental Rugs & Carpets	Meik & Ian McNaughton
Needlepoint 1/12 Scale: Design Collections for the Dolls' House	Felicity Price
The Secrets of the Dolls' House Makers	Jean Nisbett

CRAFTS

American Patchwork Designs in Needlepoint	Melanie Tacon
A Beginners' Guide to Rubber Stamping	Brenda Hunt
Blackwork: A New Approach	Brenda Day
Celtic Cross Stitch Designs	Carol Phillipson
Celtic Knotwork Designs	Sheila Sturrock
Celtic Knotwork Handbook	Sheila Sturrock
Celtic Spirals and Other Designs	Sheila Sturrock
Collage from Seeds, Leaves and Flowers	Joan Carver
Complete Pyrography	Stephen Poole
Contemporary Smocking	Dorothea Hall
Creating Colour with Dylon	Dylon International
Creative Doughcraft	Patricia Hughes
Creative Embroidery Techniques Using Colour Through Gold	Daphne J. Ashby & Jackie Woolsey
The Creative Quilter: Techniques and Projects	Pauline Brown
Decorative Beaded Purses	Enid Taylor
Designing and Making Cards	Glennis Gilruth
Glass Engraving Pattern Book	John Everett
Glass Painting	Emma Sedman
Handcrafted Rugs	Sandra Hardy
How to Arrange Flowers: A Japanese Approach to English Design	Taeko Marvelly
How to Make First-Class Cards	Debbie Brown
An Introduction to Crewel Embroidery	Mave Glenny
Making and Using Working Drawings for Realistic Model Animals	Basil F. Fordham
Making Character Bears	Valerie Tyler
Making Decorative Screens	Amanda Howes
Making Fairies and Fantastical Creatures	Julie Sharp
Making Greetings Cards for Beginners	Pat Sutherland
Making Hand-Sewn Boxes: Techniques and Projects	Jackie Woolsey
Making Knitwear Fit	Pat Ashforth & Steve Plummer
Making Mini Cards, Gift Tags & Invitations	Glennis Gilruth
Making Soft-Bodied Dough Characters	Patricia Hughes
Natural Ideas for Christmas: Fantastic Decorations to Make	Josie Cameron-Ashcroft & Carol Cox
Needlepoint: A Foundation Course	Sandra Hardy
New Ideas for Crochet: Stylish Projects for the Home	Darsha Capaldi
Patchwork for Beginners	Pauline Brown
Pyrography Designs	Norma Gregory
Pyrography Handbook (Practical Crafts)	Stephen Poole
Ribbons and Roses	Lee Lockheed
Rose Windows for Quilters	Angela Besley
Rubber Stamping with Other Crafts	Lynne Garner
Sponge Painting	Ann Rooney
Stained Glass: Techniques and Projects	Mary Shanahan
Step-by-Step Pyrography Projects for the Solid Point Machine	Norma Gregory
Tassel Making for Beginners	Enid Taylor
Tatting Collage	Lindsay Rogers
Temari: A Traditional Japanese Embroidery Technique	Margaret Ludlow
Theatre Models in Paper and Card	Robert Burgess
Trip Around the World: 25 Patchwork, Quilting and Appliqué Projects	Gail Lawther
Trompe l'Oeil: Techniques and Projects	Jan Lee Johnson
Wool Embroidery and Design	Lee Lockheed

MAGAZINES

WOODTURNING ◆ WOODCARVING
FURNITURE & CABINETMAKING ◆ THE ROUTER
WOODWORKING ◆ THE DOLLS' HOUSE MAGAZINE
WATER GARDENING ◆ EXOTIC GARDENING
GARDEN CALENDAR ◆ OUTDOOR PHOTOGRAPHY
BLACK & WHITE PHOTOGRAPHY ◆ BUSINESSMATTERS

The above represents only a selection of titles currently published or scheduled to be published. All are available direct from the Publishers or through bookshops, newsagents and specialist retailers. To place an order, or to obtain a complete catalogue, contact:

**GMC PUBLICATIONS,
Castle Place, 166 High Street, Lewes,
East Sussex BN7 1XU, United Kingdom
Tel: 01273 488005 Fax: 01273 478606
E-mail: pubs@thegmcgroup.com**

Orders by credit card are accepted